ROBERT FROST HANDBOOK

ROBERT FROST HANDBOOK

James L. Potter

The Pennsylvania State University Press
University Park and London

"It Bids Pretty Fair"   "Neither Out Far nor In Deep"
"The Pasture"   "Dust of Snow"
"For Once, Then, Something"   "Fragmentary Blue"
"The Oven Bird"   "Questioning Faces"
"The Silken Tent"   "Not All There"

From *The Poetry of Robert Frost* edited by Edward Connery Lathem. Copyright 1916, 1923, 1939, 1947, © 1967, 1969 by Holt, Rinehart and Winston. Copyright 1936, 1942, 1944, 1951, © 1962 by Robert Frost. Copyright © 1964, 1970, 1975 by Lesley Frost Ballantine. Reprinted by permission of Holt, Rinehart and Winston, Publishers.

Library of Congress Cataloging in Publication Data

Potter, James Lain.
  Robert Frost handbook.

  Includes bibliography and index.
  1. Frost, Robert, 1874–1963.   2. Poets, American—
20th century—Biography.   I. Title.
PS3511.R94Z88   811'.5'2[B]   79-9145
ISBN 0-271-00230-1

For Pitman B. Potter

Because I've wanted to
emulate him, I've tried to be as
good a scholar and teacher as he
—yet he is still the best.

Contents

Preface

This handbook is intended to provide the basis for a sound general comprehension of Frost as a poet. I have tried to furnish the kind and the amount of background information and critical analysis of the poetry that will be useful to general readers or students who have Frost's work at hand. My chapters should help them to a valid and reliable understanding of the poet, and should also indicate how to pursue further their knowledge of the poet and his work.

The chronological table lists the main externally observable events of Frost's life. It provides an overview of his life at a quick glance, and will serve as a reference for dates and similar information.

Part I of the text, Frost's Life and Works, provides a basic biography and an account of Frost's career as a poet, including analyses of the general character and structure of the principal volumes of poetry he published. Frost's life provides a great deal of insight into the nature of the man and his work, for we can observe the same general tendencies in both areas, perhaps more than in the case of most poets. Those who wish to investigate Frost's life further should read Lawrance Thompson's three-volume biography, to which any present study of Frost, including mine, must be greatly indebted.

Part II is an overview of the poetry, taking into account both the works themselves—virtually all of Frost's poetry—and most of the important critical and scholarly analyses of Frost's life and work. It is time to try to understand the poetry as a whole in the light of all the sophisticated critical work that has been done, especially since 1960. This book is an attempt to find a valid conception of the persona and of the implicit as well as explicit patterns of thought and predisposition embodied in the poetry. We can now reasonably hope to perceive the basic patterns of Frost's poetry. I have tried to read the mind of the poet only as it appears in his poems in all its complexity and apparent inconsistency, though I have correlated this reading with evidence from external sources such as the letters and biographical material. The purpose of Part II is to help us understand Frost's work; it does not pretend to offer standards of evaluation for the poetry. I have preferences and opinions that will no doubt be evident enough, but these are not central to the study, which is concerned with the prior task of comprehension.

The main thesis argued here is that beneath all its other charac-
teristics the poetry manifests a fundamental tension between two dif-
ferent conceptions of the universe and man's role in it: a secular or
even agnostic view, and a more religious one. At the same time, the
poetry embodies a more familiar dichotomy, that of a "dark" sense
of things on the one hand, and a more optimistic one on the other,
each of which finds expression in both the secular and the religious
conceptions of the universe and man.

These dichotomies would seem irreconcilable, and in fact Frost
usually swings back and forth between the two sets of poles. In his
work as a whole, however, and in a few particular poems, he
achieves a balance, though an uncertain one. This should become
evident in Part II as a whole, but particularly in Chapter 8, where
some of Frost's most complex poems are discussed, such as "West-
Running Brook" and "Directive." In these Frost achieves not merely
a "momentary stay against confusion" but a substantial resolution of
his continuing metaphysical and creative problems.

The myth of the farmer-philosopher suggests that Frost was an
unliterary, conventional poet. No one now doubts that he was origi-
nal in many ways, but it is also important to know that he had sig-
nificant literary antecedents, that he was far from ignorant about his
poetic heritage, and, further, that he experimented with and focused
in important new ways on various aspects of poetic technique. In
fact, it is now becoming increasingly evident, as Part III will show,
that Frost's role in our poetic heritage is most significant. His rela-
tionship with Wordsworth, Emerson, and Thoreau and his critical
and creative concern with form, voice, and metaphor are discussed
in this section to indicate just how much of a conscious artist Frost
was.

Finally, the Bibliography provides an annotated list of works by
and about Frost. It is not exhaustive, but should satisfy the need for
a full and informative working bibliography. Here the reader can
find where to look first for information and analysis of Frost and of
particular poems by him.

I intend and expect that this handbook will be useful and informa-
tive. I believe it constitutes the kind of guide to Frost that will always
be needed, and that it will provide a fundamental understanding of
his work to begin with.

I should like to thank all those who have helped me as I worked
on Frost. I cannot list every one of them, for they include all the stu-
dents in my Frost classes at Trinity College to begin with, as well as
those who made Frost the subject of their MA theses here. These

students often provided fresh insights which I might well have missed. I also owe considerable debts to Robert D. Foulke of Skidmore College and Gordon J. McKinley of Westminster School for their critical readings of the manuscript. Their sharp eyes and sense of style helped me a great deal. To Laurence Perrine, James L. Woodress, and other readers for The Pennsylvania State University Press, go my thanks for suggestions that led me to improve the study in many ways and to expand its scope to a much more useful format. And, as he knows, John M. Pickering of Penn State Press deserves great thanks for persistence and encouragement over a considerable time. Thanks, too, to Mrs. Delores Noonan for all her work, and of course to Judy, my wife, for her faith and patience.

Robert Lee Frost: Chronology*

1874–1912: Birth to age 38

1874–1895: Childhood and youth
1874 – Robert Lee Frost born to William Prescott Frost, Jr., and Isabelle Moodie Frost, San Francisco, March 26
1876 – Isabelle Frost returned to Massachusetts for several months. Jeanie Florence Frost, R's sister, born, Lawrence, Mass.
1885 – William P. Frost, Jr., died. Isabelle Frost returned with children to Lawrence, Mass., then to Salem, N.H., where she began teaching
1888 – Enrolled in Lawrence High School; began friendship with Carl Burrell
1890 – Frost's first poem, "La Noche Triste," and others
1892 – Met Elinor Miriam White, graduated co-valedictorian with her from high school; attended Dartmouth College for a few months
1893 – First teaching job, Methuen, Mass. (8th grade); worked in Arlington Mill, Lawrence
1894 – "My Butterfly" published by *The Independent;* poems published occasionally in periodicals through 1912, then increasingly thereafter. Had two copies of *Twilight* printed; one copy given to Elinor, one subsequently destroyed. Went to the Dismal Swamp, Virginia, area
1895 – Worked as reporter; taught in school owned by his mother

1895–1912: Early married life
1895 – Robert Frost and Elinor White married
1896 – Elliott, first son, born
1897 – Entered Harvard
1899 – Withdrew from Harvard, settled in Methuen where he began chicken farming. Lesley, first daughter, born
1900 – Elliott died. Moved to Derry, N.H., farm. Isabelle Frost died
1901 – Frost's paternal grandfather died, leaving him an annuity
1902 – Carol, second son, born
1903 – Irma, second daughter, born
1905 – Marjorie, third daughter, born. Began going to Bethlehem, N.H., during hay-fever season (family went in August, 1906–1911)

---

*This chronology is based on information from Frost's letters and biographies of Frost by Thompson, Thompson and Winnick, and Gerber (see Bibliography for complete sources).

1906 – Began teaching at Pinkerton Academy, Derry
1907 – Elinor Bettina, fourth daughter; died within two days. Suffered serious case of pneumonia
1909 – Frosts moved to Derry Village
1911 – Taught at N.H. State Normal School, Plymouth, N.H., for academic year; Frosts moved to Plymouth

1912–1930: Development of Frost's poetic career

1912–1915: Residence in England
1912 – Frosts moved to Beaconsfield, Buckinghamshire. Met Ezra Pound
1913 – *A Boy's Will* (London: David Nutt & Co.) published. Met Edward Thomas
1914 – Frosts moved to Dymock, Gloucestershire. *North of Boston* (London: David Nutt) published
1915 – Frosts returned to United States

1915–1930: Teaching at Amherst and Michigan
1915 – Frosts lived in Bethlehem, then bought farm in Franconia, N. H. *North of Boston* and *A Boy's Will* (both New York: Henry Holt & Co.) published. Met Amy Lowell, Louis Untermeyer, Edwin Arlington Robinson. Phi Beta Kappa Poet, Tufts
1916 – Phi Beta Kappa Poet, Harvard. *Mountain Interval* (Holt) published. Elected to membership in National Institute of Arts and Letters
1917 – Began teaching at Amherst
1918 – Honorary M.A., Amherst
1920 – Resigned from Amherst. Jeanie Frost committed to State Hospital, Maine. Frosts moved to South Shaftsbury, Vt.
1921 – First lecture/reading at Bread Loaf School of English. Began as Poet in Residence at University of Michigan; Frosts moved to Ann Arbor
1922 – Honorary M.A., Michigan. Continued at University of Michigan as Fellow in Creative Arts
1923 – First southwestern lecture tour. *Selected Poems* and *New Hampshire* published. Honorary L.H.D., University of Vermont. Carol Frost and Lillian LaBatt married. Became Professor of English at Amherst
1924 – *New Hampshire* awarded Pulitzer Prize. Honorary Litt.D., Middlebury and Yale
1925 – "Fiftieth" birthday party, New York City. Elinor miscarried. Became Fellow in Letters at University of Michigan
1926 – Honorary Litt.D., Bowdoin. Spoke at first Bread Loaf Writers' Conference. Irma Frost and John Cone married. Became Professor of English at Amherst
1928 – Lesley Frost and James D. Francis married. Visited England with Elinor and Marjorie. *West-Running Brook* published
1929 – Jeanie Frost died. *A Way Out* (one-act play) published. Robert and Elinor moved to Gully Farm, Bennington, Vt.

1930–1963: The culmination of Frost's career

1930–1938: Major personal troubles
 1930 – Honorary Litt. D., University of New Hampshire. *Collected Poems* published. Elected member of American Academy of Arts and Letters. Marjorie and Carol's wife, Lillian, found tubercular
 1931 – *Collected Poems* awarded Pulitzer Prize. Helped establish Rocky Mountain Writers' Conference, University of Colorado. Honorary L.H.D., Wesleyan University
 1932 – Phi Beta Kappa Poet, Columbia. Honorary Litt.D., Columbia; Honorary L.H.D., Williams
 1933 – Second southwestern lecture tour. Marjorie Frost and Willard E. Fraser married. Honorary Litt.D., Dartmouth
 1934 – Marjorie died of puerperal fever. Elinor suffered heart attack; Frosts first visited Florida
 1936 – Appointed Charles Eliot Norton Professor of Poetry, Harvard. *A Further Range* published; Book of the Month Club Selection. Honorary L.H.D., St. Lawrence University, University of Pennsylvania, Bates
 1937 – Elected member of American Philosophical Society. *A Further Range* awarded Pulitzer Prize. Honorary Litt.D., Harvard. Elinor had operation for cancer
 1938 – Elinor died of heart attack. Resigned from Amherst. Moved to Boston to be near Theodore and Kathleen Morrison

1938/39–1949: Various activities, various places
 1939 – Awarded Gold Medal for Poetry, National Institute of Arts & Letters. *Collected Poems* (enlarged) published. Honorary Litt.D., Colorado. Appointed Ralph Waldo Emerson Fellow in Poetry, Harvard. Purchased farm in Ripton, Vt. (to summer there regularly). Appointed Lawrance Thompson his official biographer
 1940 – Sold *Twilight* to Earle J. Bernheimer. Purchased land in South Miami, Florida, for winter home. Phi Beta Kappa Poet, Tufts. Carol Frost committed suicide
 1941 – Awarded Gold Medal, Poetry Society of America. Moved to Cambridge, Mass. Honorary Litt.D., Princeton. Phi Beta Kappa Poet, Harvard, William and Mary
 1942 – Built "Pencil Pines" in South Miami. *A Witness Tree* published
 1943 – *A Witness Tree* awarded Pulitzer Prize. Became George Ticknor Fellow in the Humanities, Dartmouth. Suffered severe case of pneumonia
 1945 – *A Masque of Reason* published. Honorary Litt.D., Kenyon
 1947 – Irma divorced, institutionalized. Honorary LL.D., University of California. *Steeple Bush* and *A Masque of Mercy* published
 1948 – Honorary Litt.D., Duke, Amherst

1949–1963: Involvement in public affairs
 1949 – *Complete Poems 1949* published. Appointed Simpson Lecturer in Literature for life, Amherst. Awarded Gold Medal by Limited Editions Club for *Complete Poems 1949*

1950 – Received "felicitations of the nation" on his "seventy-fifth" birthday from U. S. Senate. Bernheimer collection of Frostiana sold at auction. Honorary Litt.D., Colgate, Marlboro. Nominated for Nobel Prize in Literature

1951 – Honorary Litt.D., University of Massachusetts, *in absentia* University of Durham, England

1953 – Honorary Litt.D., University of North Carolina

1954 – Celebrated eightieth birthday: reception at White House, banquets in New York City and Amherst. Represented USA at World Congress of Writers, São Paulo, Brazil. Honorary Litt. D., University of Cincinnati

1955 – Honorary LL.D., Dartmouth; Honorary Litt.D., University of Rhode Island

1956 – Honorary LL.D., Colby

1957 – Went on "good-will mission" to England. Honorary Litt.D., Oxford, Cambridge, National University of Ireland. Honorary Litt.D., Ohio State. Dined at White House with President Eisenhower

1958 – Gold Medal for Distinguished Service from Poetry Society of America. Appointed Consultant in Poetry in Library of Congress. Huntington Hartford Foundation Award ($5,000). Helped secure Ezra Pound's release from St. Elizabeth's Hospital for the criminally insane

1959 – Attended eighty-fifth birthday party, New York City: Trilling speech, "A Cultural Episode." Honorary L.H.D., Miami University; Honorary Litt.D., Syracuse, Tufts

1960 – Honorary LL.D., University of Florida; Honorary L.H.D., Hebrew Union College

1961 – Participated in President John F. Kennedy's inauguration. Honorary LL.D., U. of Miami; Honorary Litt.D., Windham College, Boston University. Lectured at Hebrew University, Jerusalem, and in Athens, Greece; visited London. Participated in the "Evening with Robert Frost" reception at State Department. Designated "Poet Laureate of Vermont"

1962 – Suffered severe case of pneumonia. Presented with Congressional Gold Medal (authorized by President Eisenhower in 1960) by President Kennedy; attended large birthday dinner, Washington, D.C. *In the Clearing* published. Honorary LL.D., University of Michigan; Honorary L.H.D., University of Detroit. Went on "goodwill mission" to Russia; spoke with Premier Khrushchev. Participated in first National Poetry Festival, Washington, D.C.

1963 – Received Bollingen Prize in Poetry. Died after month-long illness, operations

I

Frost's Life and Works
(1874–1963)

Frost's Early Growth
(1874–1912)

Robert Frost's life, like his poetry, shows him to be very humanly contradictory. For many years—in fact, until he was nearly forty—he seemed to flounder uncertainly, not feeling sure of his talents, his nature, or the direction he should pursue. Then he made his mark as a poet, becoming more and more widely known until at the end he was the United States' *de facto* poet laureate.

Frost's early difficulties left him unsure of himself in many respects. He was often very vulnerable to adverse criticism, especially since he was fundamentally warm and loving, intense and sensitive. At times he felt quite insecure, professionally and as a husband and father, giving way occasionally to jealousy of other poets on the one hand, and perhaps to vague thoughts about suicide on the other. He was able to survive because he was determined, practical, and tough, both mentally and—despite his bouts with sickness—physically. Charismatic, intellectually stimulating, personally charming, he made numerous friends wherever he went and influenced a great many more, directly and indirectly. And he continued writing his poetry with such success because he was in addition idealistic, fundamentally religious, retaining a searching, hopeful cast of mind until the very end.

Of the first thirty-eight years of his life, Robert Frost spent his childhood in San Francisco, his youth around Lawrence, Massachusetts, and his early married life there and elsewhere in northern Massachusetts and in New Hampshire. The major influence on him through the first few years of his marriage was that of his mother. Her devoutness and mysticism, her loving sensitivity and courage, and her idealistic refinement did much to shape Frost's basic nature. Later, Frost also felt the influence of Carl Burrell, an older comrade from high school days, who encouraged Frost's interest in wildflowers, in philosophical speculation, and in writing poetry. The third and eventually the longest influential relationship was that with

Elinor White, whom Frost married in 1895. Her influence was always great, but problematic: Frost was possessive, and resentful of her independence of mind, but admired her greatly and was very devoted to her. Learning to adjust his relationship with her was probably one of the main means by which he came to maturity. During this formative period he vacillated a good deal, searching for a satisfying identity and a way of life. Only gradually did he develop into a poet; most of the time he seemed destined to be primarily a teacher. Not until 1912 did he fully realize that his main commitment was to poetry.

Robert Lee Frost was the first child born to his parents, William Prescott Frost, Jr., and Isabelle Moodie Frost. Robert's mother and father had had a rather disturbed relationship and were to continue thus; they hardly seemed well suited to each other. Each had a significant effect on their son, but Isabelle Frost was by far the most influential; Robert and his sister Jeanie lived with their mother from their father's death in 1885 until Robert's marriage ten years later. Even after that he maintained close ties with his mother until her death in 1900.

Robert's father was brilliant (at Harvard he had been a member of Phi Beta Kappa and had graduated with honors), energetic, and ambitious, but also restless, erratic, and given to drink.[1] He had come west from New England, meeting and winning his wife on the way, in Columbus, Ohio, where they were both teaching. In San Francisco he became a newspaperman—an exciting life, especially in a small raw city not yet far from gold-rush days. Soon he became involved in politics and was led into the usual (at least for that time and place) adventurous and convivial excesses that helped to destroy him. Up through the birth of his son (his Copperhead sympathies led him to name the boy after the Southern general) he was very solicitous of his wife, but this concern gradually became disrupted by an increasing wildness as well as by physical illness. When the second child was almost due in 1876, Isabelle took Robert and returned east partly to escape her husband and partly to visit his family to explain her plight. She returned to San Francisco many months later with the new baby girl, Jeanie.

As Robert grew into an active boyhood he found his father's activities exciting. His father took him on many political errands and sent him alone on others, often having kept him out of school because he seemed sickly, at least to his parents. Frost said later that he grew up in saloons, and that he served as a kind of political kid about town.[2] His father suffered from tuberculosis, however, and the disease as well as the alcohol undermined his heroic stature in Robert's eyes. In

1885 William Frost died and his widow took the two children and once again returned east.

Several other particular aspects of his life in San Francisco affected Robert significantly. One storm on the coast was so memorable that it furnished the basis for the later famous sonnet "Once by the Pacific," and the gold-rush tradition of the city that Robert lived in until he was eleven is recalled in "A Peck of Gold." One other episode seems especially revealing. Although Robert was considered delicate—he never emulated his father's long, exhausting "health" swims in the Pacific—he decided he wanted to join a tough gang in the vicinity, and in order to prove his worth fought two of the boys at the same time. He lost, but was accepted for his bravery, and took part in some of the gang's adventures, including the pilfering. Looking back, Frost considered this victory of bravery over fear a kind of "growing up"; it must have helped his self-confidence considerably at the time, and when he recalled it later.

Back in the East, the small family now settled in Lawrence, Massachusetts; they found it hard to endure the funeral and the brief stay with William's parents. To the sensitive eleven-year-old Robbie his grandfather seemed harsh, even cruel, forbidding him and Jeanie to play on his lawn or to approach his flower beds. And their grandmother nagged and scolded just as much, it seemed to them. Isabelle Frost eventually found a teaching position in nearby Salem, New Hampshire. Neither Robert nor Jeanie liked this new part of the country nor the people they met there—including the relatives—but they became more content when settled in as a family with their mother.

Isabelle Frost remained a teacher on and off until within a year of her death, but her achievement was very mixed. Her refined manners and speech usually appealed to the better students but she was almost always having disciplinary problems with the rougher boys in that farming and manufacturing area. She was very different from her husband: quiet, sensitive, imaginative, and very religious, even mystical. Early in her years in San Francisco she had become interested in Swedenborgianism. Robert was baptized in that faith and, with his sister, was greatly influenced by his mother's moralistic Bible stories and romantic tales of heroes of many kinds, all shaped to demonstrate opposed moral values.[3] She gradually led Robert to see the earth—indeed all physical things—sometimes as a reflection or refraction of spiritual, heavenly qualities. Both he and Jeanie naturally adopted the general social values of their mother as well: restraint, refinement, unworldliness.

Robert was not interested in school at first even though he and his sister were in their mother's classes and she continued to expose them to folklore, poetry, and religious tales by reading to them at home. Robert was shy and apparently lazy; eventually, however, he began to enjoy reading and started to interest himself in his school-work. At the same time, he became more active physically: he played baseball and even got into a fight on a school picnic.

High school in Lawrence became the first arena for Robert's intellectual and poetic activities; here his intense and inquisitive mind began to reveal itself. In the course of his career there he became the leader of the debating society and the editor of the school news-paper. Some of his reading had very significant effects on him. His studies in Latin and Greek resulted in a particular interest in classical subjects and verse forms which he experimented with later at various times (see "For Once, Then, Something," for example). Richard A. Proctor's *Our Place Among Infinities* stimulated Robert's interest, which became lifelong, in the relation between religion and science; this was an especially significant development, for it reflected Frost's growing ambivalence toward spiritual and earthly attractions. He was truly religious, but felt the claims and the appeal of the world on its own terms as well. Further, W. H. Prescott's *Conquest of Mexico* helped lead Robert to write his first poem, "La Noche Triste," about Cortes's escape from Tenochtitlan. And during the summers he was introduced to farm work, including sharpening scythes and mowing hay, familiar activities in his later poetry. One summer he took a girl for a rowboat ride and was prevented from becoming involved with her only by his characteristic prudishness and idealism.

Perhaps the most important event in Robert's first three years of high school was his friendship with Carl Burrell. Some time before, Burrell had left school to work but he had returned when he was nearly twenty-five, ten years older than Frost.[4] He was friendly and easygoing, and although he did not seem cultured he helped reveal several new dimensions of the world to his younger friend. He introduced Robert to such great American humorists as Artemus Ward, Josh Billings, and Mark Twain, whose influence can be seen in Frost's pervasive humor; he loaned Robert his copy of *Our Place Among Infinities*; he conveyed his interest in "botanizing"—observing wildflowers—which stayed with and profoundly influenced Frost during most of his life; and, a dedicated though not very talented poet himself, he set Frost an example that first bore fruit in "La Noche Triste." Burrell had poems printed in the school newspaper; Frost's poem was accepted also, much to the benefit of his self-esteem, and this led to further work. The friendship remained close for several years, through Robert's courtship of Elinor White, their marriage and honeymoon, and their early years at Derry, New Hampshire.

Elinor and Robert met first in their senior year at Lawrence High School. For Robert it was a year filled with activity. In addition to editing the newspaper, he joined the football team, read and studied intensively (he was especially impressed by Edward Rowland Sill and Emily Dickinson, according to Lawrance Thompson), and continued to write both prose and poetry for the newspaper. At this time he began "Trial by Existence," which indicates the heavenly provenance of human souls, but emphasizes the pain and uncertainty of their earthly existence. The poem reflects his metaphysical preoccupations and perhaps also the unhappiness in his family caused by his sister's serious case of typhoid fever and her increasing moodiness and instability. The strain on Robert this year seems to have been fairly severe, but he was successful enough to become co-valedictorian—with Elinor White. Characteristically, he was both pleased and jealous; when he learned that her grades were virtually as high as his, he suggested that they share the honor, but then found it hard to remain self-denying. He also was extremely nervous when the time came to give his speech; the episode indicates clearly how Robert needed to bolster his confidence through intellectual and artistic attainments, and how his consequent vulnerability to rivals sometimes conflicted with the warmer, more generous side of his nature.

After graduation, Robert sold his valedictorian's medal in a whimsical gesture of iconoclastic defiance, but continued planning to attend college, just as Elinor did. They spent much of the summer together, though their relationship was no more easy then than in the rest of their shared life. Robert's physical passion dismayed Elinor —as "The Subverted Flower" suggests[5]—but they enacted a "marriage" ceremony to represent their commitment to each other.

When Elinor left for St. Lawrence University in Canton, New York, Robert went to Dartmouth, though not for long. Impatient with the regular regimen, uncertain of Elinor, and worried about his mother's disciplinary problems in school, he left quietly before the first semester was over. The next few years were a mixture of achievement and frustration.

Robert returned home to live, and was hired to take over the most unruly of his mother's classes. This beginning of his long teaching career was difficult. He had to face down and even punish physically several boys bigger and stronger than he. His determination made it possible, but the job lasted for only a few weeks. For the next four years (1893--1897) he held a succession of odd jobs—teacher, mill worker, reporter. Relations with Elinor continued to worry him; there were several disputes, partly because he had no set-tled career and partly because of his jealousy over her. He felt inse-cure; he didn't know what direction his life was to take yet, whereas Elinor was purposefully engaged in academic work. She also seemed to Robert to be involved with at least one other attentive suitor be-sides himself. During this period he was working on his poetry, how-ever; in 1894 he had "My Butterfly" accepted by *The Independent,* a magazine published by the distinguished clergyman, the Reverend William H. Ward, assisted by his sister Susan as a literary editor. This encouragement was the first objective reinforcement of his hope of a future as a poet. Robert's paternal grandfather offered to support him for a year so that he could try to establish himself in his vocation. But Robert had little affection for the old man despite the considerable help he had provided Isabelle Frost and her family in the past. Robert responded flippantly, posing as an auctioneer and calling out, "I have one, who'll give me twenty . . . ?" No doubt Robert imagined a certain condescension in the offer which his natural independence would resent.

"My Butterfly" also figured in the most disturbing and revealing episode in Robert's courtship. He had the poem and four others printed and bound in two copies of a booklet he entitled *Twilight,* and traveled to Canton, New York, to offer it to Elinor and talk out their troubles—his jealousy and her apparent indifference. She seemed to receive him and the gift coldly, however, and he bitterly tore up his own copy and left on another trip, this time to the Dismal Swamp in Virginia, perhaps to lose himself in it. Whether this was merely a gesture at escaping his despair or a real suicide attempt is hard to say, but it did put him in considerable danger not only in the swamp, but also among the hoboes he encountered in his subsequent wanderings, at least according to some of his later accounts of the episode.[6] There are indications later in his life and his writing that he was occasionally preoccupied with the idea of death, simulta-neously as an escape and as something fearful personally and theolog-ically. "Into My Own," though written later, reflects the kind of im-pulse that may have impelled him into the Dismal Swamp.

Frost returned to the same personal situation he had left—living at home with his mother, working at odd jobs, and maintaining an un-certain relationship with Elinor. He wrote for a newspaper in Law-rence; he made up with Elinor, had another serious dispute with her and fled to Cambridge, to visit former high-school friends. On the way home he first read Francis Thompson's "Hound of Heaven," an event he later came to consider personally significant, symbolically.

The year 1895 nevertheless turned out to be a turning point for the better in Frost's life. When his mother expanded the private school she had begun informally a few years earlier, both he and later Elinor joined the staff. They spent a very happy summer in the White Mountains with friends (marred only by the incident on which "The Lockless Door" is based). Their relationship had settled down and they were married shortly before Christmas. Robert seemed to have achieved a measure of stability in his personal life and his profession as a teacher; the direction of his career seemed clear, despite his continuing interest in poetry. The following summer they spent a delayed honeymoon in New Hampshire near Carl Burrell, Frost's close high-school friend. Burrell led them on many "botanizing" expeditions, which figure in "The Quest of the Purple-Fringed" and "The Encounter." "The Self-Seeker," based on a serious accident that happened to Burrell, reveals much about his personality, his interests, and his charm.

The Frosts' first child, Elliott, was born in September 1896. Robert had returned to his mother's school, and the family seemed well established. Nevertheless, Frost seems to have felt frustrated anew, both in his career and as a husband. This may have been one underlying reason for his becoming involved in a minor scandal. Frost started a fight with a man who had implied he was a coward, and was taken to court and fined ten dollars. Subsequently the affair was featured in a newspaper report, and Frost was thoroughly humiliated and ashamed. Frost's uncertainty about his career no doubt also lay behind his decision to enter Harvard in 1897 in hopes of better preparing himself to teach. His experiences at Harvard affected him more profoundly than those at Dartmouth earlier, even though he again left rather soon. In the year and a half he was there he continued to write some poetry, though not very much. "The Tuft of Flowers" may have been finished, at least, as a paper for English A, though it was based on an experience of the summer of 1891. He took a course with the young (eleven years older) George Santayana, who made a very favorable first impression but came to represent a repellent skepticism and cynicism to Robert.

Much more to Frost's liking and more important to his spiritual and intellectual development were the views of William James. Frost read and was strongly influenced by *The Will to Believe,* and took a philosophy course that used James's *Psychology.* Frost often acknowledged the influence of these books and the later *Pragmatism* (1907) on his theological and ethical views as well as his practical behavior and personal attitudes such as his self-confidence and sense of identity. In James, Frost evidently found enunciated and clarified many views he himself had held vaguely and uncertainly. James's pluralism and developing pragmatism, and his combination of skepticism with a belief in God, particularly appealed to Frost, but the young man's personal diffidence responded most strongly to James's assertion of the need to be somewhat selfish in the interests of self-fulfillment, as well as to his affirmation of the value of effort, will, and courage in such fulfillment. This was the kind of encouragement and reassurance Frost needed especially now.[7]

Frost withdrew from Harvard honorably and in good standing near the end of his second year, for two kinds of reasons. He had again become impatient with academic restrictions and conventions. He dropped George Lyman Kittredge's Milton course, for example, because he was disgusted with the students who took notes so assiduously that they seemed not to respond to Kittredge's insights with any literary pleasure. Moreover, he became exhausted and ill in his sophomore year from his work as student, as father (Elinor, her mother, and the baby Elliott had come to live with him), and as principal of an evening school, since the money Frost's grandfather was providing was not really sufficient. Frost's illness was a recurrence of what had seemed to be a touch of tuberculosis suffered the previous summer.

The Frosts settled in Methuen, near Lawrence, where Robert began raising chickens in accordance with the advice of a doctor to find a more outdoor, active occupation. Frost's chicken farming continued, with the help of a nearby experienced poultryman, for several years even after the Frosts moved to Derry, New Hampshire. The year or so around the turn of the century were, again, a mixture of happiness and sadness, and again the sadness seemed to predominate. Lesley, the Frosts' first daughter, was born in Methuen, but a few months later Elliott became very ill and died. His death was a severe blow; for a long time Robert felt guilty virtually of murder for not calling a doctor sooner. The poem "Stars" stems from this time, as does "Home Burial," to some extent.[8] The image of the cold indifference of the heavens to man's difficulties in the one poem, and the evident lack of understanding between husband and wife in the other, reflect Frost's sensitivity and psychological insecurity at the time. During the same period, Frost's mother was becoming obviously weak; she was terminally ill with cancer, though she maintained her usual fortitude and serenity until the end in 1900. The strain on Frost's basically warm nature was more than considerable; he must have had to develop a certain toughness of spirit at this time which was to stand him in good stead later.

The move to Derry in the same year was one of the Frosts' most fortunate and beneficial decisions. Although the first year was darkened by Isabelle Frost's death, the Derry period became a generally happy time for the family and a stable and encouraging period for

Robert Frost because it was fertile in material for his poetry and led also to real success in teaching. Robert's grandfather bought the Derry farm for the Frosts' use, and arranged for Carl Burrell and his grandfather to live there and run the place. The first few months of unhappiness were characterized by the sonnet "Despair" and, much later, the bitter poetic tribute to his mother, "The Lovely Shall Be Choosers." In the years between 1901 or 1902 and 1906, however, Frost recovered from his depression to a large extent, enjoying family and country life more than ever before: "Mowing," probably written early in the period, shows the peace of mind he was able to attain.[9]

Burrell was efficient at farming and relieved Frost of most such worries. He also led the Frosts on botanizing expeditions again, which helped greatly to assuage their unhappiness and added much to Robert's liking for and knowledge of the plants and flowers that figure in so much of his poetry. Frost also came to know the people in that farm area; his admiration of their courage and independence and his affection for their idiosyncrasies show in many of his poems, especially in *North of Boston* (1914). One of his neighbors in particular, Napoleon Guay, figured in "Mending Wall" and "The Axe-Helve." Frost came to know Henry David Thoreau's *Walden* and the work of Ralph Waldo Emerson, both of which reinforced the respect for originality and independence, as well as for natural surroundings, that Frost developed most fully at Derry. He was nevertheless subject to the old familiar misgivings about strangers, storms, the dark, and death, as "The Fear," "Storm Fear," and "Spoils of the Dead" reveal; his general moodiness and the occasional desire for escape persisted, too, as we can see from "Tree at My Window" (written later) and "Into My Own."[10] Toward the end of the period, "The Trial by Existence" was finally completed, and was accepted by *The Independent*; the poem shows both how incomprehensibly difficult Frost sometimes found life to be and how determined he was to face it courageously.

For the most part, though, the Derry years were highly rewarding and pleasant for Frost. His financial situation improved considerably when his grandfather died and surprised Robert by leaving him a very generous bequest, including the farm and a sizable annuity—enough at least for him and his family to subsist on. This was especially welcome since Frost fell out soon with Carl Burrell—Frost evidently had felt slighted by what he considered the condescending "conspiracy" that his grandfather and Burrell had entered into to run the farm. As a result, Frost had to try to run the farm himself when Burrell left. Frost was not really much of a farmer, as he later admitted, for he was disorganized and had little understanding of farm animals, and was thus not very successful at managing the place.

Perhaps the happiest aspect of the Derry period was the Frosts' family life. Three more children were born: a son, Carol, in 1902; a second daughter, Irma, in 1903; and a third girl, Marjorie, in 1905. As the children grew, Frost enjoyed playing with them and teaching them poems and religious stories, and led them, too, to enjoy the flowers, trees, and brooks around them. And at the same time, the relationship between Robert and Elinor was at its best: many of the poems of or about this period are love poems for Elinor, such as "A Prayer in Spring," "A Dream Pang," and "The Pasture."

In 1906, Robert Frost decided to stop trying to be a farmer and obtained a part-time teaching job at nearby Pinkerton Academy, a small private boys' school. One event that helped him obtain the job was the reading of "The Tuft of Flowers" before a meeting of the Men's League of the Congregational Church in Derry. Lacking self-confidence, Frost was much too nervous to read it himself, so the pastor obliged; the poem pleased the audience, and Frost was highly gratified.

Robert Frost's teaching at Pinkerton (and later, too) was unconventional. He was informal, even casual, in class, but he demanded originality and thoughtful effort from his students. As one would expect of someone with his active and searching mind, he intended them to develop ideas of their own, ideas that meant something, rather than to perform meaningless rote tasks. He worked hard, especially in coaching debaters, organizing and directing plays that he had personally condensed from Shakespeare, and reorganizing the English curriculum. This last achievement led to his speaking at a teachers' convention—a feat he would hardly have been capable of a few years earlier. His health sometimes suffered, as usual. He had a serious case of pneumonia in 1907, and began to suffer severely from hay fever in late summer—so much so that the family started going up to Bethlehem and, later, Franconia, in the White Mountains, each August. One summer they traveled as far as Lake Willoughby in the "Northeast Kingdom" of Vermont. These summer vacations bore fruit. In Franconia, Frost learned of the people and the story that figure in "The Fear," while Lake Willoughby provided the locale and the speaker of "A Servant to Servants," one of Frost's most moving dramatic monologues. In both cases, characteristically, it was the isolation and vulnerability of the people that he felt most keenly.

For several years while Frost was teaching at Pinkerton, the family lived at the farm. They finally decided, over Elinor's objections, to move to a rented apartment in Derry Village. She liked the solitude in the countryside, despite the unhappy memory of their fourth girl, Elinor Bettina, who was born in 1907 but lived for only a few days.

Frost was now gaining self-confidence as a teacher and a poet. His colleagues respected him, and he managed to keep writing despite his other work, allowing a few poems—"A Late Walk," for example—to be printed in the school literary journal, though none appeared elsewhere. When a new young principal, Ernest Silver, was appointed, Frost found him congenial and appreciative. They became good friends in the two years of Silver's stay, and when he moved to Plymouth, New Hampshire, to be principal of the State Normal School there, he asked Frost to join him as a teacher. Reluctantly, though the move represented a step up, Frost agreed. There he continued his casual style of teaching, pleasing students also with the "country" dress, manner, and style of speech he had grown into; perhaps he was developing an identity to reinforce his self-confidence. He made friends with Sidney Cox, later the author of reminiscences of the poet in *A Swinger of Birches*. At the same time Frost began to feel cooler toward Silver, mainly because he had seemed to criticize Elinor's casual housekeeping in the Frost house where Silver had rooms. As usual, Frost was defensive about whatever shared his identity.

During the year at Plymouth, Frost developed a significant aspect of his poetry, the emphasis on "voice," particularly on natural speech as the poetic medium. He became interested in William Butler Yeats and the plays of his Abbey Theater in Ireland, where Irish mores and idiom were featured. This development, added to other incentives toward independent, original, creative work, helped lay the groundwork for his coming full-time commitment to poetry. He had continued to correspond with Susan Ward, the literary editor of *The Independent*, even sending her poems occasionally, for she was an understanding audience. Her brother, the general editor, the Reverend William Ward, was evidently not. Frost once described to him in glowing terms the views expressed in Henri Bergson's *Creative Evolution*. The impulse in the life force—especially when abetted by the creative mind—is to resist the normal flow of matter down toward nothingness and to push upward toward the source. Ward, however, considered Bergson's books atheistic; in dismay, Frost found support for a more flexible, broader religious perspective in William James's *Pragmatism*. Eventually he sent to Susan Ward his great ironic sonnet "Design," aimed at her brother's narrowly literal conception of divine providence.[11]

The intensity as well as the means of Frost's reaction offers evidence of his growing intellectual and poetic initiative at this time. He

First Flowering
of Frost's Poetic Career
(1921–1930)

In the eighteen years between 1912 and 1930, Frost seriously began his career as a poet and developed into one of America's most popular and highly regarded writers, the winner of two Pulitzer Prizes. He published his first six major volumes, including his *Collected Poems* of 1930. He developed his most famous poetic personality, that of the rural New England farmer-sage, and then went beyond it to approach the role of the opinionated "bard." At the same time, he pursued his career as a college teacher and a lecturer. He made many literary friends, some of whom profoundly influenced his growth as a person and a poet—Ezra Pound, Lascelles Abercrombie, Edward Thomas, Amy Lowell, and Louis Untermeyer, for example. And as his children matured, his relations with them and with his wife became more problematic. The complexities and difficulties of his personality became increasingly evident in his personal life.

The Frosts sailed to England in late summer of 1912 to begin the poet's quest for fulfillment and recognition. They managed to find a small house in Beaconsfield, Buckinghamshire, about halfway between London and Oxford. Typically, Frost noted the local flora—laurel and dogwood; he also expressed his pleasure in the poetic associations of the vicinity, "within a mile or two of where Milton finished *Paradise Lost* on the one hand and a mile or two of where Grey lies buried."[1] Perhaps Frost felt he belonged, or at least wanted to belong there, too.

Frost was ready to publish. Within a month or so he had assembled thirty-odd poems into a manuscript to submit to the firm of David Nutt and Company in London, to which an acquaintance directed him. The manager of the firm, Mrs. Alfred Nutt, quickly accepted the Frost poems for publication and his career thus began in earnest. He wrote to friends in America about the achievement with justifiable pride.[2]

Before the volume, *A Boy's Will* (1913), appeared in print, Frost began to prepare the ground for its favorable reception by readers and critics. This became a regular part of his process of developing a poetic career: before each volume appeared, Frost prepared for its acceptance as well as he could—by alerting reviewers and urging friends to publicize the volume, for example. The procedure reflects his personality very clearly; although he believed his poetry was good, indeed original in its style and voice (see Chapter 10), his sensitivity to others' opinions made him afraid that his work would be rejected. It is important to note how similar this attitude in a human sphere was to his worry that his work might not be acceptable to God. In England, he made friends with the poets Harold Monro and F. S. Flint, and through the latter came to know Ezra Pound and eventually to meet William Butler Yeats. Pound, eleven years Frost's junior, was already widely respected, and it was greatly to Frost's advantage that Pound wrote a very favorable review of *A Boy's Will* for the American *Poetry* magazine published by Harriet Monroe. Pound also loaned a copy of the book to Yeats, who liked it so much he had Pound bring Frost to one of Yeats's evening "salons." Frost had admired Yeats's plays and poetry since the years at Pinkerton Academy, and hoped not merely that the Irish poet could help advance his career but that the two could become friends. Neither, unfortunately, was the case—Frost was unable to establish any lasting contact with Yeats.

A Boy's Will was a selection of some of Frost's first poems, such as "My Butterfly," written in 1894, as well as his latest. He arranged them to represent a personal psychological progression "out of self-love and into his love for others":[3] Part I began with the theme of withdrawal from the world and ended on a note of one kind of return to it; Part II represented some principal areas of experience the poet wished to be concerned with; and Part III represented the resignation and acceptance necessary in a mature person's confrontation of life. This progression is reinforced by a seasonal movement from autumn through winter to spring in Part I and, finally, through summer back to autumn again by the end of Part III. At the same time, there is a dramatic progression in the voice tones and the moods of the persona, moving from the defiant and impulsive adolescence of "Into My Own" to the slightly melancholic maturity of "Reluctance."[4] This progression foreshadows the combination of the lyric and the dramatic that became characteristic of Frost's work. Further to emphasize the progression in the volume, Frost added glosses to the titles of the poems in the table of contents.[5]

A Boy's Will is one of Frost's most personal selections of lyrics. He said that it reflected his own growth; it seems to represent his psychological development from the destructive escapism of the Dismal Swamp episode to the more confident and responsible maturity of the Pinkerton years. The themes and moods are dramatized and distanced by the progressive structure and the glosses because of Frost's personal emotional reticence, but many of the poems have endeared him to successive generations of readers, such as "Into My Own," "Storm Fear," "Mowing," "Revelation," and "Reluctance."

The book was generally well received despite some preliminary adverse or perfunctory notices: In addition to Pound's praise in *Poetry*, Frost received serious approbation from his friend F. S. Flint in *Poetry and Drama*, and from others as well. Frost clearly made a mark with this, his first volume of poetry, and was pleased indeed with the public acceptance.[6]

The friendship between Frost and Pound did not remain warm even though Pound continued to help publicize Frost. Frost had objected to Pound's repeating some personal stories Frost had told when they first met, especially since they were not completely accurate. Throughout his life, Frost tended to slant his accounts of past events for personal advantage or dramatic flavor, or both. This was evidently one way he reinforced his shaky self-confidence—even if he did not improve his image directly by his imaginative revisions of the past, he would profit psychologically by the dramatic flavor he infused into it. The main hindrance to the friendship between Frost and Pound, however, was the clash of their personalities, for both were self-centered and independent. Although they met occasionally thereafter, and Pound reviewed Frost's next volume, *North of Boston* (1914), favorably, they never were friends.

While waiting for *North of Boston* to appear, Frost began preparing for its reception as usual, by circulating the poems among friends and acquaintances. These included Monro, Flint, and Pound, and also several literary figures he had met recently: W. W. Gibson, Lascelles Abercrombie (the leader of the "Georgian" poets, a group of well-known English pastoral poets), Ralph Hodgson, Edward Thomas (the Welshman who became Frost's closest friend), T. E. Hulme (with whom Frost shared an interest in Bergson), and the new poet laureate, Robert Bridges.

Like *A Boy's Will*, *North of Boston* consisted of both old and new poems. Several—"The Death of the Hired Man," for example—had been written at Derry, while others were composed after *A Boy's Will* was accepted by Mrs. Nutt. Even though many poems in *North of Boston* were contemporaneous with those in *A Boy's Will,* the later book embodies a mature perspective on northern New England people and their existence that contrasts sharply with the adolescent at-

titudes traced in the earlier volume. There, the poems reveal that
Frost was feeling his way toward a conception of himself as a poet.
In *North of Boston* we see that he has found his subject—New England
and its people—and has developed the plain-spoken, rural persona
that became his public image for so long. The tone is neither naively
optimistic nor pessimistic and despairing. Frost here acknowledged
the bleak social and economic conditions of the region. He sym-
pathized with the people who endured them stoically and with wry
humor, while at the same time he objected to the rigid and stultify-
ing life patterns they accepted.[7] Poems like "A Servant to Servants,"
"Home Burial," and "The Wood-Pile" clearly demonstrate the dual
response manifested in the book as a whole. A major achievement of
the book is the representation of rounded characters in complex and
problematic situations. To accomplish this Frost had drawn on and
developed his interest in making his poetry sound like talk rather
than sheer music. At about the time *A Boy's Will* was accepted for
publication, Frost was formulating his conception (though it was not
really original) of the "sound of sense," the prosodic and stylistic
principle fundamental to his work from the first. The principle in-
volved embodying or at least suggesting the basic meaning expressed
by a speaker or persona in the intonations and sentence rhythms of
the language riding on and cutting across the formal meter.[8] In
1914, a new friend, Lascelles Abercrombie, made clear the impor-
tance of Frost's prosodic accomplishment in *North of Boston* when he
reviewed the volume for *The Nation*.

Abercrombie also pointed out that Frost's use of simple and
common people and events, especially in a rural setting, made him
seem to many readers a strictly regional and a nature poet. This is
true only in a superficial sense, for the symbolic implications of the
North of Boston poems are very wide, even though the scope of the
subject matter was more restricted here than in later books. On the
whole, *North of Boston* was very well received indeed by critics, some
of them friends, others equally influential strangers like Ford Madox
Hueffer and, later, Edward Garnett.[9]

Before *North of Boston* appeared, Frost and his family moved, in
April 1914, from Beaconsfield to the town of Dymock in Gloucester-
shire, near the houses of his friends W. W. Gibson and Lascelles
Abercrombie. The Frosts first rented a small house, then shared the
Abercrombies' rambling combination of houses. This time in
Gloucestershire became memorable for the good literary and per-
sonal fellowship in the group that included as long-term visitors
Rupert Brooke, Edward Thomas, and the tramp-poet W. H. Davies.
Despite Frost's occasional jealousy of the other, established, poets, he

found their company congenial and supportive, as did Elinor. Edward Thomas and Frost became particularly close friends. Frost evidently saw a good deal of himself in Thomas, became very attached to him, and helped him combat his profound and persistent melancholia partly by urging him—quite successfully—to develop his poetic powers. Thomas, like Rupert Brooke, was killed three years later in World War I, which broke out in the fall of the year. Frost felt, and continued to feel, that he had lost his closest friend.[10] The depth and intensity of Frost's affection are indicated later by poems about or addressed to Thomas, such as "Iris by Night," and "To E.T." Normally reticent about his emotions, he there expressed his feelings even more directly than in the poems about his mother.

When the war broke out Frost realized that his career in England would be severely curtailed and, since he had already been more or less surreptitiously trying to arrange for American publication of his work, he decided to return to the United States—especially since the whole Frost family had been feeling very homesick for many months. Mrs. Nutt arranged for Henry Holt and Company to publish an American edition of *North of Boston*. With that indication of prospective success at home, the Frosts left for America in February 1915.

Upon arriving in New York, Frost sent his wife and children up to Bethlehem, New Hampshire, to stay with their friends from the Derry years, the Lynches. He himself stayed in the city briefly, paying visits to Henry Holt and Company and otherwise furthering his career in America. Then, after a quick trip down to see his sister Jeanie, teaching in New Jersey, he left for Lawrence and Boston, where he spent most of his time again on his career. He looked up Ellery Sedgwick, the editor of the *Atlantic Monthly*, who evidently preferred to forget his earlier rejection of Frost's poems. He introduced Frost to several well-known Boston literary and intellectual figures, including the poetry editor of the *Evening Transcript*, William S. Braithwaite. All of them were eager to meet the new poet whose work was attracting so much attention. Frost was "summoned" to a dinner by Amy Lowell, the poetess and sister of the President of Harvard College, when he called to thank her for her review of *North of Boston*. She helped Frost to understand the current conflict between the "older" and the "new" poetry in America. Although Frost was flattered by her attention, and extremely pleased by the general interest in his poetry and himself, he felt that he and his work should stay outside the conflict, for he was no novel "Imagist" à la Pound, although, at the same time, his unusual "common" subjects and intense conversational style were unconventional. Stubbornly, he

stuck to his individuality, believing in his own perceptions and refus-
ing to risk losing the identity through which he was building his
self-confidence.[11]

Much literary and critical activity stemmed from these brief con-
tacts Frost made in New York and Boston at this time. Most im-
mediately, they led to public readings and talks about his poetry
which enabled him to earn money for his family and later his chil-
dren's families, and at the same time provided a stage where he
could shape his public image of the kindly, humorous farmer-phi-
losopher.

After going up to spend a few months with his wife and children
in New Hampshire, and buying a farm almost out from under a
farmer in Franconia, Frost returned to Boston. Thanks to friends he
had recently made, he had been invited to speak at a meeting of the
Boston Authors' Club, and to read at the annual meeting of the
Tufts chapter of Phi Beta Kappa, both on the same day in May 1915.
Despite his nervousness both events went well enough. It was a long
time before he was really confident on such occasions, but his per-
formance as a public speaker was developing satisfactorily. He had
spoken very nervously indeed as valedictorian at Lawrence High
School, and later at Derry he had been too nervous to read one of
his poems in public at all. Not much later, however, he spoke suc-
cessfully at a teachers' convention; perhaps he was most insecure
when exposing himself to the public in his own poetry. Not until
much later did he develop fully enough self-assurance to feel at
home on the podium, though he always enjoyed the attention.

At the same time, Frost continued to develop his literary friend-
ships. He cooperated with Braithwaite on an article for the *Evening
Transcript*, renewed his acquaintance with Sedgwick of the *Atlantic
Monthly*, and, most important, met Louis Untermeyer, the leftist New
York poet and critic, thus beginning a lifelong friendship. Frost also
met Edwin Arlington Robinson, though Frost's sense of rivalry with
the already established poet never allowed a friendship to develop
between them. Untermeyer was almost the only poet of Frost's own
generation with whom he developed a close relationship. The lack of
self-confidence engendered by the years of uncertainty about his
career, poetic and otherwise, no doubt lay behind his jealousy. Yet at
the same time, Frost was often very generous with help and advice to
younger poets, such as students in the colleges where he taught.

Back in Franconia, in the summer of 1915, Frost took up his av-
ocation of farming again while his literary position continued to de-
velop. He encouraged Untermeyer to attack those whom he himself
considered literary "enemies";[12] he was unhappy with Untermeyer
and Braithwaite for praising Edgar Lee Masters and other contem-

poraries. These were somewhat less attractive reflections of Frost's insecurity and his determination to achieve recognition. An important article by the British critic Edward Garnett appeared, in which the author again raised the then vexed question why an American poet had to be discovered in England. Other issues raised early in Frost's career were whether he had any humor and whether his work was not really prose in verse form. These annoyed Frost and of course seem rather improbable now. He left Franconia for a time to give readings and talks in Boston, Lawrence, New York, at Dartmouth and Amherst, and elsewhere; some of these went well, some poorly. When he returned home he was ill for a week—a pattern that unfortunately became common in the course of his life. What with the illness, and the pressure of reading commitments as well as that of preparing for a new volume of poems, *Mountain Interval*, Frost became depressed even to the point of worrying whether the poetry in him had died.[13] His morale and his poetic stature were both considerably improved, however, by a very successful reading at Harvard as the Phi Beta Kappa poet, and shortly after that he received an invitation from Amherst College to join their faculty for at least one term starting in February 1917.

Frost accepted the position at Amherst for several reasons. He liked to teach and considered this his vocation aside from poetry—toward the end of his stay in England he has written to a friend that he dreamed of teaching writing in a small college. He also appreciated an assured income, small though it was. And he hoped he would have time on the side to write. Thus began Frost's long teaching association with colleges and universities, and with Amherst in particular, where the new president, Alexander Meiklejohn, seemed to be fostering a humanistic spirit in contrast to the general educational thrust toward science.

Just before Frost began at Amherst, his third volume of poetry, *Mountain Interval* (1916), was published. The "Interval" (or more conventionally, "intervale") in the title means lower land between hills, usually with some kind of stream. Frost said he was using the word for its double meaning— to recall to Elinor, as the dedication indicates, both the physical location and probably the special quality of their life on their various farms in New Hampshire.[14] The volume had particular significance for Elinor, as well as for Robert, with good reason. Twenty-four of the thirty-two poems were written or at least begun on one of the Frosts' farms—eleven came from Derry, thirteen from Bethlehem and Franconia.[15] Almost all, in any case, derive their subject matter and atmosphere from the Frosts' mountain interval farms. One Derry poem, "In the Home Stretch," is the dialogue of a couple moving into an isolated farm. They must derive directly from Robert and Elinor's experience. The dominant genre also is appropriate for this volume. About three quarters of the poems are lyric rather than narrative or dramatic, so that we seem to be hearing the voice of a farm-dweller himself. This is the persona of *North of Boston*, certainly, but at the same time it is almost impossible to avoid believing it is Frost's own voice for the most part. The tenderness and sensitivity of poems like "An Old Man's Winter Night," "The Oven Bird," "Birches," and "The Hill Wife" manifest the warmer side of Frost most clearly—although the tougher side is evident, too, in " 'Out, Out—' " and "The Vanishing Red."

Frost's first years at Amherst confirmed the pattern set during his earlier teaching experiences and developed it further. During the near-decade 1917 to 1926, he moved from Amherst to the University of Michigan twice, drawn by each institution in turn, yet impatient with various conditions in each, as well as with the constraints of college teaching in general. Finally, in 1926, Frost was to settle at Amherst for a twelve-year stretch. That college became his academic home despite other brief associations with Michigan and, later, Harvard and Dartmouth.

At Amherst as at Michigan, Frost's class procedures were informal, not to say loose. He would lounge in his chair and speak about almost anything that crossed his mind in connection with the general topic of the course. When his students read their papers, he would treat them gently, becoming impatient only when the writing was pretentious or empty. His courses were neither demanding nor "tough," and students often considered them "gut" courses. He made himself easily available to students, encouraging them to stay after class or drop in at the Frost house to talk—or rather listen. Often certain students became especially devoted and received particular attention, sometimes remaining friends whom Frost saw at various times in later years. He almost always responded warmly to students, at the same time thoroughly enjoying their admiration. He taught courses in literature, writing, and after the United States entered the war, a seminar called simply "War Issues"; he was perhaps a particularly good person to teach such a course, for he admitted "liking the fight,"[16] even though the death of Edward Thomas at the front in 1917 saddened him very greatly.

At Amherst Frost soon became impatient and even disgusted with the regime. He found President Meiklejohn's liberal and experimental "Amherst Idea" too radical, he had moral objections to other features of Amherst life—such as the reputed homosexuality of some teachers—and he was anti-intellectual enough to mistrust academic experience in general. Despite Meiklejohn's attempts to make the poet's tenure agreeable (including awarding him his first honorary degree), Frost resigned in January 1920, and went to Franconia, where the family spent the year.

This year began very badly: Robert's sister Jeanie was arrested for breach of the peace, and eventually had to be committed to a state hospital in Maine, for she had become increasingly subject to dementia praecox. She was to die in the hospital nine years later. Frost was evidently torn between feeling sorry for Jeanie, in whom he could see some of his own troubles, and divorcing himself emotionally from her plight for his own self-protection. As often happened, his sympathy conflicted with his need to protect his vulnerable ego.

Most of this Franconia year was pleasant and rewarding, however. The family played at farming and otherwise enjoyed life together in the mountains, despite growing internal tensions caused by Lesley's resistance to her father's dominance, and Carol's attempts to retreat from it. A young poet friend, Raymond Holden, spent a good deal of time with them. In the fall of the year, the Frosts were able to move to Vermont, thanks to Holden's buying their farm (at a considerable profit for Frost) in order to be near a literary group including Dorothy Canfield Fisher and other friends. The year was fruitful in terms of Frost's writing. At Amherst he had had little time or inclination to write, with the notable, and sad, exception of certain poems related to Edward Thomas and his death (for example, "Not to Weep," 1917; "To E.T.," 1919). In contrast, Franconia offered much material for his poetry then and later. A story about one local woman went into "The Pauper Witch of Grafton," maple sugaring provided the basis for "Evening in a Sugar Orchard," and perhaps partly from a recurring argument between Robert and Elinor about the existence of God came "Good-by and Keep Cold."[17] The two of them often disputed the question of God's existence; Robert was fundamentally religious, while Elinor professed to be atheistic, and sometimes accused her husband of cowardice for not acknowledging the validity of her views.

The Frosts' new house was in South Shaftsbury, Vermont, near Bennington. Nearby, Dorothy Canfield Fisher and her neighbor Sarah Cleghorn had helped organize the Poetry Society of Southern Vermont, which contributed to a congenial environment for Frost. The Stone Cottage, as the new farm was to be called, became the family home and refuge for many years. The move exhausted Frost, however, and added to his burden of financial uncertainty. Still, his writing seemed to be going well—especially pleasing was his newly developed talent for epigrammatic compression, as in "Fire and Ice" and "Dust of Snow."[18] And there were other encouraging signs as to his career: *Harper's* had requested and printed groups of poems on two occasions, and a thoughtful and favorable study of Frost's work by George R. Elliott, a teacher at Bowdoin College, had appeared recently. At about the same time, a shake-up in the editorial staff of Frost's publisher resulted in his being awarded a regular stipend of $100 a month as "consulting editor" for remaining with Holt. Frost believed the family could manage financially with this added to the annuity from his grandfather and the income from lectures and books, though *Mountain Interval* had not proven popular. The year 1921 was filled with readings and lectures in many different places, most notably at the summer Bread Loaf School of English, founded by Middlebury College, in northern Vermont. During his performance there. Frost suggested the establishment of a writer's conference at Bread Loaf; some five years later this occurred, and Frost became closely affiliated with it.

At intervals, Frost returned to relax in Vermont, "farming" at the Stone Cottage, but clearly this kind of existence could not continue indefinitely, especially since the University of Michigan had invited Frost to be "poet-in-residence" for the coming year for $5,000. The prospect of a "year-long picnic" and a relatively sizable salary was too attractive.[19]

Frost spent two years at Ann Arbor, busy ones. He became very popular at the university, but eventually found the experience frustrating. He had no formal duties but acted as advisor to the student literary magazine, socialized, and in particular helped organize and run a series of lectures by writers each year—all this supplemented by his own lecture tours.

Writers of the first series were Padraic Colum, Carl Sandburg, Amy Lowell, Louis Untermeyer, and Vachel Lindsay. The lectures were extremely popular, and Frost enjoyed both his work behind the scenes and his meetings with the writers, with the exception of Carl Sandburg, whose Whitmanesque, folk-poet image he found affected. Amy Lowell and Frost had a humorous time on the platform together, however, and he could hardly avoid being pleased by Untermeyer's lecture, for it was largely devoted to praise of Frost himself.[20]

Family problems beset the Frosts again in the course of the first year. Lesley developed a dislike for her teachers and the university (thanks partly to her father's criticism of academia, perhaps). Irma was miserable, Marjorie was lonesome back in school in Vermont, and Carol became so unhappy that after one quarrel with his father he simply left without notice to hitchhike back to the Stone Cottage, where he remained. Lesley and Irma soon followed. It was becoming increasingly clear that Frost was a difficult father; as his children grew, they evidently felt the strain of his intense and stubborn personality. He evidently loved them very much but tried to dominate them, and they responded often with defiance—especially Lesley—or by simply retreating into their own selves and ways—Carol's characteristic behavior. No doubt the simple fact of Frost's growing fame caused some of the difficulty, for it put them in shadow to some extent. Things were better between them all in the summer of 1922, when they (except for Irma and her mother) hiked along much of the "Long Trail" in Vermont—though Frost was rather chagrined to find that his children could outwalk him. They could hardly outtalk him, however, as his lecture tours made clear. Particularly satisfying, though so exhausting that he fell ill at the end, was a southern trip of ten lectures in fourteen days, including an almost triumphal experience in Dallas, Texas. Frost was becoming increasingly well known and liked by the public for his humor and his combination of strength and gentleness.

At the same time, there were indications of Frost's continued problematic social relations besides his family troubles. He was offended —rather naturally—by Amy Lowell's satirical portrait of him in *A Critical Fable*. He was taken to task by Joseph Warren Beach (not yet a famous scholar) for Frost's stories about pushing Beach into marriage. And Frost quarreled sharply with a columnist for repeating some remarks he had made, purportedly in confidence, about T. S. Eliot's *The Waste Land* and James Joyce's *Ulysses*, which had recently been causing a literary stir.

Frost's efforts on behalf of students and the college community in general at Ann Arbor were greatly valued, on the other hand, even though the second series of writers' lectures was less successful and he was unable—partly because of recurrent bouts with the flu—to participate as much in college life as before. He did not want to stay there longer, however, and readily accepted an invitation from Amherst to rejoin their faculty. The trustees had dismissed President Meiklejohn, several objectionable faculty members had resigned, and Frost was again attracted to the college.

Frost had misgivings about going to Amherst because he still felt he had too little time for writing at college, even when he had no formal duties. During the time at Michigan, nevertheless, he had managed to create and assemble enough material for a new volume, entitled *New Hampshire* (1923) after the long Horatian poem that formed its core. This volume consisted of the title poem followed by two other parts called in the book's subtitle "Notes" and "Grace Notes." "New Hampshire" discussed in mock serious tones the peculiar qualities of the state—especially its purported lack of commercialism and the individuality of its people. The poems from "A Star in a Stoneboat" to "I Will Sing You One-O," called "Notes," illustrate one or another feature of New Hampshire life in more detail;

mock-serious footnote references to these poems appeared at various points in the title poem. The "Grace Notes" consist of short lyrics supposedly added to the volume just for decoration. The volume was also enhanced by woodcuts by J. J. Lankes, whose work Frost had seen recently in the form of illustrations Lankes had made for poems he had liked in *Mountain Interval*.

In *New Hampshire* we can see a shift taking place in Frost's general method which amounted to a more explicit, even discursive concern with broad issues. In this volume there are fewer dramatic and—in John Lynen's sense—"pastoral" poems than before, and more explicitly philosophical poems. That is, Frost was coming to address larger issues more directly than he had earlier when he typically used dramatic techniques—as in dialogues like "The Death of the Hired Man"—to embody "country" life that represented more general issues implicitly. In "Hired Man," Frost's general concern with human sympathy and understanding (among other themes) is embodied objectively in the playlet involving Warren and Mary. Beginning with *New Hampshire*, Frost was increasingly inclined to identify the issues and talk about them explicitly; when dialogues occur, they are between voices representing philosophic or social positions rather than between characters. This change in Frost's poetic focus and method was allied to a partial change in his persona, from a New England farmer to a poet whose vision is broader than other men's, a change that had been developing for many years.[21] The quality of Frost's work was just as great. Indeed this volume contained not only "New Hampshire," one of his very best long poems, but also some of his greatest shorter ones: "The Grindstone," "Fire and Ice," "Nothing Gold Can Stay," "The Need of Being Versed in Country Things," and best of all, "Stopping by Woods on a Snowy Evening." The book was very well received by the public and the critics. It was awarded the Pulitzer Prize as the best volume of poetry published during the year.

Back at Amherst, Frost first taught a course in literature of his own devising and one in philosophy on "judgments in History, Literature, and Religion." Family life was not uneventful: Carol married Lillian LaBatt, to whom he had been engaged since the Long Trail hike. Frost continued his lectures and readings and received additional honorary degrees, from Middlebury and Yale. One lecture trip led to a new offer from Michigan of a permanent appointment as poet in residence; Frost could not resist, even though his position at Amherst was also supposedly permanent.

The last year at Amherst (for the time) also marked the unfortunate end to the long friendship between Frost and Amy Lowell. She was unable to attend his "fiftieth" (actually his fifty-first)[22] birthday party, so Frost refused to attend the dinner in honor of her recent and popular book on John Keats. He had never thought much of her poetry, and this was one way to express his feelings. Unfortunately, Miss Lowell was almost chronically ill, and was made worse by the dinner; she died only a few weeks later. Frost was of course shocked and contrite and paid tribute to her at Amherst and in an article for a newspaper.[23] The episode reflects the kind of conflict that sometimes arose in Frost. His innate insecurity and his desire for recognition and independence led him impulsively to deny his essential human warmth and sense of fairness. The results were sometimes perversely satisfying but often embarrassed him and made him feel guilty.

At the end of the academic year, Frost was to receive yet another honorary degree, from Bowdoin, but at the last minute had to refuse. Elinor had a miscarriage and was very ill. She recovered slowly and they left for Michigan despite her weakness and their joint worries over other difficulties in the family. Indeed, during the one year at Ann Arbor, both Carol and Marjorie were seriously ill, while Mrs. Frost continued to be worried and tired. Frost enjoyed some aspects of the life at Michigan—he found his added poetic eminence pleasing, and met young people he liked, one of whom, John Cone, quickly became engaged to Irma. But the poet and the rest of his family were homesick for New England, and when President Olds of Amherst made a new and attractive offer of a part-time position, Frost accepted happily.

The new position was especially pleasant because it paid well yet allowed him most of the year to work on his own poetry. On this basis, Frost remained at Amherst for the next twelve years, until 1938. Not only was the arrangement convenient, but he had come to feel affection for and loyalty to the college. He had many friends among the faculty, and enjoyed working with the students. He felt at home in that part of the country and particularly in the town of Amherst.

The year Frost made this move (1926) was also eventful in terms of his family life, not always fortunately. During the fall and winter, almost all the Frosts were quite ill at one time or another, sometimes for long periods, Marjorie especially. More pleasantly, Irma and John Cone were married. Most significant in terms of Frost's career were the founding of the Bread Loaf Writers' Conference, in which he was instrumental, and particularly certain developments intended to lead toward biographical studies of the poet. There were at one time three different people working in this direction. Two of these, for further complication, had the same name: Wilfred Davison, the director of the School of English at Bread Loaf, and Edward Davison, a young English poet. Rather confusingly, Frost alternately encouraged and discouraged both of these (both eventually dropped their projects), while enlisting and helping Gorham B. Munson to write a booklet entitled *Robert Frost: A Study in Sensibility and Good Sense* (1927). An article by Munson, "The Classicism of Robert Frost," had pleased Frost for the image of the classic poet it projected, but the new book—and a subsequent article by Munson—annoyed Frost by characterizing him as a thorough "humanist," anti-Romantic, and almost anti-Christian.

In 1928, the persistent illness of Marjorie Frost led her parents to take her to Europe, in hope of a change. The experiment was not very successful, but it did lead to interesting events for Frost himself. In England they revisited some familiar places and a number of old friends such as Edward Thomas's widow and Lascelles Abercrombie. They also made the acquaintance of several eminent literary figures, including T.S. Eliot and Robert Bridges, experiences that should have been pleasing and rewarding to Frost. Unfortunately, neither kind of experience proved satisfactory. Most of the old friends seemed to have changed, and the literary notables seemed uninterested in Frost or his poetry. Otherwise the general reception accorded Frost in England, once his presence became widely known in literary circles, was flattering, but the pace of the activities exhausted him and his wife, and they were glad to return home.

Frost's latest volume, *West-Running Brook* (1928), had just appeared (again with woodcuts by Lankes) and showed Frost still at the height of his powers. Here "the philosophic tendency" first evident in *New Hampshire* had become dominant: The persona of the poet with his wider vision transforms itself somewhat into that of the "bard"—the public poet— who expresses opinions on everything, especially religion and public affairs.[24] No doubt Frost was encouraged to express himself thus by public acceptance and his own successful performance. Increasingly he was to voice his wide-ranging and penetrating—though sometimes quirky—thinking. This persona of the bard became more and more evident in the rest of Frost's work, and is most fully realized in the last volume of his poetry in 1962. The poems in the present volume were grouped in six sections as follows: I, Spring Pools, with the epigraph, "From snow that melted only yesterday"(the first eleven poems);II, Fiat Nox, with the epigraph, "Let the night be too dark for me to see/Into the future. Let what will be, be." ("Once by the Pacific" through "Acquainted with the Night"); III, West-Running Brook (the title poem); IV, Sand Dunes (that poem through "The Flower Boat"); V, Over Back ("The Times Table" through "The Birthplace"); VI, My Native Simile, with the epigraph, "The sevenfold sophie of Minerve" (the last seven poems). The title poem evidently is intended to suggest the basic theme of the book, that of contraries, and the various sections seem to focus on variations of that theme, although the structure is not clear as that of *A Boy's Will* or *New Hampshire*. Lawrence Thompson sees a kind of progression through the book, up to a realization in Part VI that "the poet had begun to approach the sevenfold wisdom of Minerva only after he had suffered through a jarring and disillusioning experience; that this experience . . . had given freshness and originality to all the subsequent poetic comparisons he made, all the implied or stated analogies between seemingly dissimilar things."[25] This thematic structure aside (the section headings were eventually dropped), the book included several of Frost's finest and most interesting poems: "Spring Pools," "Acceptance," "Once by the Pacific," "Bereft," "Acquainted with the Night," "The Lovely Shall Be Choosers," and of course "West-Running Brook" itself. It is worth noting, too, that Frost negotiated an especially advantageous contract with Holt for this book and subsequent work; he enjoyed being a shrewd businessman.

While the Frosts were in Europe their eldest daughter, Lesley, married a young man in Pittsfield, Massachusetts, where she managed a bookstore. Even before her parents returned, however, Lesley wanted a separation. At the same time, Irma and John Cone were also on the verge of separating; their difficulties had already begun earlier in the year. These difficulties disturbed the elder Frosts, especially since they were too conservative to approve of divorce. Their own marriage had not been easy, but their love for each other held them loyally united. Moreover, they had seen and felt the stress of Louis Untermeyer's marital problems. Untermeyer had for years been involving his friends in his emotional entanglements. He married and divorced his first wife at least twice, eventually taking three other wives and—as Frost saw it—causing the suicide of his son. The marriages of Lesley and Irma also eventually ended in divorce, despite Robert's and Elinor's attempts to salvage them. Another family problem, that of Robert's sister, came to a sad end soon after Lesley's and Irma's first marital crises: Jeanie died in 1929. The strain on both the Frosts of all these experiences was considerable. Robert in particular suffered from the fact that people he loved were having profound difficulties while at the same time his idealistic conception of marriage was violated. And he was equally torn between a desire to involve himself in his children's and friends'—not to mention his sister's—difficulties, and a need to protect himself and Elinor from the stress of unhappy and insoluble problems. He did try to influence his children, but there was little to do about Louis Untermeyer or Jeanie. One of the few consolations Frost had at this time was the

Triumphs and Troubles
(1930–1963)

The last thirty-three years of Frost's life presented first a series of devastating family tragedies for the poet and his family, including the death of Elinor in 1938. The pain of these events was eventually negated by Mrs. Kathleen Morrison's care of him and by his continued growth in stature until he became the "grand old man" of American letters, reading at President John F. Kennedy's inauguration and representing the nation on goodwill missions to Russia and elsewhere. Honors came to him steadily, even increasingly —honorary degrees, medals, prizes, and positions. He published five more major collections of poetry, including some of his very best poems, and wrote his best critical prose. He lectured and taught until the end. When he died, the nation lost its "poet laureate."

The family troubles Frost suffered had been foreshadowed by the illnesses and the psychological problems already suffered by members of the Frost family. A critical period began in 1930, when Marjorie fell ill with tuberculosis and had to be taken to a sanatorium in Boulder, Colorado. At almost the same time, Carol's wife, Lillian, was found to have the same disease; she and her husband decided to move to the drier climate of southern California. Frost and his wife combined a trip to see Marjorie settled with a lecture stint in Colorado (where Frost helped establish another writers' conference), and then they went on to visit Carol and Lillian and their young son, Prescott, as well as the state of Frost's birth, which he celebrated in "A Record Stride."

To help support his children and to pay for a new house in Amherst, he undertook extensive lecture tours in the next few years which were partly responsible for a succession of illnesses, mostly flu, that periodically incapacitated Frost. He managed to fulfill his obligations—not only his readings but various honors as well: He was Phi Beta Kappa poet (reading his new poem "Build Soil") at Columbia and received his ninth honorary degree there, as well as his tenth at Williams College in Massachusetts. He attended a dinner honoring

T. S. Eliot in Boston. Again he found Eliot affected, and when Eliot consented to read one of his poems Frost topped him by pretending to compose one himself ("A Record Stride") and read it on the spot. Many years later, however, in 1947, Frost's feelings changed when Eliot dropped in on Frost and the two poets chatted cordially and unaffectedly.[1]

Periodically, the Frosts went to visit their children and Marjorie's new fiancé. Marjorie's and Lillian's health were evidently improving greatly although Frost's own continued to be bad. Marjorie was married in 1933, and almost immediately there occurred a major blow. Upon giving birth to her first child, she contracted puerperal fever and after suffering badly for weeks, she died in May 1934. Her parents were desolated – they had loved Marjorie very much indeed, admiring her courage and sharing her suffering. Exhausted, they returned to Amherst where, to make things worse, Mrs Frost suffered a severe heart attack. This at least had the effect of prompting the Frosts to follow earlier advice from their doctor to go to Florida for the worst of the winter. Thereafter, the southern stay became a regular event; later, Frost bought land and built a house in South Miami as a permanent winter refuge.

Despite these crises and tragedies, Frost's career remained active. He taught and lectured, wrote poetry, and traveled a good deal, meeting many people and becoming better and better known. In 1935 he wrote an introduction to Edwin Arlington Robinson's long narrative poem, *King Jasper*, published just after the poet's death. This prose piece had relatively little to do with Robinson's own work. Instead, Frost became involved in expressing his thoughts and feelings about a number of things that had concerned him recently – the fear that his work might not prove worthy, the need to voice griefs rather than grievances in poetry, the irresponsibility of experimental modern poetry, the need to balance seriousness and humor in writing. Later, he said the piece revealed more of himself than any other single source, and this is true both directly and indirectly.[2] The acute and searching sensitivity of Frost's mind showed itself here, as elsewhere, in his thoughts about poetry. We have now come to value his discussions of poets and poetry highly; although he was not a systematic critical theorist, he was an important one in certain respects.

Another occasion the same year, Frost's trip to the Rocky Mountain Writers' Conference, was equally revealing; there he found much to object to and be objectionable about, especially since he was not always the featured speaker. A couplet he had composed represented his views on this subject: "I only go / When I'm the show." One evening after a lecture later in Frost's tour, a hotheaded young poet took great exception to some of Frost's remarks and emptied a mug of beer over his head. Clearly Frost's attitude toward other writers, especially rival poets, was always problematic—as he himself indicated.[3]

Frost's next volume of poetry was *A Further Range* (1936), and although it came in for considerable criticism, it was chosen by the Book of the Month Club and received a Pulitzer Prize as well. This was particularly satisfying, for Frost had been especially "wiley," as he spelled it, in preparation for the book's reception and to defend it against criticism afterwards.[4] The dedication indicates the general scope and focus of the book and suggests why it was so severely attacked by leftist critics: "To E. F. for what it may mean to her that beyond the White Mountains were the Green; beyond both . . . range beyond range even into the realm of government and religion."[5] In this volume Frost emphasized more explicitly than before his social, religious, and political opinions, sometimes aphoristically, as in the "Ten Mills," elswhere in the long "political pastoral," "Build Soil."

As usual, the poems were grouped in sections: Taken Doubly ("A Lone Striker" through "A Record Stride," all of which were given subtitles pointing up their broader social or political significance), Taken Singly ("Lost in Heaven" through "Provide, Provide"), Ten Mills (originally eleven very short poems, but the contents varied in later editions), The Outlands ("The Vindictives" through "Iris by Night"), Build Soil (that poem and "To a Thinker," which was originally called "To a Thinker in Office") and Afterthought ("A Missive Missile"). This pattern seems more of an aesthetic arrangement than a developing structure, though the earlier sections do lead up to the long "Build Soil" climactically if not thematically. Almost all of the poems carry social and political implications, more or less obvious.

Frost's views seemed naively and irresponsibly reactionary to the critics of such periodicals as *The New Republic, The Nation*, and *New Masses*. Always very sensitive to attacks on his work or views, Frost often pretended in self-defense not to pay much attention to criticism, favorable or adverse; this time, fortunately, his friend Bernard DeVoto, editor of *The Saturday Review*, replied to the critics vehemently in a long article in 1938.

Before the uproar about *A Further Range* came to this point, other major activities and honors demanded Frost's attention. Particularly, he was asked to deliver an ode on the occasion of the Tercentenary Celebration of Harvard College, to be the Phi Beta Kappa poet there, and finally to serve as Charles Eliot Norton Lecturer, all in the same year, 1936. When the time came Frost delivered the six lectures to capacity crowds, speaking informally about everything from prosody to religion. The lectures were recorded stenographically;

unfortunately, all the copies have disappeared.[6] The poet hoped for a while that the lectureship would lead Harvard to offer him a permanent position, but this was in vain. He fell ill again, with shingles, and gave up—quite gratefully, since his stubborn individualism disliked turning out verse on demand—the idea of writing the poems for Harvard. He also was unable to return to Amherst in time for the fall term of 1936, to his regret, since he felt he had generally neglected his duties there.

The next year was occupied with the usual activities of writing, teaching, lecturing, and reading. A commencement address in 1937 at Oberlin revealed publicly for the first time some of his deeply felt religious beliefs. The critical attacks and rebuttals of *A Further Range* occupied his mind most of the time. The Frosts' health seemed generally good, but then, in the fall of 1937, Elinor had to have an operation for breast cancer. Her heart proved strong enough on that occasion, though she had had a number of attacks. When she and Frost went house-hunting in Florida in March 1938, however, she suffered several severe attacks and died within a day or so. For Frost, who was himself ill, the loss was almost unbearable; he felt that he had never been fair to his wife, that he had sacrificed her to his career and had nurtured his ego at her expense. His sense of guilt was intensified, moreover, by Lesley's hysterical accusations of thoughtlessness and cruelty. Yet Frost had been devoted to and dependent on Elinor despite the difficulties between them, and it took a long time for his spirits to revive. He resigned his position at Amherst and returned to the Stone Cottage to stay with Carol and his family.

Frost recovered only gradually from his depression. Friends at Harvard managed to have him elected to the Board of Overseers and tried to get him a position at the university similar to that at Amherst, though to no avail. Most important was the help of Kathleen Morrison. Mrs. Morrison had first made Frost's acquaintance when he read at Bryn Mawr while she was an undergraduate there. Since then she had married Theodore Morrison, an English instructor at Harvard, a poet, and director of the Bread Loaf Writers' Conference. These two helped care for Frost, and eventually Mrs. Morrison came to serve as a kind of business manager and part-time companion for the poet. The Morrisons persuaded Frost to read and speak at Bread Loaf that summer. He caused considerable uproar there—which blew over fairly quickly—by heckling Archibald MacLeish and offending other friends like Bernard DeVoto. Frost was still suffering from the emotional turmoil caused by Elinor's death, not to mention a recently awakened attachment to Kathleen Morrison. Shortly after he moved to Boston to be near the Morrisons, he wrote and presented to her the fine sonnet "The Silken Tent" which he first entitled "In Praise of your Poise."[7]

Frost resumed his public readings and began to think about the enlarged *Collected Poems*, to appear in 1939; as a preface, he wrote, "The Figure a Poem Makes," one of his richest and most suggestive critical essays. Also that year, he received the Gold Medal for "distinguished work in poetry" from the National Institute of Arts and Letters. He was concerned, however, about the psychological and financial difficulties of his son Carol. Irma, too, not only was emotionally disturbed, but had to have a tumor removed. These concerns, added to the strenuous lecture tours, exhausted him and left him ill periodically. In the summer of 1939 Frost was back at Bread Loaf, this time with Untermeyer. He bought a farm in Ripton, Vermont, near the Writers' Conference, on the understanding that the Morrisons would occupy the farmhouse and he the cottage behind it; this arrangement lasted for many years. That fall Frost went to Harvard as Ralph Waldo Emerson Fellow in Poetry, a two-year appointment created by Frost's friends the poets David McCord, Robert Hillyer, and others. He held a weekly "seminar" for students interested in poetry, in his usual informal manner.

Late in the year, Frost again was ill and eventually went to the hospital for an operation. Because of financial pressures, he agreed during this period to sell to a wealthy collector the unique copy of *Twilight*, made for and given to Elinor just before he went to the Dismal Swamp so long ago. This relationship with the collector Earle J. Bernheimer had begun some years earlier and was to continue for many more, though other collectors, including various libraries, became active.

After a visit to Florida, another lecture tour, and a summer in Ripton, Frost returned to Boston. There he was confronted with another family crisis, one that had been building for many years: Carol was extremely depressed. He had suffered from a form of paranoia with occasional deep depression throughout most of his life. This time neither his wife nor his father could help; particularly apprehensive about an operation Lillian was to undergo, Carol shot himself. Again, Frost felt he had failed his family. Carol and he had long had a difficult relationship. The son had tried many occupations, and had even written poetry, all with little satisfaction; he had rejected his father's influence, having resented his fame and his attempts to direct—or dominate—his children. Evidently Carol came to feel that he did not measure up to his father's expectations, and the worry about Lillian was the last straw. Frost seemed to have recognized Carol's difficulties, but too late; now he tried to reason with him and console him, but without success. No doubt Frost felt that if he had been more understanding before, things might have been different.

Still, Frost had to continue his work. He prepared two new volumes for publication the following year (1942), one of prose and one of poetry (though the former never appeared). He resumed his duties as Emerson Fellow at Harvard and accepted the invitation to spend an additional year there as "Fellow in American Civilization." He spoke at an exhibit of his work at the Library of Congress. When the United States entered World War II, however, Frost worried about the curtailment of his lectures and the possible lessened demand for his poetry books. He received some help from a small monthly stipend offered by Bernheimer, the collector, in return for future consideration in regard to manuscripts and the like, and Holt reassured him about the sale of his books.

Frost's attitude toward the war, at first unenthusiastic, changed gradually after Pearl Harbor as various friends and relatives entered the service. Lawrance Thompson, appointed Frost's "official biographer" in 1939; Willard Fraser, Marjorie's widowered husband; and Carol and Lillian's son Prescott were among those who gave Frost a sense of personal involvement. Some of Frost's colleagues, like Untermeyer, MacLeish, and Sandburg, wrote for the Office of War Information, but Frost refused to let himself be hired to produce official propaganda and remained independent as always.

A Witness Tree, a collection almost entirely of lyrics, appeared in 1942. Not so obviously aimed at public social and political issues as *A Further Range*, it nevertheless reflected his concern with the relationship between "inner and outer weather," between personal standards and public problems. The volume opened with two introductory poems, "Beech" and "Sycamore," which provided keys to the meaning of the book's title and to the focus of the poems in it. "Beech" presents a tree at a corner of the farm in Ripton, Vermont, defining the line between Frost's personal property and the outer world; "Sycamore" quotes an old New England primer to represent a tree that serves as a means of transcending material limitations and perceiving the spiritual:

> Zaccheus he
> Did climb the tree
> Our Lord to see[8]

Again, the volume is divided in sections for aesthetic reasons if not on the basis of themes or subjects. The first section is entitled One or Two and consists of the first fourteen poems; it may be unified by a concern with love in various forms, or it may—perhaps at the same time—indicate that the poems in the section focus on only one or two symbols of the contact between inner and outer dimensions.[9] The next section, Two or More, seems to consist of poems whose scope is rather broader ("The Gift Outright" through "The Lesson for Today"). The three remaining sections are Time Out (that poem through "It is Almost the Year Two Thousand"), Quantula (epigrams and other brief poems from "In a Poem" to "An Answer"), and Over Back (the last six poems). The volume sold extremely well, and was favorably reviewed as "vintage" Frost—as it deserved to be, containing as it does "The Silken Tent," "All Revelation," "Come In," "The Most of It," "The Subverted Flower," and "The Gift Outright." Frost received an unprecedented fourth Pulitzer Prize for it, thanks to Untermeyer's plea that the poet not be denied a well-deserved prize merely because he already had three.

The same year Frost received this prize, he also resumed his college teaching. The Emerson Fellowship at Harvard was now merely honorary, so Frost looked elsewhere. He was offered the Ticknor Fellowship in the Humanities, a position created for him at Dartmouth College, where he had had his first abortive undergraduate experience in 1893. He was to meet students regularly, though informally, during the autumn and early winter. He held this position for the next six years.

Among the faculty at Dartmouth, Frost found an old friend, Sidney Cox, whom he had first met in 1911 when teaching at the New Hampshire State Normal School. Cox was devoted to Frost and remained a close friend for the rest of his life. A newer friend at Dartmouth, Ray Nash, had helped to bring Frost to the college, and now collaborated with the librarian to set up the most important exhibition of Frost's work yet. Thanks to Earle Bernheimer, it included even the unique *Twilight*.

During this same period and for the next few years, however, Frost's relationships with other friends and relations deteriorated in various ways. He alienated Bernard DeVoto by recounting false stories about him—they had been estranged since the time in 1938 when Frost created an uproar at the Bread Loaf Writers' Conference—and they were not reconciled until several years later. Even more disturbing were Frost's strained relations with his close friend Louis Untermeyer over Frost's refusal to work for the Office of War Information. Frost was able to demonstrate in a long verse epistle of 1944 to his friend that he was really not suited to that kind of work and secured Untermeyer's forgiveness. More complicated were the relations with Earle Bernheimer, partly because of misunderstandings, partly because of Frost's neglect of the collector, and partly because of Bernheimer's financial problems. The two remained on fairly good terms, but eventually Bernheimer had to sell his large collection at auction in 1950, much to Frost's chagrin, for he had hoped that it could be left intact to some library.

Frost's family problems continued to beset him. His daughter Irma separated from her husband John Cone in 1944, and continued to be unstable despite the poet's persistent efforts to find living circumstances that would suit her. She was declining emotionally; finally, in 1947, she had to be institutionalized. Yet again Frost felt guilty about his offspring's difficulties; even though he tried to explain to Irma and secure her understanding, she rejected him.

Despite Frost's personal problems—sometimes, indirectly, because of them—his poetry continued to develop. Major works of the middle forties were his pair of short plays, *A Masque of Reason* (1945) and *A Masque of Mercy* (1947), and another collection of poems, *Steeple Bush* (1947). Frost's interest in drama is well known. His major achievements were the dramatic monologues and dialogues like "A Servant to Servants" and "The Death of the Hired Man," but he also wrote one-act plays like "A Way Out" (1929), and a full-length play *The Guardeen* (written c. 1941, published 1943). Most of these were in prose, but the two *"Masques"* were in loose and flowing conversational verse. Although they have been produced at times—and Frost even thought briefly of a Broadway production—they are primarily closet drama. Frost at first sometimes called *A Masque of Reason* "The Forty-Third Chapter of Job," and it concerns Job's rather comic attempts to wrest an explanation from God for the afflictions visited on him. None of God's explanations make sense to Job, however, and the conclusion is inevitably that we cannot expect God to be comprehensible in human terms. *A Masque of Mercy* is a sequel and culmination to the theme of the relations between God and man. The rather devastating conclusion to this more serious play is that man can only live and work in uncertainty, never knowing if his best is good enough; all he can do is rely on God's mercy. Both plays have disturbed readers because of their tone; the comic treatment in the *Masque of Reason* in particular seemed not to suit the subject and theme. They are nevertheless extremely important works in Frost's canon. They embody in religious terms the kind of uncertainty he had always felt about his work, manifesting his fundamental insecurity—as well as his searching and sensitive thought about man's function in the world.

Steeple Bush was not one of Frost's best-liked collections of lyrics. The reviews were generally kind, but a few were unfavorable enough to make the poet suffer what seemed a heart attack, but was actually only a reflection of emotional strain, albeit a severe one.[10] The poems in the volume focus largely on religious or scientific and technological concerns, and reflect Frost's personal preoccupations and beliefs to an even greater degree than before. Several poems, such as "The Fear of God" and "Beyond Words," offer particularly valuable insights into Frost's mind; the former expresses the point of the *Masque of Mercy* (echoing the preface he had written for E. A. Robinson's *King Jasper* at the same time), and the latter shows how intensely Frost could hate. One of the poems, "Directive," is among his very best and most profound works.

During his six years at Dartmouth, Frost enjoyed the teaching, continued his lectures and readings, and received more honorary degrees. He was incensed, however, when Ezra Pound received the Bollingen Prize for poetry in 1948, although he himself was not eligible, for he had published no poetry that year; he simply felt that a "traitor" should not be awarded such a prize.[11] That same year, President Charles Cole, a former student of Frost's, asked the poet to return to Amherst as Simpson Lecturer in Literature, a position for life with minimal duties, and he accepted gladly. Occasionally, later, he filled other temporary positions, but from 1949 on he was officially a member of the Amherst faculty.

In the same year, Holt published a second general collection of Frost's poetry, *The Complete Poems of Robert Frost*. Like the earlier *Collected Poems* (1939), it opened with "The Figure a Poem Makes," but it culminated in the two *Masques* at Frost's request. It became a best seller and received the Gold Medal of the Limited Editions Club. In 1950 he was nominated for the Nobel Prize in literature, but this honor eluded him—it was one of the few he never received. As he approached his "seventy-fifth" birthday, the United States Senate passed a resolution extending him "the felicitations of the Nation." The year held some unfortunate events, such as the auction of Bernheimer's collection (for a total of nearly $15,000), but these were overshadowed by Frost's honors and achievements.

In the next five years Frost's life followed an even tenor. Writing, occasional lectures, additional honorary degrees, and communication with friends filled most of his time. He had successful operations for skin cancer in 1951 and 1953; otherwise his health was good. Some friends of his died, but he gained others. One new friend was Andrew Wyeth, who was planning to illustrate a new edition of *North of Boston*, which unfortunately never came to pass. In 1954 Frost celebrated his eightieth birthday (Lawrance Thompson's research had revealed the truth about his age), a busy occasion, filled with honors and praise for Frost. He attended a reception at the White House (without President Eisenhower, however) and banqueted in New York and Amherst. Though Frost was almost ill from exhaustion, the event was certainly satisfying. It marked the ultimate stage in the poet's life and career. Frost was now the "grand old man" of American letters.

The last decade of Robert Frost's life was just as active as the rest of it. He not only continued to teach and lecture but developed an increased interest in public affairs founded on activities he was asked to undertake as a representative of the nation.

The first such mission was to Brazil in 1954 as an official representative of the United States at a writers' congress. His talks and readings were very popular, no doubt partly because the outward simplicity of his poetic style and the inherent "sound of sense" made the poems easier for the South Americans to appreciate. Frost also used the occasion to make a few political observations and pronouncements, as one would expect; this tendency was to grow steadily in the coming years. The poet also managed to avoid the other United States representative at the congress, William Faulkner, whom he evidently disliked; he was perhaps somewhat jealous of the novelist's eminence, and he was also too puritanical to approve of Faulkner's drinking.

Before the next mission abroad Frost received further honors at home, including some honorary degrees. By 1955, he had accumulated well over a score of hoods for these degrees, and found the collection awkward to store. His amusing—and sensible—solution was to have them cut up and made into a patchwork quilt.

In 1957 came an episode that added more to Frost's "glory" (as he called it, deprecatingly but with delight) than almost any other. He was asked to represent the nation at an exhibition of his works at the American Embassy in London. He accepted and the trip became almost a triumphal tour, though an exhausting one. He met many old and new friends and acquaintances, such as T. S. Eliot, F. S. Flint, the scholars Basil Willey, Nevil Coghill, and Maurice Bowra; the poets C. Day Lewis, Stephen Spender, and W. H. Auden; the writers Graham Greene and E. M. Forster; Adlai Stevenson; Lord Beveridge (the architect of the British welfare state); and the Prime Minister of Ireland, Eamon de Valera. He gave talks and readings, and revisited his old haunts in the Dymock area where he had come to know Lascelles Abercrombie, Edward Thomas, Rupert Brooke, and others. And he was awarded honorary degrees from Oxford, Cambridge, and the National University of Ireland. Tired though he was by the activity, he greatly appreciated his renown; from now on, it would seem, he began to take it more for granted, no longer needing to react quite so defensively to imagined slights, and indeed feeling enough confidence to apply the weight of his eminence to good purpose.

One such occasion began in 1957, though its roots went back as far as 1912. This was the freeing of Ezra Pound, who had been held in a hospital for the criminally insane since 1945. It had become clear that Pound would never be fit to stand trial for treason and thanks largely to the initiative of Archibald MacLeish, efforts had begun to have him released. Frost agreed to sign a letter jointly with T. S. Eliot and Ernest Hemingway requesting reconsideration of Pound's status. The fact that Frost's attitude toward Pound had changed is also evident in his writing and consulting with such people as his friend Sherman Adams, as well as Attorney General William Rogers and others, on Pound's behalf. The indictment against Pound was dropped and he was finally released in 1958.

When this affair was successfully concluded, Frost became further involved with Washington affairs; he was appointed Consultant in Poetry in English at the Library of Congress, succeeding Randall Jarrell. The eight-month position offered him a chance through lectures and press conferences to express opinions on many different aspects of public life and to complain, too, that as a resource he was not being used enough. The job also led, two years later, to a position devised specifically for him, that of Honorary Consultant in the Humanities at the Library of Congress, which he was to hold for three years. Again he hoped to exercise political influence and to some extent he did so, helping to foster the recognition of the importance of art in the nation.

In addition to this semipolitical activity, Frost was also involved in more strictly literary and personal affairs. He visited his friend J. J. Lankes, whose woodcuts had illustrated some of Frost's books, just before he died of cancer. He had another half-friendly encounter with his old rival, Carl Sandburg. Most important, he celebrated his eighty-fifth birthday at a banquet in New York City attended by many eminent friends and admirers, among them the well-known critic Lionel Trilling. As the principal after-dinner speaker, Trilling caused a stir that went beyond the particular occasion. Calling Frost a "terrifying" poet, he reemphasized an aspect of Frost's poetry that had almost been lost sight of behind the grandfatherly image, the fact that there is a dark or tragic side to Frost's work, as "Design," "The Lovely Shall Be Choosers," and similar poems reveal. Many people at large objected to this profanation of the myth of the kindly rural philosopher, but others were prompted to look at Frost's poetry as a whole more closely and candidly.[12] Frost was intrigued, even amused, by Trilling's comments. Not many years earlier he might have been annoyed, but he was evidently beyond that now.

In 1957, while Frost was involved with helping free Ezra Pound, he had one of his long-time ambitions fulfilled when President Eisenhower invited him to dinner at the White House. Frost had admired General Eisenhower and was delighted by the honor, but within a few years an even greater honor was accorded him. Thanks to Frost's friend Stewart Udall (soon to be Secretary of the Interior), President-Elect John F. Kennedy requested that Frost participate in the inauguration ceremony in 1961 to make clear the importance of the arts in our culture. Frost wrote the poem "Dedication" for the occasion, but was unable to read it in the glare of the winter sunlight, and presently recited "The Gift Outright." His commanding presence and appearance as well as his personal charm received wide publicity; in fact, he almost "stole the show," as Kennedy had earlier predicted he might.

That same year, Frost went abroad again, this time to Israel, Greece, and England. He was invited by the Hebrew University of Jerusalem to be the first lecturer in a new program on American Culture and Civilization. In the company of Lawrance Thompson, he toured Israel and participated in several talks with students in his usual informal style. In Athens he gave very successful public lectures, but he was suffering increasingly from homesickness as well as digestive trouble. When he reached England his heart was found to be erratic and slow and the doctor ordered him home almost immediately. Fortunately, he recovered quickly once he was back in the United States, and was soon active again. His intellect was just as acute as ever, his interests just as wide-ranging, but physically he was obviously aging–though he seemed amazingly tough and resilient.

His next important event was the "Evening with Robert Frost," a reception and reading that took place in the State Department Auditorium. It was a major triumph. Although President Kennedy was prevented from attending by a political crisis, many well-known Washington figures were there to hear Frost voice his opinions on the opposition of poetry and science and to hear him read his poems. The enthusiastic reception, including several standing ovations and personal compliments from important people, must have helped greatly to make Frost feel he was important to the nation. Not long after, he learned that he was important to Vermont, too, when that state designated him its official poet laureate.

In February of 1962, Frost almost died. At his home in South Miami, Pencil Pines, he contracted an extremely serious case of pneumonia and survived only because of quick and expert medication. He recovered thoroughly, however, and was quite well when his last collection of poetry, *In the Clearing*, was published. It had no particular structure except for two sections entitled Cluster of Faith (five poems: "Accidentally on Purpose" through "Forgive, O Lord ...") and Quandary (the last ten poems). Like *Steeple Bush,* the next preceding volume fifteen years before, it had a general concern with religious attitudes and beliefs and their relationship with scientific ones, as the epigraph to the book suggests. This consists of lines from "Kitty Hawk" which praise the process of "risking spirit / In substantiation" (lines 23–24), or embodying the spiritual in the material. This evidently seemed to Frost to represent the relationships between religion and science, and it may well also represent his projection of his mind into the concrete form of verse.[13] Here in his last book we find an echo of the theme of "The Trial by Existence" in his first—as he said himself, he remained much the same throughout his life . And at the same time, as we have seen, his persona, as well as his subject matter, had changed during his career from New England farmer to poet and finally to "bard." It is in such a poem as "Kitty Hawk" that this last is most fully realized. That some of his concerns date from early in Frost's life as well as from the later stages is also evident in the fine poem "The Draft Horse," written around 1920. In addition, the book contains several important works, ranging from penetrating aphorisms like "It takes all sorts of in- and outdoor schooling / To get adapted to my kind of fooling," to the long meditative "Kitty Hawk" on which Frost had worked on and off since 1953.[14] As a poetic valediction, the book leaves little to be desired. On the same day *In the Clearing* appeared—the poet's eighty-eighth birthday—Frost received from President Kennedy a Gold Congressional Medal that had originally been authorized by President Eisenhower.

The last and most dramatic mission Frost undertook was to Russia in 1962. He was to be a good-will ambassador, especially in presenting his idea of "the right kind of rivalry" between the two nations.[15] At first the trip was rather disappointing for Frost, mainly because of the language barrier, and his lack of familiarity with modern Russian writers. He met many of these, including the well-known "angry young poet" Yevgeny Yevtushenko. Frost's readings and literary discussions were successful enough, however, although there were those on both sides of the Berlin Wall who believed that his reading "Mending Wall" (beginning "Something there is that doesn't love a wall") was a tactical error. One is nevertheless inclined to applaud this evidence of his persistent sense of humor and of his stubborn determination to say what he thought even if indirectly.

The most dramatic moment of the trip was Frost's meeting with Premier Khrushchev. Frost had fallen nervously ill, as he sometimes did under stress, when he learned that the meeting would finally take place, and the Premier came to talk with Frost at his bedside. Khrushchev seemed to like Frost's concept of a noble rivalry between their two nations, but felt that the United States was economically and politically devitalized. Frost was much impressed with the Premier even though he was far from sure that the conversation helped achieve the national rapprochement he had hoped for. And afterward, his distortion of Khrushchev's remarks into a statement that the United States was "too liberal to fight"—reflecting his own conservatism— led to an unhappy estrangement from President Kennedy, himself considered liberal.[16]

Frost continued to be active until the end. He received more honorary degrees and other honors, and gave further readings and lectures, most notably at the first National Poetry Festival in Washington. D.C. (in the midst of the Cuban missile crisis, so that President Kennedy could not have attended). But he was not very well—his prostate was causing trouble as well as his persistent cystitis. He seemed on the whole to be facing calmly the prospect of death, although as always he had misgivings about the ultimate acceptability of his life's work (he had originally intended to call *In the Clearing*, "The Great Misgiving.")

In December 1962, Frost fell gravely ill, and had to undergo an operation for cancer of the bladder. He survived well, but soon suffered pulmonary embolisms and died in January of 1963, at nearly ninety years of age.

Frost must have felt that he had had a good and fulfilling life, we may be inclined to believe—and this may well have been the case at the end. Yet clearly he never rested on his laurels. He never seemed content with past achievements, but "lived in turning to fresh tasks" ("The Woodpile"), and the reasons for this are most characteristic of the man as an individual, a husband and father, a public figure, and a poet: he was impelled in two distinct ways, equally strong.

Both his life and his poetry were the result of a need to prove himself to other people (as he indicated in "The Fear of Man"), to himself in particular, and especially—as the *Masque of Mercy* reveals—to God. At the same time, they were the product of a desire to express his ideas and feelings, to share his perceptions with other human beings; it is significant that he chose "The Pasture" as the epigraph to his collected poems, for it reflects his warmth, thoughtfulness, and sensitivity, and its refrain, "You come too," indicates his desire for human sharing. These two motives often conflicted, so that at times he would swing uncertainly between them: sometimes he would appear to be the mythic Frost—everyone's grandpa—while at other times he would seem a "terrifying" poet and a "bad man," as Lionel Trilling and Bernard DeVoto, respectively, had called him. He was, of course, both and neither myth and/or monster—in other words, he was a complex and contradictory man and poet.

II

Uncertain Balance:
Frost's Poetic Stance

[4]

"My Kind of Fooling":
The Deceptiveness of Robert Frost

If the public image of Robert Frost as a man and as a poet is decep-
tive, the fault is partly his and partly ours. He helped to foster his
image as a kindly and humorous rural sage in his public appearances
and his poetry, and many people have been unable or unwilling to see
anything else. Thoughtful readers of Frost are inevitably distressed
by the limitations and falsifications of the Frost myth in its sim-
ple form; it persists mainly because many readers find comfort in it,
because it answers a need to preserve various myths, some merely
popular, some central to our culture.[1] Fortunately it has been re-
vised by increasing knowledge about Frost and his work. Anyone
who reads much of his poetry intently, or who has read the studies
of his poetry by such critics and scholars as Lawrance Thompson,
Reginald L. Cook, John F. Lynen, Reuben A. Brower, and Frank
Lentricchia, knows how much more complex Frost is than the simple
myth indicates.

Thompson's biography of Frost has made clear that the myth was
partly created and significantly developed and propagated by the
poet himself.[2] We have learned of many episodes in Frost's life when
he deliberately worked up his public image directly or indirectly.
Certainly that image corresponded to much that he actually was—but
not to all that he was. He was often kind, thoughtful, and helpful,
and even more, often wise; frequently he seemed most content with
the simplicities of the rural life—as his persistent "botanizing" sug-
gests—in contrast to the difficulties of urban existence. Thus the
Frost myth is valid to a significant degree. But at the same time,
Frost was often riddled with doubts about his position, his role in re-
lation to his family and friends, and even his poetic powers. Evi-
dently, he was often angry and bitter, sometimes despairing, and
perhaps even suicidal at moments. One is reluctant to consider Frost
a "tortured soul," but the mixture in him of attitudes, motives, and
often unacknowledged characteristics leaves no doubt that a more
complex image is needed than that of the Frost myth. As one comes
to know the poet and his work well, one becomes uncertain of his
basic character, and of the stance manifested in the poetry. Thomp-

son has shown in biographical terms that Frost often concealed much of himself, good and bad, from many people, even from himself. Certainly, we have learned, he wore a mask in public much of the time, concealing his personal problems and complexities from his reading and listening audiences. Most accurately, we can say that Frost tried simultaneously to reach out to others and to hide from them. In his writings, too, he tried to put himself forward and remain in the background at the same time, and as a result produced poetry that is often quite deceptive—sometimes half-intentionally—for many readers.

Our concern is with Frost's poetry; the main question is, "Are we reading his poetry correctly?" To begin with, if we accede to the Frost myth, we oversimplify our reading. The myth implies, for one thing, that Frost's work is explicit, that everything in it is immediately available on the surface. Further, it suggests that his work is not so much "poetry" as "verse" (to make the snobbish distinction), hence less worth critical attention. It may be taken as simple stuff, casually tossed off—or at least not as painstakingly wrought as the poetry of Eliot or Yeats—and therefore not worth as much aesthetic attention.

Let us consider "Mending Wall" as a kind of test case, for there the speaker seems to be the very image of the Frost myth. Here we find the typical rural activity of mending a stone wall in the spring, one shared by the poet and a neighbor, both farmers:

> Something there is that doesn't love a wall,
> That sends the frozen-ground-swell under it
> And spills the upper boulders in the sun,
> And makes gaps even two can pass abreast.
> The work of hunters is another thing:
> I have come after them and made repair
> Where they have left not one stone on a stone,
> But they would have the rabbit out of hiding,
> To please the yelping dogs. . .
> I let my neighbor know beyond the hill;
> And on a day we meet to walk the line
> And set the wall between us once again. . . .
> There where it is we do not need the wall:
> He is all pine and I am apple orchard.
> My apple trees will never get across
> And eat the cones under his pines, I tell him.
> He only says, "Good fences make good neighbors . . ."
>   I see him there,
> Bringing a stone grasped firmly by the top
> In each hand, like an old-stone savage armed.

He moves in darkness as it seems to me,
Not of woods only and the shade of trees.
He will not go behind his father's saying,
And he likes having thought of it so well
He says again, "Good fences make good neighbors."

On the simplest level, the poem pictures the activity clearly, in plain language, and makes gentle fun of the neighbor for insisting that "good fences make good neighbors" when it is clear that there is no practical reason for this one, and that in addition there is something unnatural about walls in general. This simplistic interpretation is hardly all there is to it, however, as experienced readers know. The Frost "myth" of the benevolent country thinker who "says" his poems straight out as if for people who don't like poetry has been sharply modified by our growing consciousness of Frost's complexity. Inevitably, as his poetry is read more closely and thoughtfully (and as we acquire information about Frost himself like that in Thompson's biography in support of our literary insights), further implications and problems in his work emerge more fully. In "Mending Wall," it becomes clear that the speaker really favors mending the wall—he initiates the process every year, and inveighs against the destructive hunters, even though there seems little overt reason for this particular wall. Thus the speaker accepts the activity as a ritual, restoring a symbol of manmade barriers that have the general function of restricting the chaos of ungoverned nature. The poem may be taken mainly as an attack on the neighbor's mindless "darkness"—yet he seems, as a "natural" man, essentially sound in his inherited respect for walls.

In the last analysis the wall is both good and bad. The barrier serves both to separate the men and to bring them together, and each of these functions is ambivalent. Individuation, maintained by barriers, is necessary to personal integrity, but understanding and cooperation are just as humanly important. The neighbor farmer simply sees that barriers are necessary without understanding why, while the speaker knows why they are and sees the defects of barriers, too. He accepts the paradox and works within it.[3]

Yet a further dimension to the poem is offered by psychoanalytic analysis. Few now deny that poetry is always to some extent a projection of the author's psyche, unconscious as well as conscious, although there is much dispute about particular interpretations. The number of images in the poem concerning the mouth, eating, and speech suggest to Norman Holland an oral "nucleus of fantasy" that embodies the desire to destroy all barriers between the self and the outside world—an impulse at the root of much that is consciously expressed in the poem.[4] Whether one accepts such interpretations or not, many critics acknowledge the validity of the approach as a means of providing further insight into poetry that has all too often been taken superficially as the work of a kindly old farmer-philosopher.

This Frost myth is also modified by the "darkness" in his poetry that Lionel Trilling emphasized when he called Frost a "terrifying" poet.[5] His vision is not only of pleasant farmland, gentle deer, and friendly people, but also of a darker universe:

Once by the Pacific

The shattered water made a misty din.
Great waves looked over others coming in,
And thought of doing something to the shore
That water never did to land before.

. . . .

It looked as if a night of dark intent
Was coming, and not only a night, an age.
Someone had better be prepared for rage.
There would be more than ocean-water broken
Before God's last *Put out the Light* was spoken.

The style here has much the same conversational flavor as "Mending Wall" (e.g., "It looked as if . . . ," "Someone had better be prepared . . ."), for this is not portentous rhetoric or plangent lamentation. But despite the implicit complexities in "Mending Wall," it is relatively optimistic—there, man and his world are acceptable and stable. "Once by the Pacific," however, is a prophecy of doomsday. Frost always considered himself something of a prophet, and on at least one occasion referred to this poem as a vision of the horrors of World Wars I and II.[6] Whether the poem is prophetic or not, the natural world he describes here is far from benevolent. On the contrary, the emphasis is on the darkness and violence which man regards fearfully but powerlessly.

More important, the vision is of nature personified. The clouds and waves become savage embodiments of a universal enmity. Metaphysically, the poem suggests not merely an indifferent universe, but a brutally malevolent one, which is—since the poem indicates no justification for the "dark intent"—incomprehensible to us human victims. And what is perhaps worst, the last two lines indicate that God himself is using this savage embodiment as His instrument, or is at least sanctioning its violence, as a preparation for the end of the world: God's command here is a counterpart of "Let there be light" in Genesis, but in contrast, there is no reason man can understand for the violent destruction of the world. This vision almost goes beyond the Old Testament God of Wrath or the Puritan's harsh deity, especially considering the dark humor of God's saying "Put out the light" as if to children, to signal the end of the world. Certainly, Frost is "terrifying" in much of his best poetry.

It is true that on one level Frost's work is easily available to readers. The casual reader can "get a lot out of" most of the poems on the first reading, and the style and technique seem simple and natural. Thus the poetry reinforces the myth and conceals to some extent other aspects of Frost's work. For this reason we must be conscious of the poet's elusiveness. Frost himself indicates this in "Revelation":

> We make ourselves a place apart
>> Behind light words that tease and flout,
> But oh, the agitated heart
>> Till someone really find us out.

Typically, Frost wishes simultaneously to conceal and to reveal, to be credited with subtlety and elusiveness and at the same time with warmth and a real desire to "communicate."

When we acknowledge that Frost's work is more elusive than it appears, we begin to recognize how complex and indeed ambiguous it is. We find it difficult to identify his poetic stance with certainty. No doubt other contemporary poets are more profound; certainly many are more obviously complex. But Frost, because he hides behind a simple front, has proven more difficult of access in practical terms. His superficial simplicity is being deeply penetrated, however, and the implicit tension that lies beneath the surface of much of his work is making itself felt more acutely. His work embodies opposing or inconsistent attitudes and impulses of many kinds, and out of this opposition comes the uncertainty that modern readers have become so sensitive to.

Frost is deliberately elusive in some cases, as "Revelation" has indicated, partly to hide his most personal and intimate thoughts and feelings. For a lyric poet he is extraordinarily reticent in some ways. With this reticence goes a desire to be found out, however, so that his real self—his depth and perhaps his cleverness—will be appreciated.

Thanks partly to Thompson's biography, we know of a number of

occasions when Frost allowed or even encouraged readers to be con-
fused by his poems, sometimes hinting at the deception—as he saw
it—and sometimes not. A typical case is "The Road Not Taken."
Many readers, we can be sure, still take the poem to be autobio-
graphical, to be a direct expression of the author as persona. It was
easy to see it thus almost from the first, for even his friend Edward
Thomas took it this way, not realizing that he himself was supposed
to be the speaker until Frost explained.[7]

The last stanza in particular sounds personal to Frost:

> I shall be telling this with a sigh
> Somewhere ages and ages hence:
> Two roads diverged in wood, and I—
> I took the one less traveled by,
> And that has made all the difference.

If we take Frost to be the speaker, however, we are likely to ignore
the irony in the poem and see it as a sentimental justification of fol-
lowing one's personal bent, of being an individual. We may well
focus on the last two lines almost to the exclusion of the rest: The
speaker has chosen an individual, uncommon way of life. But this
reading leaves us with some troublesome questions about internal
consistency: Why does the speaker insist in stanzas 2 and 3 that the
roads are really pretty equally worn? And why does he sigh, since
that might imply regret over the choice? These questions can lead us
to perceive the irony if we pursue them (though many readers fail to
do so). They do not need to be dealt with, however, if we understand
that the speaker is Edward Thomas. Instead, we see at once that
Frost was mocking Thomas's habit of fretting over choices, present
and past. One key to the poem comes early, in lines 2–3: The
speaker wants to have both choices. He sees little real difference be-
tween them and hates to give up either one, telling himself futilely
that he may be able to avail himself later of the one he lets go. The
style and tone suggest hesitancy and a rather wistful indecisiveness
mixed with a faint consciousness that dithering is silly. In the last
stanza, the speaker becomes realistic—he looks to the future when, he
knows, he will dramatize the choice in retrospect (he will tell it "with
a sigh" and will pause and repeat himself dramatically as in "and
I— / I took . . ."). He realizes that he will transform the memory of
his actual hesitancy into an account of how he once made a crucial
and uncommon choice which determined the rest of his life.

Frost is ironic in this poem, pretending to sympathize with the
speaker, and in those terms he is deliberately deceptive. He didn't

intend to be *that* mystifying, however, and may well have found it
embarrassing to explain himself to Thomas. But he subsequently al-
lowed the mystification to continue for the public. In his readings
and conversations Frost occasionally specified that he was making
fun of Thomas, but more often he merely hinted more or less
broadly that the poem was not as obvious as it seemed.[8] He evidently
wanted the poem to succeed in the manner intended, and this en-
tailed allowing it to be understood, but not *too* easily. The public
should be led to take it rightly as the words of Thomas, but they
should recognize that Frost was being a little "tricky" about it. Typi-
cally, Frost urged his point restrainedly, trying to avoid obviousness
while seeking appreciation.

An equally deceptive poem is Frost's powerful sonnet "Design":

> I found a dimpled spider, fat and white,
> On a white heal-all, holding up a moth
> Like a white piece of rigid satin cloth –
> Assorted characters of death and blight
> Mixed ready to begin the morning right. . .
> . . . .
> What had that flower to do with being white,
> The wayside blue and innocent heal-all?
> What brought the kindred spider to that height,
> Then steered the white moth thither in the night?
> What but design of darkness to appall? –
> If design govern in a thing so small.

From the circumstances of its composition we know that "Design"
was originally aimed at the Reverend William Hayes Ward, who
maintained a very rigid and narrow conception of divinity and of
God's relationship with man and the world.[9] The version of the
poem we have is poetically superior to the original, but thematically
it is almost the same. The only significant difference in meaning ap-
pears in the last line, which first read, "Design, design! Do I use the
word aright?," thereby leaving the theme just a little more uncertain
than in the revision. The original reason for the hedging here, then,
was to conceal the mockery aimed at the distinguished clergyman.

There are other equivocations involved in the history of the poem,
however, revolving around the fact that most readers now interpret
"Design" rather differently from the way Frost intended it. Usually
see the poem as one of two things, either a suggestion that darkness
or evil does design the universe, or that there is no design at all,
merely chance. If design does govern in these particular small

things, then it would seem to be evil. Or there may be no design at all—it may be simply long-worked-out odds that set up the white spider-flower-moth combination. "Natural selection," a refinement of chance, evidently may determine the colors of insects, with due allowance for "sports" like the white heal-all.

In a way, however, we are "deceived" in these two interpretations—they are not what the poem evidently meant to Frost. What he wanted to suggest to the Reverend Ward was: "If you insist that God's design governs every minute detail in the universe, you may find that some details suggest a dark and malevolent God." This argument is based on Frost's confidence in the goodness of God's design, which is nevertheless a general one, subject to partial and momentary anomalies. He was not seriously suggesting that God was evil, nor that He did not exist. By revising the last line Frost tried to make clearer his basic point, but the sonnet still was ambiguous—and, surprisingly, Frost allowed it to remain so. Our common interpretations are perfectly legitimate, of course, when we take the poem by itself; the "deception" lies in Frost's tacitly permitting those interpretations by refraining from further revisions and explanations to clarify his original point (which he sometimes provided for "The Road Not Taken"). Frost may have sympathized with our interpretations; as Thompson suggests, he sometimes felt the power of darkness strongly enough to do so.[10] In any case he refused to be more explicit about the theme of "Design," either because he felt it was clear enough as it stood, or because he was reticent about his intimate thoughts and emotions. Perhaps both motives were involved.

We can see Frost's fundamental reticence operating in much more of his work, as well as in the cases just described. We know, for example, that he arranged the sequence of the poems in *A Boy's Will* quite carefully to show stages in his earlier psychological and social progression.[11] Indeed he went so far as to provide rather unclear explanatory notes to the poems in the table of contents of early editions. But he dropped these notes, and subsequently said little about the pattern—he would not make a display of himself.

Frost's poem "The Lovely Shall Be Choosers" shows the same reticence. He acknowledged that he wrote it about his mother, but its allusions to her difficulties are usually so veiled and abstracted that we need to have considerable knowledge of her life to understand the poem. The first two "joys" are a good case in point:

> Be her first joy her wedding,
> That though a wedding,
> Is yet—well, something they know, he and she.

And after that her next joy
That though she grieves, her grief is secret:
Those friends know nothing of her grief to make it shameful.

Behind these lines is Frost's mistaken notion that his parents had had to be married because he himself had already been conceived, but he certainly did not make this clear publicly.[12] The last "joy" in the poem is equally obscure, and has remained so. We still do not know who is represented by the "one" to whom her heart will go out as this last joy. In the last analysis, we may well wonder why Frost would expose such personal thoughts and feelings about his mother, especially when they sprang from some circumstances he considered shameful. Typically, as much as he revealed himself—and her—to his readers, he concealed just as much by deliberate vagueness and dissimulation.

The combination of self-exposure and reticence is in fact a keynote to much of Frost.[13] The cases just cited are perhaps the clearest indications of the tendency, but one almost always needs to read his work with some qualification, with a grain of salt.

One typical way Frost conceals himself is by his wit and humor. His work is pervaded by his sense of humor—he is continually joking, punning, indulging in what seems like sheer whimsy. Very few of his poems lack some touch of fooling, or at least of wittiness, sardonic though it may be at times. Occasionally the humor seems almost pointless. In *A Masque of Reason*, when Job's wife asks what God is doing as He pulls His collapsible prefabricated plywood throne upright, Job says, "Pitching throne, I guess." There seems little specific reason for the flimsiness of the throne or for the pun, and this episode like others has rather disgusted a number of readers. It takes a broad and tolerant perspective to allow this kind of joking its validity. Frost recognized the problem himself, saying, "It takes all sorts of in- and outdoor schooling / To get adapted to my kind of fooling."

There are two basic reasons for this fooling. It is often a weapon, first of all, as in "A Hundred Collars" and "Departmental," where we are made to laugh at a stuffy professor on the one hand and at mankind in general, represented by the ants, on the other. Secondly, and more generally, Frost uses humor as a mask, to prevent others from seeing where he is most vulnerable. When he uses humor or wit as a weapon in irony, it also serves as a shield; "Irony is simply a kind of guardedness," he said. But he added, "So is a twinkle. It keeps the reader from criticism."[14] In other words, both aggressive wit and good-humored fooling enable him to hide from the reader. During his life he generally felt threatened; this would explain his wanting to hide in his poetry the real intensity of his feelings. More important, in many of his poems we can feel that intensity if we penetrate the surface humor. The perceptive reader can see beneath the tonal mask to the fundamental seriousness. In the *Masques*, even when the humor seems merely one aspect of a general good humor, and inconsequential in particular instances (as in "pitching throne"), it conceals somewhat the intense concern with the relations between God and man that Frost manifested virtually all his life. At times he professed to be purely "secular," but this, too, was a smoke screen, meaning at most that he was not a churchgoer. Only occasionally did he emerge to let himself be seen clearly. In the *Masques* he hides behind the humor quite consistently, for he would be embarrassed to be caught preaching—and could be tragically disturbed, personally, if he confronted his doubts about man and God too directly.

In general, Frost hides behind three different kinds of humor. First, there is the levity, the good-humored fooling that we noted in connection with God's throne in the *Masque of Reason*—this is the "twinkle" that Frost mentioned. Then there is the sharper humor, the wit, which seems more immediately pertinent in its context, and which is often ironic. And third is a laconic quality, a "New England farmer" type of understatement which verges on both humor and irony, and is faintly amusing because of the inconsistency with its context. Usually we find these three kinds combined, often inextricably, but there are enough "pure" cases for us to see the various motivations for his choice of humorous masks.

The mask of levity, of good-humored fooling, appears in a great many of Frost's poems, but more and more often in his later years. We first see it clearly in three or four poems in the early *North of Boston* (1914). In "The Mountain," the line "all the fun's in how you say a thing," indicates the kind of pleasantries exchanged by the two speakers. Particularly, the farmer whom the poet interviews is something of a "grand liar" type. To begin with, he tells about a spring supposedly right at the top of the mountain that is " 'always cold in summer, warm in winter.' " The narrator joins the fun, saying, " 'There ought to be view around the world / From such a mountain.' " It becomes clear that the mountain and their attitudes toward it develop into a symbol of poetry and poetic endeavor (and more.)[15] The levity is carried through to the end of the poem: All the joking illustrates the "fun" in how a poet says—and sees—a thing. The farmer and the narrator exercise their metaphoric and verbal imaginations on the mountain and its spring, making only a passing concession to the commonsense approach to their subject when the farmer says that the water probably remains about the same temperature, winter and summer. But literal truth is quickly pushed aside by metaphoric truth when the farmer finally breaks off the conversation by saying that he had lived there " 'ever since Hor [the mountain] was no bigger than a −.' " In "A Hundred Collars," also in *North of Boston*, we have a half-farcical spectacle in the professor's nervously confronting the amiably massive salesman who complains that his shirt collars are too tight:

> "Number eighteen this is. What size do you wear?"
>
> The Doctor caught his throat convulsively.
> "Oh−ah−fourteen−fourteen."
>
>   "Fourteen! You say so!
> I can remember when I wore fourteen.
> . . . .
> You act as if you wished you hadn't come.
> Sit down or lie down, friend; you make me nervous."
>
> The Doctor made a subdued dash for it,
> And propped himself at bay against a pillow.

Some poems of Frost's middle years manifest his sense of fun, such as "Departmental," "A Considerable Speck," and "The Literate Farmer and the Planet Venus." The rhythm of "Departmental," for one thing, is "good fun" and helps to set a similar tone for the poem; and then there are the phrases like "feelers calmly atwiddle," not to mention the general imagery of the earnest little ants, all going about their business.

In Frost's later volumes, from the forties on, the fooling seems to increase, but at the same time it is mixed more thoroughly with ironic notes. Typical is "It Bids Pretty Fair":

> The play seems out for an almost infinite run.
> Don't mind a little thing like the actors fighting.
> The only thing I worry about is the sun.
> We'll be all right if nothing goes wrong with the lighting.

This version of "all the world's a stage" is presented tongue-in-cheek, but it also has a satiric point at the expense of mankind in general and social critics in particular. Also typical, and more highly wrought, are the *Masques*. These annoy certain readers because the humor in the *Masque of Reason* seems too broad and inconsequential, and the tone in *A Masque of Mercy* at first too light to fit the serious themes of the plays. The *Masque of Reason* is after all an exploration of the nature of religious faith, and the *Masque of Mercy*, of the relation between God's mercy and His justice. The *Masques*, like many of Frost's poems, lack the "high seriousness" of the Romantics and the Victorians on the one hand, and the ironic bleakness of moderns like Eliot on the other. Some readers have therefore found it hard to perceive the seriousness of the concern beneath the surface; they can neither enjoy the "fooling" nor appreciate the serious matter it is joined with.

This broader humor of *A Masque of Reason* and the poems we have just looked at is at one extreme for Frost: here he goes as far as he can to avoid being caught preaching. More usually he simply allows his inborn wit to serve as part of his poetic medium. Except in some of his earliest poetry, his work is pervaded by his wit, sometimes wry, sometimes frivolous. Though he professed to be anti-intellectual, he could always keep enough intellectual detachment from his material to establish an almost equal aesthetic distance for the reader.

Often, Frost's wit takes the form of puns. Sometimes these are so inconsequential and awkward, like "pitching throne," that they seem whimsical. But usually Frost's puns are functional, helping to develop the themes of his poems fairly directly. In "Mending Wall," for instance, lines 31–33 raise the question of giving "offense" in building the wall. The pun on "a fence" directly concerns the validity of stone walls—the word play may be outrageous but it keeps the focus on a main issue in the poem. The same is true in a better-known case, that of "morning right" in "Design." There, "right" suggests "rite," and "morning" may suggest "mourning," both appropriately. Indeed, the conception of a ritual effectively intensifies the problematic question of universal design: If the white spider-flower-moth collocation embodies a ritual (as it must if only to the extent of being a breakfast scene), then what a design there may be for us all!

Puns are only one manifestation of Frost's wit, however, for his poetry abounds in clever phrasing and unexpected figures of speech. The epigrams represent the most obvious exercise of verbal cleverness, and it is tempting to chuckle at the phrasing without seriously considering Frost's meaning. The lines about his "fooling" quoted earlier are a case in point; the following are equally good:

(Forgive, O Lord)

Forgive, O Lord, my little jokes on Thee
And I'll forgive Thy great big one on me.

The neatly turned parallel phrasing reinforces and partly exemplifies the point of the explicit statement: This epigram itself is one of Frost's "little jokes" on God, and because he has made it, he can better endure God's "big joke," the difficulty and uncertainty of satisfying Him. The interrelated concepts that the two lines embody could serve as keys to Frost's moral and poetic philosophies, as we shall see later.

Epigrams printed separately appear more often in the later poetry, but like most wits, Frost tended throughout his life to think epigrammatically. Readers will recall many brief passages that can stand alone. Some favorites are the following:

> The fact is the sweetest dream that labor knows.
> > (from "Mowing")

> "Home is the place where, when you have to go there,
> They have to take you in."
> > (from "The Death of the Hired Man")

> Better to go down dignified
> With boughten friendship at your side
> Than none at all. Provide, provide!
> > (from "Provide, Provide")

Frost's wit is not simply epigrammatic, however, for it is evident in the basic medium of his poetry, his imagery and figures of speech, and his diction, even in passages where he is at his most serious. He gives the woman speaker in "A Servant to Servants," who knows she is slowly going insane, a wry sense of humor:

> Bless you, of course you're keeping me from work,
> But the thing of it is, I need to *be* kept.
> There's work enough to do—there's always that;
> But behind's behind. The worst that you can do
> Is set me back a little more behind.
> I shan't catch up in this world, anyway.

This speaker is like many others in Frost's dramatic pieces—they have a flair for a half-humorous, neat, and rather original turn of phrase, like Frost himself. And like Frost, they try to dissipate their worries by joking about them. They are exemplars of mythic rural New Englanders, whom Frost has adopted as his type. His public and literary image is founded partly on this type, and as personae in his poetry, they are partly him, despite their individual differences.

A similar rural New England wit comes more directly from Frost in the monosyllabic opening of "Directive": "Back out of all this now too much for us. . . ." Equally wittily, in a different way, he later writes, "if you'll let a guide direct you / Who only has at heart your getting lost" (to the complexities of the modern world, of course). This kind of mild wit very often appears simply as understatement appropriate to the myth of the laconic Yankee, and is one of the most effective ways Frost's wit operates in serious contexts to shield him from the eyes of the reader. The severely understated ending of " 'Out, Out—,' " for instance, has seemed to some altogether too callous:

> They listened at his heart.
> Little—less—nothing!—and that ended it.
> No more to build on there. And they, since they
> Were not the one dead, turned to their affairs.

But one point of this conclusion is that it tries to mitigate the tragedy, as the woman in "A Servant" accepts hers, by accepting its inevitability and underplaying it. We get an even flatter understatement in "Acquainted with the Night," where the anti-emotional line "I have been one acquainted with the night" is the keynote and frame of the poem. And in "The Draft Horse" we get a particularly notable case of this common technique of Frost's. After the stranger stabs the horse, Frost describes the buggy riders:

> The most unquestioning pair
> That ever accepted fate
> And the least disposed to ascribe
> Any more than we had to hate,
>
> We assumed that the man himself
> Or someone he had to obey
> Wanted us to get down
> And walk the rest of the way.

It is hard to imagine a more neatly, almost humorously, noncommittal way of suggesting the terror and helplessness of the pair's position—with other overtones suggesting that the two are not very perceptive, and are too trusting, placing too much faith in the benevolence of the "someone." It is further suggested that the supernatural power in question was really unsympathetic and irrationally demanding since there is no evident reason to want the pair to walk. This poem is an objective mythic indictment of God's treatment of mankind, in contrast to the *Masques,* where the case is argued explicitly and is resolved ultimately in God's favor. Frost does not identify explicitly any of the emotional or psychological elements in this passage; since he states only what seem to be obvious facts, it is only by inference that we can perceive his own feelings in relation to the experience described. He acts the part of a straight-faced comedian; what he accomplishes by joking in the *Masques* he achieves here by understatement. The effect is rather like that of the knocking on the gate in *Macbeth*.

Frost never allows his poetry to become a *cri du coeur*. For one thing, he often adopts a dramatic method, producing monologues and dialogues as well as the *Masques*. Here he is able to hide in the supposedly objective point of view of the playwright. But even when he speaks in his own person, as he evidently does in most of his lyrics, even to the point of talking directly to the reader, he keeps his distance from his material and from us partly through his wit and humor. This is a "classical" quality in his poetry, perhaps, that contrasts with the emotionality associated with romanticism—a kind of urbanity or restraint that may seem strange in a lyric poet. As a lyricist, he writes about himself, about his own experiences, his thoughts, and his feelings. But at the same time, he conceals or diffuses these by joking, playing, and teasing.[16]

Self-consciousness was an important element in the deceptiveness of "Design" and "The Road Not Taken" and in Frost's use of wit and humor. He held himself back knowingly, enjoying the fact that his more private or deeper thoughts and feelings were hidden from the reader. But this process must have become just as much a habit of mind as a deliberate technique. If it was a response to a real need he felt, it must have become second nature—and indeed it persisted and increased throughout his life.

Even more clearly, the element of irony is basic in Frost. Here, he does not try deliberately to deceive or maintain a pretense. Rather, most of the irony in his poetry reflects his cast of mind. There are some poems in which he establishes the classic ironic position of saying the opposite of what he really means, but for the most part, he is in the position of Northrop Frye's *eiron,* the persona who "makes himself invulnerable . . . , appearing to be less than [he] is."[17] Frost's use of understatement achieves a wit that often partakes of this kind of irony. But there are further examples which indicate that it is more than merely a manner of speaking. It is, one comes to realize, a central position for Frost, enabling him on the one hand to show the inadequacy of man's expectations of life and the universe, and on the other to maintain one kind of defense against the incomprehensible powers and conditions surrounding him.[18]

The most obvious uses of irony are the classic ones, where the poet says the opposite of what he means, leaving the reader to perceive the real point. This is the case in a few of Frost's poems, like "The Most of It," "Haec Fabula Docet," and "The Subverted Flower."

In "The Most of It," a man tries to evoke a loving response from the natural world, and fails. The man's position is analogous to Adam's in *Paradise Lost* before the creation of Eve: he finds nothing in nature that is near enough to his level, or enough like him to offer a comprehensible response. But there is an additional and more significant analogy between this poem and various others of Frost's, such as "Two Look at Two" and "The Need of Being Versed in Country Things," which suggest strongly that it is up to man himself to comprehend and accept nature on its own terms if he is to achieve any real contact with it. In "The Most of It," the poet says, "nothing ever came of what he cried / Unless it was the embodiment . . ." and then describes the buck's manifestation in detail, so that it becomes quite obvious that something did come of it: an "embodiment" of nature. Irony lies in the contrast between nature's failure to respond in the terms the man desired or expected, and the significance of the response as we perceive it. The man has asked for "counter-love, original response"; the great buck that appears is certainly original, but hardly loving—it is a brute animal, an embodiment of the power and indifference of nature, so much so that the man is not quite certain that it was a response (note the hesitant "unless it was" and the disconcerted "and that was all"). When one is "versed in country things," one knows that nature is independent, self-sufficient, and often brutal; this is what the man is to learn from the ironic contrast between his expectations and nature's fulfillment of them.

"Haec Fabula Docet" is even more obviously ironic. We realize this partly from what we know of Frost's feeling about "do-gooders" and overly solicitous humanitarian impulses. Another poem, "A Roadside Stand," makes these feelings plain, but even without knowing that poem we can see the irony in the contrast between Frost's attack on the officious interference that causes LaFontaine's death and the moral that the proud and independent are doomed to trouble. If the Blindman had been left alone, the poem suggests, he probably would have found the trench with his cane and avoided it; in addition, the "overanxious" helper provokes his rage, causing him to fall. We are apparently intended to endorse the Blindman's stance of fierce independence, yet Frost calls him "the apogee of human blind conceit," and indicates in the moral that independence like his has disastrous consequences. Nevertheless, the workmen are gruesome in the glee with which they bury the Blindman; our sympathies are with him despite his pride. The "Moral" is ironic; Frost is evidently arguing in a hard-nosed fashion that one should be allowed to try to "go it sole alone" without interference—and this is what he argued for, one way or the other, throughout his life.

Most often, Frost's irony, even in a classic form, is not so clearly spelled out. In "The Subverted Flower," for instance, one may argue about who is at fault, the boy or the girl. The boy seems to be guilty of a certain sensuality (Frost could be prudish enough to see it thus), as we can see from the flower symbolism and from certain relatively direct descriptive touches like "another sort of smile / Caught up . . . his lips," and "with every word he spoke / His lips were sucked and blown." But most of the description is as the girl sees it, overreacting to the boy's hesitant passion. The boy is forced to flee like a cowardly beast, but the ending makes us see the girl as irrational and indeed almost as bestial in a way as the boy: "Her mother wiped the foam / From her chin, picked up her comb, / And drew her backward home." On the surface, the poem describes a boy's trying to subvert an innocent girl, but to a sensitive reader it suggests that the girl has distorted the boy's motives and the nature of the episode. We should not be surprised to learn that the poem reflects an episode in Frost's early courtship of Elinor White. Thompson has shown that their relationship was seriously disturbed by Elinor's very shy reaction to Frost's physical passion, and Frost's resentment reflects itself in the subtle slanting here in the boy's favor.[19]

These poems of "classic" irony are few, however. Most usually Frost's ironic position appears in his unwillingness to spell out the main point of his poems. Although he has the reputation of being explicit, it is only partly deserved—and in only a superficial sense. He does often describe scenes and actions, if not usually people, in some detail, and he may well draw some clearly expressed thematic conclusions from them, but these are usually only part of the whole point. It is a mistake to think of Frost as another Aesop, even though he sometimes wears that mask. In "Haec Fabula Docet," he is mocking the fable form, and perhaps the reader a bit.

Frost wrote a significant number of poems, moreover, in which no themes are explicitly stated at all, in which the meaning must be elicited primarily by the reader. This literary method is of course common in modern literature, even characteristic. Frost's use of the method indicates the importance, to him and to us, of the subtext, the themes worked out implicitly, even though he may in other poems bring part of the themes to the surface.

"The Pasture" is a good example of the method:

> I'm going out to clean the pasture spring;
> I'll only stop to rake the leaves away

> (And wait to watch the water clear, I may):
> I sha'n't be gone long. — You come too.
>
> I'm going out to fetch the little calf
> That's standing by the mother. It's so young
> It totters when she licks it with her tongue.
> I shan't be gone long. — You come too.

This seems such a simple poem — and of course it is, in a way. All it does is extend an invitation to join the poet in performing a couple of pleasant farm chores that are briefly but specifically described. There hardly seems to be any "meaning" here, until we begin to recognize the implications of the actions and the poet's attitude toward them and toward the reader. Then we realize that Frost is inviting us to share archetypal experiences of the search for truth, purity, and the source of all natural vitality on the one hand, and for love on the other. Since Frost used "The Pasture" as the epigraph to his collected poems, he is suggesting what his poetry is all about and is also indicating a whole way of reading it. He is suggesting that a reader should take his poetry as humanly shared experiences rather than the pronouncements of a seer.[20] But Frost does not make this explicit; he embodies it symbolically in the objects, actions, and tone of the poem. "The Pasture," in an important sense, is unpretentious, for Frost does not permit himself to make grandiose claims for his work out loud — it's safer that way.

We find the same situation to some extent in a number of other poems like "The Vantage Point," "After Apple-Picking," and "All Revelation." Here he provides more specific hints about the implications of the poems, but that is all. We are still left with the job of exploring them. In "After Apple-Picking," for instance, Frost does say:

> For I have had too much
> Of apple-picking: I am overtired
> Of the great harvest I myself desired.

and he concludes,

> One can see what will trouble
> This sleep of mine, whatever sleep it is.
> Were he not gone,
> The woodchuck could say whether it's like his
> Long sleep, as I describe its coming on,
> Or just some human sleep.

On top of the description of apple-picking and its aftermath, these hints make it obvious that the poet is talking about considerably more than simply picking apples. We understand that he is concerned profoundly with the nature of man's life and his work and perhaps of his death, and even with further metaphysical considerations. But it is up to us to explore these. Frost is too reticent, even too diffident, to impose them on us explicitly.

Finally, the dramatic poems and the plays evidence Frost's ironic position by virtue of their inherently objective point of view. Even in the *Masques* we do not get Frost's views directly, although all the characters are to some extent his mouthpieces, so we cannot know just how much to allow for dramatic exigencies. When Job's wife manifests so strongly her impatience with God in *A Masque of Reason,* for example, we can be sure that this is not just Frost speaking, but rather a character being played off against the others for dramatic purposes. And to the extent that all of the characters in the *Masque* represent Frost, there is that much of a balance between them. Since they are played off against each other, we finally come to see a complex mixture of views rather than a single personal view that we can take to be that of Frost himself. Paul's words at the end of *A Masque of Mercy* are certainly Frost's:

> We have to stay afraid deep in our souls
> Our sacrifice—the best we have to offer,
> And not our worst nor second best, our best,
> Our very best, our lives laid down like Jonah's,
> Our lives laid down in war and peace—may not
> Be found acceptable in Heaven's sight.

He made the same point in his introduction to Robinson's *King Jasper*: "There is the fear that we shan't prove worthy in ourselves. That is the fear of God." But this is not all of Frost, for the Keeper's attitudes, not to mention Jonah's, also reflect Frost and qualify Paul's views. As usual, Frost avoids setting himself clearly and definitely in the reader's sight.

This objectivity and balance is even more obvious in the dramatic poems. Monologues like "A Servant to Servants" and "The Pauper Witch of Grafton" are almost completely objective character studies; Frost keeps himself out of them. There are, too, dialogues like "Home Burial" and "West-Running Brook," and a few dramatic poems with three or more speakers, like "Snow," all of which are considerably more objective than the *Masques*. In "Home Burial," typically, each speaker is partly at fault and partly justified in his attitude toward the other. The husband is rather callous, though not hard-hearted, and considerably more sensible; the wife is warmer and more sensitive, but almost neurotically unrealistic as well as imperceptive of her husband's real grief. In "Snow," similarly, we find ourselves sympathizing with each of the three *dramatis personae*, even Meserve for responding to the challenge of the storm.

"A Servant to Servants" is one of Frost's most strikingly successful dramatic monologues; the speaker, a farmer's wife, tells a silent interlocutor about her situation, which she can perceive all too well, and manifests half-consciously in the course of the narration the desperate effects of her entrapment, especially as it reflects the entrapment of the whole society of isolated farmers which she represents. She is imprisoned particularly by the work:

> It's rest I want—there, I have said it out—
> From cooking meals for hungry hired men
> And washing dishes after them—from doing
> Things over and over that just won't stay done.
> By good rights I ought not to have so much
> Put on me, but there seems no other way.

She is trapped also by the insanity in her family:

> I have my fancies: it runs in the family.
> My father's brother wasn't right. They kept him
> Locked up for years back there at the old farm.
> I've been away once—yes, I've been away.
> The State Asylum . . . .

She feels she cannot avoid these traps, but she does want to prevent her family's falling into the one that the "old-fashioned way" of keeping the insane at home represents.

> I've heard too much of the old-fashioned way.
> My father's brother, he went mad quite young.
> . . . .
> They soon saw he would do someone a mischief
> If he wa'n't kept strict watch of, and it ended
> In father's building him a sort of cage,
> Or room within a room, of hickory poles,
> Like stanchions in the barn, from floor to ceiling—
> . . . .
> Cruel—it sounds. I s'pose they did the best
> They knew. And just when he was at the height,

Father and mother married, and mother came,
A bride, to help take care of such a creature,
And accommodate her young life to his.

She recognizes some of the effects on herself of her imprisonment, but only some of them—she knows that she can feel little, emotionally, but she is not conscious of her neurotic vagueness and uncertainty:

I promised myself to get down some day
And see the way you lived, but I don't know!
With a houseful of hungry men to feed
I guess you'd find . . . It seems to me
I can't express my feelings, any more
Than I can raise my voice or want to lift
My hand (oh, I can lift it when I have to).
Did you ever feel so? I hope you never.
It's got so I don't even know for sure
Whether I *am* glad, sorry, or anything.

Without a single word from her interlocutor, she is allowed to ramble through her thoughts and stories and emerge as one of Frost's most thoroughly individualized and realistic characters, as well as one of the most uncomplaining yet pathetic victims of circumstance. Frost makes no direct appeal for our sympathy; he stays in the authorial background and lets the woman speak for herself. This objectivity of Frost's, coupled with the woman's stoicism, keeps the poem from being sentimental.

What makes it truly difficult for readers of Frost is that he stays in the background and puts himself forward simultaneously. He is a writer with marked character—we can recognize his style and tone easily, and we are familiar with his typical subjects. And in his lyrics, he seems to be speaking in his own person. Yet he is elusive. Sometimes he seems to confront us directly and explicitly, as in "Two Tramps in Mud Time" or "Birches," where the conclusion is practically a spelled-out moral. But usually he withholds or conceals himself to some extent. He may seem on the surface to be saying one thing, while implying another; he may seem to be half-joking, while really being serious; he may even half-deliberately allow us to be misled for a time in interpreting certain poems.

What we see on the surface is certainly Frost, and we are sometimes deceived, like the man in "The Most of It," into thinking that that is all. The more closely we examine Frost and his work, however, the more clearly we see that much lies beneath the surface, that his work is complex and ambiguous. The inconsistency between the surface impression of his poetry and the subtext is in itself a mark of that complexity.

[5]

"Speaking of Contraries":
The Tension in Frost's Poetry

Frost's reluctance to expose himself to criticism often resulted in ambiguous poetic expression, sometimes quite deliberate. He felt particularly vulnerable about his religious views, and did not like to discuss them seriously, at least in public; indeed, his poetry seldom confronts religious issues straightforwardly.[1] Rather than argue about them in plain terms (as in the exceptional *Masques*), Frost usually implies, suggests, or hints ambiguously. He likes to leave a choice of interpretations to the reader, as in "For Once, Then, Something." What does the speaker perceive here beyond the vision of an anthropomorphic Deity in the surface reflection? Either he achieves a glimpse of a neoplatonic reality, or he can see no more than an ordinary material level of reality.

> Others taunt me with having knelt at well-curbs
> Always wrong to the light, so never seeing
> Deeper down in the well than where the water
> Gives me back in a shining surface picture
> Me myself in the summer heaven, godlike,
> Looking out of a wreath of fern and cloud puffs.
> *Once*, when trying with chin against a well-curb,
> I discerned, as I thought, beyond the picture,
> Through the picture, a something white, uncertain,
> Something more of the depths—and then I lost it.
> Water came to rebuke the too clear water.
> One drop fell from a fern, and lo, a ripple
> Shook whatever it was lay there at bottom,
> Blurred it, blotted it out. What was that whiteness?
> Truth? A pebble of quartz? For once, then, something.

Frost pointedly does not say what he saw—as persona he does not know—and our imaginations remain stretched between the two possibilities.

69

This ambiguity and the resulting tension are characteristic of Frost's work. They appear in various forms and dimensions, sometimes as deliberately as in "For Once," often less so. Sometimes Frost appears inconsistent or uncertain, and it may be for this reason that Yvor Winters considered him a "spiritual drifter."[2] The point is that Frost was not of a single mind, nor did he often concentrate on single, unified methods and effects in given poems. Some readers have taken this as diffidence, but it would be more accurate, I think, to see it as the reflection of a multivalence, and a strong sense of the inherent complexity and multiplicity of human and cosmic affairs. Frost's ambiguity manifests itself in two general dimensions, that of depth, and that of tone or attitude. In the first, we can see an opposition between the simple, the particular, and the superficial on the one hand, and the complex, the general, and the profound on the other. In terms of tone, we not only find lightness opposed to seriousness, but also the tolerant and subjective opposed to the skeptical and impersonal. These contrarieties appear in most of his poetry and result in a subtle but pervasive poetic tension.

In terms of the opposition between simplicity and complexity, John F. Lynen's *The Pastoral Art of Robert Frost* is especially illuminating. Lynen begins by reminding us (p. 9) that in the pastoral mode, the simple and natural rural world is almost always seen in relation to the sophisticated and complex world of urban civilization. Then he shows how this opposition is characteristic of Frost—indeed, that it is a key to a great deal of the poetry, if not all. Certainly it points directly at the opposition between the simple and the complex that we find throughout Frost.

Frost's style, to begin with, is a kind of fusion of the simple and the subtle. His sentence structure is generally direct and uncomplicated, his diction relatively plain. There are no purple passages, indeed little rhetoric; he leans toward understatement, if anything. It is a commonplace that his style is conversational. Similarly, his prosody seems simple and conventional, for he typically uses common meters like iambic tetrameter and pentameter, and follows unelaborate or loose rhyme schemes. We find little free verse, few exotic experiments in prosody. Not that Frost was ignorant or incapable of them: "For Once, Then, Something" is in classical hendecasyllabics, and "After Apple-Picking" is extraordinary for its controlled freedom of rhyme and rhythm, as Reuben A. Brower has shown.[3] We recognize that Frost was a master poetic craftsman. He deliberately chose to make his style and poetic techniques simple, and to shape his poetry into what he called "the sound of sense," in order to seem natural and direct rather than highly wrought.[4]

With this restrained medium, however, he carries a weight of suggestion, of implication. To achieve this suggestiveness, Frost at times weaves into his poetry allusions to his reading—more often, I believe, than most readers think. In general, he gives the impression of not being very heavily allusive; in contrast to Eliot, for one, he seems most unliterary. The reason is probably that many of his allusions are implicit, hence concealed except to those who recognize them.

The most explicit allusions and the heaviest concentration of them are in the *Masques,* no doubt, but even there we can find "concealed" allusions in various passages. Consider, for instance, the passages where Frost casually paraphrases Herrick's "To Daffodils," refers to the golden birds of Yeats's "Sailing to Byzantium" (*A Masque of Reason,* lines 435-437, 459-461), and quotes *Pilgrim's Progress* (*A Masque of Mercy,* lines 530-535). Elsewhere in his poetry the allusions are even less obvious. This is the case in "The Star-Splitter," for instance. The poem tells how Brad McLaughlin burned down his house and spent the fire insurance money on a telescope to satisfy his "lifelong curiosity / About our place among the infinities." This line refers, as Thompson has indicated, to Richard A. Proctor's *Our Place Among Infinities.*[5] The book had fascinated Frost when he was a boy, prompting an interest in astronomy while at the same time arguing persuasively that science and religion or metaphysics could and should be independent in a person's thinking. The importance of the covert allusion is that it resolves some of the uncertainty of the poem, for without it, we may feel that the narrator is unjustifiably scornful of McLaughlin's endeavor, especially since both of them greatly enjoy using the telescope. The allusion indicates that McLaughlin's curiosity may be admirable, although his telescope is useless as a means of answering metaphysical questions.

A somewhat clearer though still relatively covert allusion appears near the end of "The Ax-Helve," to resolve by its implications the argument about knowledge and education between the narrator and his neighbor. This neighbor, Baptiste, has been arguing that the knowledge that his children get from experience is more valuable than book-learning "laid-on" artificially in school. The ax-helve has become a symbol of "natural" education in contrast to the abstract or academic by virtue of the built-in curves of the helve "native to the grain before the knife / Expressed them," rather than imposed cross-grain on a straight stick. On this basis, the poem is a fairly straightforward account, with local color, of a pastoral dialogue.

After finally trimming the ax-helve, however, Baptiste stands

. . . the ax there on its horse's hoof,

> Erect, but not without its waves, as when
> The snake stood up for evil in the Garden.

In this allusion to *Paradise Lost,* Frost points up the difference be-
tween knowledge given in abstract terms to man, as in formal educa-
tion, and knowledge gained by him through his own experience, like
Baptiste's. When man, at the serpent's prompting, ate the fruit of
the tree of knowledge, he embarked on the human process of ac-
quiring knowledge for himself, through his own experience. As the
result of disobedience to God this has been called "evil," but its ulti-
mate result is good, according to the doctrine of the "Fortunate Fall"
which Milton held to. The implication in the context of Frost's poem
is that nonacademic experience is not simply better education but is
more valid and significant for man because it is "natural" human ac-
tivity, rather than artificial and authoritarian knowledge imposed on
man. The poem carries a humanistic implication of the worth and
validity of mankind independent of the direct control of God.

   Frost's use of the ax-helve as a symbol of man's knowledge illus-
trates why he called himself a "synecdochist."[6] He believed in con-
centrating on particular, small, often single examples of general and
broad ideas or phenomena, and his usual practice reflects this belief.
A simple thing like an ax-helve, a stone wall, or the song of a bird
points toward issues that involve man's relations with other men,
with his universe, and sometimes with God. The process is charac-
teristic of Frost, and since he concentrated particularly on the exam-
ples he found in New England, he seemed to be a local poet. He en-
joyed his pose of Yankee farmer, and he may not have realized just
how many people would be content with that and fail to perceive
further symbolic dimensions in his poems. An appreciation of the
particular, descriptive level of Frost's poetry is necessary, of course;
indeed it is the combination of this with the perception of symbolic
implications that makes his work effective as pastoral poetry in Ly-
nen's sense. "The Oven Bird" is a perfect illustration of Frost's
synecdochic method:

> There is a singer everyone has heard,
> Loud, a mid-summer and a mid-wood bird,
> Who makes the solid tree trunks sound again.
> He says that leaves are old and that for flowers
> Mid-summer is to spring as one to ten.
> He says the early petal-fall is past,
> When pear and cherry bloom went down in showers
> On sunny days a moment overcast;
> And comes that other fall we name the fall.

He says the highway dust is over all.
The bird would cease and be as other birds
But that he knows in singing not to sing.
The question that he frames in all but words
Is what to make of a diminished thing.

In style, scene, and structure, this is quite simple, and in prosody
almost equally so; thematically, however, it has significantly wider
implications. The style is concise, and almost pedestrian, from the
flat "There is" of the opening to the prosaic phrases of the final lines:
"The question that he frames," "what to make of"; this style is as ap-
propriate to the point of the poem as the bird's song is to the sea-
son.[7] The scene is restricted: woods in midsummer with the sound of
the teacher-bird echoing through the trees. This material is pre-
sented in a three-part progressive structure: the first three lines
identify the bird, the season, and the place; the next seven describe
the season; and the last four lines point up the appropriateness of
the bird's unmelodic song. This is the way the poem works in im-
mediate terms; it concerns the fact that midsummer is a falling-off
from the freshness of spring, and that the loudness and harshness of
the bird's song (sometimes described as "teacher-teacher") is one ap-
propriate way to respond to that diminishment, much more in keep-
ing with the season than the fresh and lilting songs of thrushes and
other springtime birds would be.

But it is clear that this immediate reading, valid though it is, is too
limited. Frost is talking about this bird in that season, but in doing so
he is also asking about diminishment in general and how to deal with
it. There is an analogy with "Nothing Gold Can Stay," and to some
aspects of "West-Running Brook":

Some say existence like a Pirouot
And Pirouette, forever in one place,
Stands still and dances, but it runs away;
It seriously, sadly, runs away
To fill the abyss's void with emptiness.

Midsummer, in "The Oven Bird," especially with the threat of the
coming fall, represents diminishment in general, a loss of innocence;
the song of the oven bird symbolizes a valid reaction to that loss. One
should not try to wax lyrical under conditions that derogate such an
impulse; if one must "sing," then one should refrain from sentimen-
tality. Further, however, the intensity of the oven bird's song
suggests that it amounts to a protest, a positive objection to the di-
minishment, in contrast to the other birds, which have subsided re-

signedly into quiet. And to give a special focus and power to the poem, the bird is made to represent the poet himself: As "singer" and "maker" ("what to *make* of a diminished thing"), indeed as prophet—a voice crying in the wilderness—the bird is Frost himself.[8]

Frost is not an "imagist," for he does not simply present images without comment, relying on the reader to perceive their significance; he usually provides at least a hint that his immediate subject carries wider or deeper implications. But he shares with the imagists the focus on the particular scene and object as analogue or symbol. This combination of the particular and the general, this offer of two perspectives simultaneously, is one source of a vital duality in his poetry, which, although it is not obvious or specifically identifiable in the works themselves, colors our reading. Frost must be read in a Janus-like "double-think" frame of mind, the simple and particular coexisting in our perceptions with the complex and general.

Along with this perspective, Frost's poems often provide a duality of tone, amiable or light, and serious at the same time. As we have seen, Frost often uses his wit and humor to develop his themes and further their effect, as in the puns in "Mending Wall" and "Design," and the understatement in "Directive." On the other hand, his "fooling," which bothers certain readers, especially in *A Masque of Reason*, often contributes only to the general tone, stemming as it does from Frost's wish to hide his concern. In the first case, the combination of wit and seriousness is a kind of literary ambivalence widely recognized and accepted. In the second case, the duality may involve a basic inconsistency, and the resulting tension would be much greater. In both cases, nevertheless, a perceptible tension exists between a relative lightness of tone and seriousness. If the discrepancy between the surface tone and the deeper seriousness is too great, as it sometimes seems in the *Masques,* then some readers will find it difficult to accept the work. In most of Frost's poetry, however, the conjunction of humor with seriousness is just evident enough to be effective without stretching to the breaking point.

But there are even more important reasons for the vitality in Frost's poetry. One is that the tone of his poetry reflects Frost's two typical but different general attitudes toward man and experience. On the one hand, the poetry is imbued with gentleness, benevolence, and "acceptance," while on the other, it often betrays an equally characteristic egotism and skepticism—a "hard-nosed" attitude. In terms of poetic technique or mode, the poetry may be lyrical, with a normally closer aesthetic distance from the poet to the subject and the reader, or it may be almost "antipoetic," more discursive, with a much greater aesthetic distance.

Some of Frost's best-loved poems come to mind immediately as examples of his gentler, more lyrical side: poems like "Birches" most clearly support the Frost myth. "The Silken Tent" shows many of the same tonal qualities—the sense of close involvement with and love for the subject, the woman, and the gentleness felt through the rhythm and style:

> She is as in a field a silken tent
> At midday when a sunny summer breeze
> Has dried the dew and all its ropes relent,
> So that in guys it gently sways at ease,
> And its supporting central cedar pole,
> That is its pinnacle to heavenward
> And signifies the sureness of the soul,
> Seems to owe naught to any single cord,
> But strictly held by none, is loosely bound
> By countless silken ties of love and thought
> To everything on earth the compass round,
> And only by one's going slightly taut
> In the capriciousness of summer air
> Is of the slightest bondage made aware.

The tone is reinforced by the emphasis on heavenward aspiration coupled with earthly love and benevolence. The poet here is open, warm, and trusting, and involves the reader, too, in these attitudes. "The Pasture" will clarify this tone further, especially as it is represented by a direct invitation to the reader, drawing him close to the poet.

In contrast, we have such poems as "Into My Own," "Fire and Ice," "Beyond Words," and "The Planners"; here, the poet seems to turn away from the reader, or even further, to turn against him as in "Beyond Words":

> That row of icicles along the gutter
> Feels like my armory of hate;
> And you, you . . . you, you utter. . . .
> You wait!

We would hardly consider this venomous attitude typical of Frost, but it is not essentially different from "Fire and Ice," one of his best-known epigrammatic lyrics. The emphasis there on hate and its correlative ice, and the implied antagonism in the style and rhythm, are at another extreme from "Birches" and "The Pasture." Many of the poems that manifest Frost's tougher side are less bitter than "Fire and Ice," but they can be just as "antipoetic" in a different way. "Build Soil," for example, in addition to the rather sardonic tone, has a style and rhythm much like prose. As a genre, it is more discursive than imaginative, and the same is true to a lesser degree of "The Bear," "Departmental," and most of the epigrams.

Thus in Frost's poetry taken as a whole there is a tonal duality in the kindliness and lyricism of a large number of poems, and the skepticism and bitterness found in others. It is perfectly normal, of course, for a poet to manifest different attitudes at different times. What is interesting in Frost is first that these contradictory attitudes are evidenced persistently throughout his work, and second that often they both inform the tone of single poems. Many poems are mixtures or fusions of lyricism and "antipoetry," of benevolence and skepticism. Consider " 'Out, Out—'": The boy who loses his hand and his life is certainly presented sympathetically, and early in the poem various details of the setting are pleasantly described—the sweet scent of the wood and the mountain ranges in the background. But much of the poem is more straightforward narrative, offered in a relatively discursive style and rhythm. The tonal duality is crystallized in the last two or three lines, where the understatements sound coldblooded and antipoetic, yet acknowledge the pathos indirectly. Similarly, "Neither Out Far nor In Deep" is perhaps an even closer fusion of tones:

> The people along the sand
> All turn and look one way.
> They turn their back on the land.
> They look at the sea all day.
>
> As long as it takes to pass
> A ship keeps raising its hull;
> The wetter ground like glass
> Reflects a standing gull.
>
> The land may vary more;
> But wherever the truth may be—
> The water comes ashore,
> And the people look at the sea.
>
> They cannot look out far.
> They cannot look in deep.
> But when was that ever a bar
> To any watch they keep?

The poem is lyrically poetic in its vivid images, strong rhythm, and central symbolic situation, but the flatly declarative style seems quite prosaic and thus antipoetic. The emotional tonality is thus difficult to identify; is the poet scornful of people who gaze searchingly but futilely out to sea, or does he admire them? Both attitudes are suggested simultaneously. "The people," as Frost terms them rather condescendingly—as if they were sheep, perhaps—ignore the land, their proper domain. They see very little; their view of the ship is necessarily limited because at any real distance much of it is below the horizon, and their view of the gull is simply a reflection from the surface of the watery sand. The style itself, flat as it is, suggests a lack of imagination in the watchers. At the same time, nevertheless, the poem suggests the eternal fascination of the sea and its mystery, with the implication that it may be the realm of "truth"—as water has always embodied it in some sense (witness "The Pasture" and "For Once, Then, Something"). Moreover, the watch is not entirely futile, for the people do see something, which is described in the most lyrical terms offered in the poem.[9] All in all, the poet sounds as if he acknowledges the futility of looking at the sea, but concedes that people are right to keep searching.

An especially interesting example of this dual tone is "The Need of Being Versed in Country Things." The main point of the poem is of course that the phoebes nesting in the barn are really not lamenting the burning of the house, for they are part of the natural world, rather than man's. The general tone, moreover, is relatively restrained, even matter-of-fact at times, thanks partly to the common diction and the conversational rhythm:

> For them there was really nothing sad.
> But though they rejoiced in the nest they kept,
> One had to be versed in country things
> Not to believe the phoebes wept.

The poet explicitly rejects the sentimental tone which might be suggested by such phrases as "the barn . . . forsaken," and "no more." But in the last two stanzas, while he is representing the phoebes' normal, unanthropomorphized existence, the poet employs certain words in key spots to develop a tonality invested with human emotion which becomes attached to the birds. Describing the elm as "touched" by the fire, and saying that the pump "flung up an . . . arm" and that the post "carried" the wire infuses these inanimates with a degree of humanity which inevitably involves the phoebes. More directly, although Frost says that the birds don't feel the human sadness, they do feel joy in the nest they are keeping. The general tone of "let's be realistic and face facts" in the poem is thus undercut—not necessarily in a bad sense—by a gentler and more sentimental flavor despite the explicit argument to the contrary.

These various kinds of ambiguity or duality in Frost's poems produce a certain tension, especially since the ambiguity often amounts to the opposition of apparently inconsistent perspectives and concerns. This vitality due to conflict is highly characteristic of Frost's work, as evidenced in the fact that he often adopted a dramatic mode as a means of developing his material. Whether in the specific form of plays or otherwise, he tended to develop his material as an overt conflict. The dialogues are obviously dramatic—the opposition between man and woman, for example, generates the intensity in many poems. In ones like "Home Burial," it is powerful, while in "West-Running Brook," it is moderated.

Most of the monologues, too, imply a conflict, "A Servant to Servants" and "The Pauper Witch of Grafton" being good cases in point. Even a large number of the lyrics are elaborations or reflections of some kind of opposed positions, beliefs, or attitudes. In his many sonnets, for example, Frost typically generates a certain opposition.[10] In "Range-Finding" it is between the world of nature and that of man's wars; in "Acceptance" the threat of darkness is opposed to the desire for security; in "Design" optimistic faith confronts the "design of darkness."

Most significantly in a large number of these poems based on opposed positions the tension is perpetuated because the conflict is not explicitly or fully resolved. In "The Subverted Flower," for one, the fault is shared to some extent by both the boy and the girl; and "For Once, Then, Something," "The Ax-Helve," and "The Oven Bird" all conclude with some form of question. There are poems like "Birches" and "The Road Not Taken" that end with a positive assertion, but these are relatively rare, and most of them emphasize some kind of opposition in the course of their development. In "Birches" the reality of earth is prized as highly as man's heavenly aspirations, and "The Road Not Taken" reflects a valid desire for significant choice as well as the difficulty of achieving it. The balance between opposed points of view in so many of Frost's poems is a primary source of vitality.

In a most fundamental sense, this duality is modal (in Northrop Frye's sense of "mode").[11] Specifically, Frost is divided between representing the world in "low-mimetic" or in "ironic" terms. The low-mimetic modes indicate a conception of the world as a quite ordinary place where "normal" human beings are generally competent enough to achieve satisfying lives. Literature in this mode, such as the work of most Romantic and Victorian poets, shows us people "like us" in a physical environment that is neither overpowering nor debased, where the usual domestic animals tend to figure. The poet who sees the world thus adopts an appropriate role, that of a thoughtful, introspective person who has achieved an understanding of experience that serves meaningfully to readers. The "ironic" poet, on the other hand, finds the world a frightening or repellent place, where most people are either victims or degenerates, below normal in competence. Ironic literature like Eliot's *The Waste Land* and Yeats's "The Second Coming" show nature to be disintegrating and destructive, and the poet adopts the role of a noncommittal craftsman because he cannot safely offer any reliable insights into such a problematic existence. Frost sometimes fulfills the role of an ironic poet, sometimes that of a low-mimetic one.

This ambiguity is evident in several aspects of the materials of his poetry. The various kinds of imagery and characters are split, to begin with. The divine imagery is sometimes conventionally Christian, that is, high-mimetic or even romantic, and sometimes ironic. The high-mimetic and romantic modes are progressively more idealized representations of the world; high-mimetic literature focuses on human beings who are superior in degree to most people, such as kings and statesmen, and the plant and animal imagery tends to be correspondingly "elevated" above the ordinary. The imagery in the romantic mode is even less worldly, and heroes can become superhuman—knights can slay dragons, for instance, and saints can achieve miracles. The imagery of heaven in "The Trial by Existence" is largely high-mimetic or romantic ("the light of heaven falls whole and white"); similarly, in "Birches" heaven is the ideal realm of purity and light, a place to aspire to. Modally, this is at an even further extreme than the low-mimetic level from the ironic. Yet Frost often represents God and other images of divinity in an ironic mode. "Design," for instance, suggests that the governing supernatural power is evil. More significantly, however, in the *Masques* God appears inscrutable and deceptive, even frightening in some ways; in addition, He and those who concern themselves closely with Him—at least in *A Masque of Reason*—are treated in joking, wry terms rather than with the reverence that would be appropriate in a more conventional romantic mode. It is the ironic mode here that no doubt offends readers—they must feel the tension between Frost's mode and the seriousness of the implicit conventional romantic mode.

The modal ambiguity is easy to see in the animal and vegetable imagery. Frost's birds are usually the ordinary phoebes and crows common in New England, and the horses and cows are the domestic animals of the farms. But in contrast to the ordinary horse of "Stopping by Woods" we see the ominous draft horse in the poem of that name, and in contrast to the "normal" deer in "Two Look at Two" there is the "great buck" that "appeared . . . with horny tread" in "The Most of It." And also on the ironic level are the spider of "Design," and the helpless moths of that poem and of "To a Moth Seen in Winter," as well as the significantly disparaged ants and hornets of "Departmental" and "The White-Tailed Hornet." Frost sees his New England as a pleasantly normal land of farms and pastures and domestic animals, but he also sees it as a land of dark woods, of snow and winter cold, and of animal life belonging to a darker than normal order of existence.

The most important imagery in Frost's poetry, the human, is even more clearly divided. His characters are often represented in low-mimetic terms—that is, as realistic and ordinary people. The farmers in "The Mountain," "The Ax-Helve," and "A Star in a Stoneboat" are common enough Yankee types. The married couples in "The Death of the Hired Man" and "West-Running Brook" have the normal amount of affection and understanding and disagreement. All of these, and others, are at home in the world, which is generally much like ours despite local differences, and they can cope with it satisfactorily. At the other pole, however, are the vulnerable people like Silas (the Hired Man), the protagonist of "An Old Man's Winter Night," the futile gazers in "Neither Out Far nor In Deep," the boy in " 'Out, Out—,' " and almost all the human figures in the *Masques*. The most notable victims are women like those in "A Servant to Servants," "The Hill Wife," and "The Lovely Shall Be Choosers," while over against these we can place the beautifully resolved "The Silken Tent," not to mention the more ambiguous figures of the two witches, who are resolute though thwarted. The relationships between men and women, too, are often ill-starred or inadequate to the conditions of ordinary human life. The couples in "Home Burial" and "The Subverted Flower" cannot understand each other, the marriage of "The Hill Wife" is destroyed by the isolation as well as the lack of mutual understanding, and the pair in "The Draft Horse," though evidently in accord, are clearly at the mercy of a cruel and obscure fate.

Besides the modal ambiguity of the imagery and the characters, there is in Frost's poetry an ambiguity in his use of the Eden myth, one central to Frost.[12] Dozens of poems come to mind in which the Eden myth figures explicitly or symbolically, among them "A Winter Eden," "Reluctance," "The Ax-Helve," "West-Running Brook," "The Subverted Flower," and, most prototypically, "Nothing Gold Can

Stay." In many of these poems Frost represents a longing for inno-
cence, for the green and golden Edenic state. This longing is anal-
ogous to sophisticated man's idealization of the pastoral world, so
that Frost acknowledges, albeit reluctantly, and often with despair,
that Eden has gone.

It is hard to say whether the desire for Eden or the sense that it
has gone is stronger in the poetry. In some poems, a recreation of
the Edenic state seems to have emerged from the desire for it. As
Nitchie points out, poems like "Going for Water" present "two lovers
who constitute their own world—Adam and Eve in Paradise."[13]
Similarly, "Directive" takes us on a journey back in time to a state of
innocence "beyond confusion." Often, too, the natural world, as dis-
tinct from the world of man, seems to have something of the simplic-
ity and beauty of Eden. "Dust of Snow" will illustrate the essential
quality here:

> The way a crow
> Shook down on me
> The dust of snow
> From a hemlock tree
>
> Has given my heart
> A change of mood
> And saved some part
> Of a day I had rued.

The narrator, wrapped in his human concerns, is depressed, but the
intrusion from the innocent and even playful natural world redeems
his spirits at least momentarily. Similarly, the narrator in "A Bound-
less Moment" has a momentary contact with Edenic nature, although
the illusion is self-imposed: he deliberately imagines for a moment that
"a young beech clinging to its last year's leaves" in March is " 'the
Paradise-in-Bloom.' " The natural world is a possible locus of Edenic
beauty and freshness, especially in contrast to the sad realities of
man's world. In this respect Frost has been considered a "nature
poet" like Wordsworth—he invested rural New England, at times,
with the ideality of the pastoral; that is, he saw "in the life of rural
New England a remote, ideal world which could serve the same
function as Arcadia," to serve as a standard for reference, and par-
ticularly a contrast to the "normal" human world.[14]

No matter how strong the desire for a pastoral Eden seems in
Frost's poetry, however, one is usually conscious that it can be no
more than a pretense or a saving illusion. Just as the narrator in "A
Boundless Moment" pretends to see the Paradise-in-Bloom, so the

couple in "Two Look at Two" feel as if there were a real communion between them and the doe and buck:

> Two had seen two, whichever side you spoke from.
> "This *must* be all." It was all. Still they stood,
> A great wave from it going over them,
> As if the earth in one unlooked-for favor
> Had made them certain earth returned their love.

The poem is especially pathetic because man and nature are "so near yet so far," while at the same time Frost avoids sentimentality by a strong sense of realism. The human pair are loving, but they know how rough the path is, and do not forget that they must return home. Further, although they are brought closer and closer to real contact with the buck and doe, a wall still separates them. The animals are not humanized except in pretense. "As if" is the keynote here: the humans *"almost"* feel "dared / To stretch a proffering hand," and it is only *"as if* the earth . . . returned their love" (italics added).

In many other poems, the sense is clear and strong that real and present nature is unpleasant for man, if not inimical. When one is "versed in country things," one knows that human affairs do not really trouble nature. If one thinks of storms ("Storm Fear," "Once by the Pacific"), or the desolation of winter ("Desert Places," "An Old Man's Winter Night"), one knows how vulnerable man is to natural forces. The material world is usually very different from the serenity and benevolence of Eden; it is a "diminished thing" and is subject to mutability ("In Hardwood Groves," "The Onset"). It may be a purposeless and random confusion or even essentially evil, as "Design" suggests.

Human beings and their affairs are just as ambiguously represented. Over against the recreations of Adam and Eve, like those in "Two Look at Two," we find many more couples who cannot or will not touch or understand each other.[15] The pairs in "Home Burial" and "The Subverted Flower" are extreme but representative cases. For the most part, man and woman are clearly postlapsarian. At their worst, they quarrel like Adam and Eve after the Fall in *Paradise Lost*; at best, they have only moments of closeness that recall departed bliss. What man can reasonably hope for is a relationship like that of Warren and Mary in "The Death of the Hired Man," or the pair in "West-Running Brook." These achieve a degree of communion by mutual concessions, by sorting out their differences, by mild argument, for they live in the real world where human relationships are always ambivalent and uncertain.

On the whole, then, the material in Frost's poetry—the universe, and the beings in it—is ambiguous in a fundamental sense. It is a mixture, or alternation, or fusion of the ironic with the low-mimetic (and occasionally the high-mimetic or romantic) in Frye's sense. We seem to encounter a universe which is on the one hand often inscrutable and uncontrollable, and on the other familiar and comprehensible to some degree where experience can be partly determined by human will.

Frost's conception of his own role as a poet has a corresponding ambiguity, for we can distinguish two poetic impulsions or characters.[16] In the low-mimetic mode, the poet speaks to himself in the lyric, and is overheard by the reader—this is the role of Wordsworth and Keats, and other Romantic poets in the conventional sense. The poet speaks with some confidence in himself and in the validity of his meanings because the world seems to exist on his own level, and he has some competence within it.[17] More recently, on the other hand, the poet has been less sure of his competence—his world is less comprehensible and controllable, and unless he has great self-confidence he will present his material without asserting meanings, perhaps suggesting unanswered or unanswerable questions that are implicit in the incongruities he observes—this is the poet of the ironic mode.

There is evidence of both of these roles in Frost's work. They cannot be absolutely distinguished, but certain tendencies seem clearly to point toward one or the other. The mask of levity and understatement that he hides behind, for example, as well as his reluctance at times to assert his theme directly or explicitly—as in "The Most of It" and his dramatic monologues and dialogues—manifest his more impersonal "ironic" role. So, too, does his concern with poetic technique, as reflected in explicit discussions of it and in the kinds of prosodic competence his poems embody. The tension Frost derives from real or apparent inconsistencies in poems like "The Subverted Flower" and from unresolved conflicts or oppositions as in "For Once, Then, Something" are also consistent with the ironic poet's characteristic preoccupation with unanswerable questions.

At the same time, Frost's work is enough like Wordsworth's to reveal a more personal role. He usually speaks directly as a recognizable individual; it is arguable that Frost often speaks in his own voice in his lyrics. His tone may be bitter and despairing, or gentle and accepting, and at different times he may be of different minds, as anyone is, but to the extent that the views and the attitudes found in his poetry are also reflected in his letters and in the events of his life we may consider them his. Both the "myth" and the darker side of Frost are partly fabrications, but they are more largely genuine; and although Frost maintained that "everything written is as good as it is dramatic," it is himself that he liked to dramatize much of the time.[18] For this reason, his observations about life and man assume added importance as evidence of his low-mimetic poetic role. In this role, he often establishes his main themes overtly even as an explicit "moral" at the end of poems. That is, he shows enough confidence in his ability to cope with the world to assert his meaning positively. In particular, he seems to maintain that he himself is significant enough in a broad context to warrant his introspection. Thus in many poems he is concerned with his own problems and has something important to say about them. Whether he generalizes explicitly on the basis of his personal experience ("One could do worse than be a swinger of birches") or not ("I have promises to keep"), he offers his experience as a source of information for mankind in general through the process of synecdoche.[19]

This modal ambiguity indicates clearly how basic is the division in Frost's work which creates its characteristic tension. When we considered the elusiveness of Frost and his work, we found that he sometimes liked to mystify his readers, but that he more commonly liked to assume a mask of levity or irony to hide his real and serious concerns. This deceptiveness makes us conscious simultaneously of what Frost seems to mean, and of what else or more he is aiming at. Frost's elusiveness, that is, represents the same ambiguity we found in his tone and style, and in the multiple modes of his work.

The tension resulting from this pervasive ambiguity is generally low-keyed, but it is persistent because the ambiguity is so seldom resolved. Frost is rarely of a single mind because he is so conscious of the complexity of man and his universe. His poetry embodies varying impressions of the nature of the cosmos and a consequent uncertainty about man's place in it and his proper role and stance. Frost's work indicates a mixture of faith and confidence in the cosmos and in himself on the one hand, and of uncertainty or even fearfulness about man's position on the other. Sometimes the poetry is only a "momentary stay against confusion" while at other times it reflects a confidence that "we'll be all right if nothing goes wrong with the lighting."[20] And in some ways it is often both at the same time, because Frost's problematic *Weltanschauung* is so fundamental—this we can see, though the roots of his problems are obscure.

"Something for Hope":
The Manageable World

Robert Frost's poetry shows that he believed at times, or with part of his mind, that the world and man's position in it are fundamentally satisfactory, even pleasant. It may not be the best of all possible worlds, but it seems, on balance, to be manageable. This attitude reveals Frost's "Americanism," as Henry Knepler applies the word.[1] Frost is sometimes uncertain, even despairing, but his work also often shows considerable confidence in man's function in the world. He accepts the world as basically satisfactory a good deal of the time, showing himself to be at home in it and even to consider it comprehensible to some extent. We know where we stand, he says, and conditions are at least somewhat in our favor.

There is, of course, the darker side of Frost which considers the world fearsome and incomprehensible, and man unfortunate and unhappy. The conflict between the optimistic and the pessimistic conceptions of the world is the source of much of the basic ambiguity and the tension in Frost's work. Later, we will consider the darker side in detail, for it still continues to be distorted by the popular poetic mask of the New England sage and the image of the "simple plain-spoken farmer."[2] More fundamental than the conflict between the darker and the lighter sides of Frost, however, is that he is partly religious and partly unreligious. Frost's poetry sometimes represents man and the universe as governed by God directly or indirectly, while at other times the poetry is largely secular, or even agnostic. The mode, the attitude embodied in the poems, varies from optimism to pessimism, but beneath that variation lies the more basic ontological uncertainty. There is clear evidence in Frost's work, as well as his life, that he believed in God, either a benevolent or a not-so-benevolent one, but there is also much evidence of a universe in which a God is either irrelevant or absent. Most of the secular poems can, no doubt, be considered basically compatible or consistent with the religious poems, at least when they are optimistic. What is significant is that although Frost may be fundamentally religious, he seems also to be absorbed primarily with man's worldly existence.

One of the most reassuring impressions that conservative readers form of Frost is due to those poems reflecting a relatively conventional Christianity, a faith in a benevolent and beneficent God. Sometimes man and the earth are considered difficult, but not so much as to threaten seriously the basic faith. As Frost once put it to Sidney Cox, "God . . . is that which a man is sure cares, and will save him, no matter how many times or how completely he has failed."[3]

The most obvious of the themes, motifs, and images that betoken this conventional belief is the direct representation of man's relationship with God and heaven. We find these predictably in some of Frost's most popular poems—"Birches," for instance. Everyone familiar with Frost recognizes the symbolism in the conclusion:

> I'd like to get away from earth awhile
> And then come back to it and begin over.
> May no fate willfully misunderstand me
> And half grant what I wish and snatch me away
> Not to return. Earth's the right place for love:
> I don't know where it's likely to go better.
> I'd like to go by climbing a birch tree,
> And climb black branches up a snow-white trunk
> *Toward* heaven, till the tree could bear no more,
> But dipped its top and set me down again.
> That would be good both going and coming back.
> One could do worse than be a swinger of birches.

Frost clearly is thinking in terms of a temporal world that is difficult yet still "the place for love," and of a spiritual world available at least as inspiration and consolation. The same image of heaven at the top of a tree appears in "After Apple-Picking":

> My long two-pointed ladder's sticking through a tree
> Toward heaven still . . .

The aim toward heaven sets the focus for the whole poem: It becomes increasingly evident that Frost is dealing with the relationship between man's labor and the surcease from it, between earthly life and a possible afterlife:

> One can see what will trouble
> This sleep of mine, whatever sleep it is.
> Were he not gone,
> The woodchuck could say whether it's like his

> Long sleep, as I describe its coming on,
> Or just some human sleep.

Even clearer manifestations of Frost's conventional Christianity
are "The Silken Tent" and "A Steeple on the House":

> What if it should turn out eternity
> Was but the steeple on our house of life
> That made our house of life a house of worship?
> . . . .
> A spire and belfry coming on the roof
> Means that a soul is coming on the flesh.

The woman described in "The Silken Tent" functions in a Chris-
tian context. Earth is again the place for love, and provides a loose
stability on that basis, while the aspiration toward heaven offers a
more spiritual kind of guidance, a contact with God which provides a
central orientation for the soul. Similarly, "A Steeple on the House"
explicitly deals with the relation between earth and heaven, life and
afterlife, suggesting in the reverential phrase "our house of life" a
fundamental contentment with earthly existence.

This earthly contentment is further represented by a second major
Christian motif or theme, that of the earth's direct reflection of
heaven. Early in his life Frost was introduced by his mother to the
notion of correspondences between heaven and earth, of symbolic
representations of heaven in earthly things, and later he felt the in-
fluence of Emerson and Thoreau, and of Transcendentalism.[4] Some
indications of these influences appear particularly in the religious
symbolic value that certain physical objects and phenomena have in
Frost's poetry. And thanks to this value, earth is often connected to
heaven in satisfying ways. This connection is most clearly repre-
sented by trees and by the sun, a familiar archetypal symbol of the
father principle and of creative energy. "Sitting by a Bush in Broad
Sunlight" makes a clear link between the sun and God as a means of
joining natural and spiritual worlds:

> God once spoke to people by name.
> The sun once imparted its flame.
> One impulse persists as our breath;
> The other persists as our faith.

The analogy between the actions and functions of God and of the
sun indicate at least an indirect connection between them. Religion

and science, though different, provide us in this poem with parallel perceptions of humanity: The sun is the counterpart in terms of our physical existence of God, the source of our spiritual life.

There are some trees in Frost's poetry, especially *en masse* as woods or forest, that are not so reassuring—in "Spring Pools," for example, they are more of a threat to innocence and purity, like the summer woods in "The Oven Bird." But singly they often carry positive connotations, particularly when they serve a religious role. In "Birches" and less obviously in "After Apple-Picking" a tree is a means of climbing toward heaven at least momentarily, much as Zaccheus climbed the tree, "Our Lord to see" in "Sycamore," the poem Frost took from the *New England Primer* for one epigraph to *A Witness Tree*. In "Directive," one might add, an old cedar serves to hold the drinking cup ("like the Grail") which the right ones are to use to renew their spiritual integrity at the spring. Finally, we might note Frost's use of color in "Fragmentary Blue" to connect heaven and earth:

> Why make so much of fragmentary blue
> In here and there a bird, or butterfly,
> Or flower, or wearing-stone, or open eye,
> When heaven presents in sheets the solid hue?
>
> Since earth is earth, perhaps, not heaven (as yet)—
> Though some savants make earth include the sky;
> And blue so far above us comes so high,
> It only gives our wish for blue a whet.

The pleasant details—bird, butterfly, jewel, eyes—in which the color of heaven is reflected suggest that the established link makes the earth a pleasant, though not the ultimate home for man.

In addition to the evidences in Frost's poetry of a direct tie between earth and heaven, between man and God, there are indications that the poet felt a generalized Christian love. He knew hate, we realize, but he was also personally affectionate, even benevolent. A corresponding sense of "charity"—of disinterested, spiritual Christian love for man and beast—emerges in some of the poetry, to help create a pleasant, "manageable" world. Such a generalized love in a religious context is evident in "Birches" and "A Silken Tent"; the same is most clearly the case with "A Prayer in Spring":

> Oh, give us pleasure in the flowers today;
> And give us not to think so far away
> As the uncertain harvest; keep us here
> All simply in the springing of the year.

. . . .
For this is love and nothing else is love,
The which it is reserved for God above
To sanctify to what far ends He will,
But which it only needs that we fulfill.

The shared happiness represented here as love seems to be more
than simply a personal relationship between two lovers; rather it is a
general benevolence which, in being sanctified by God, makes for a
good world.

A similar feeling is shared by the two mowers in "The Tuft of
Flowers." The speaker, finding a tuft of flowers left deliberately by a
previous mower, senses "a spirit kindred to [his] own" and concludes
that " 'men work together . . . / Whether they work together or
apart.' " And the same kind of impersonal but hopeful human con-
tact is found in "A Missive Missile" and "An Unstamped Letter in
Our Rural Letter Box." Although the first of these is concerned
explicitly with the deficient communication between the prehistoric
man who decorated the "pebble wheel" and the poet who is examin-
ing it, the speaker considers it some kind of human contact, and
there is a "mortal longing" for the "two souls" to meet. The contact is
less tenuous in the unstamped letter left by the tramp in the poet's
letter box, and both represent an attempt at contact which is a pre-
lude to Christian love.

"The Death of the Hired Man" shows most clearly the kind of
"charity" Frost was capable of believing in to the betterment of his
vision of the world. The kindness that Mary and eventually Warren
show toward Silas derives from heaven, as the passages linking Mary
with the moon suggest. Significantly, Mary's definition of "home" as
"something you somehow haven't to deserve" represents mercy "in
its deepest religious sense of undeserved grace"[5] and corresponds
almost perfectly with Frost's definition of God mentioned earlier:
"That which a man is sure cares, and will save him, no matter how
many times or how completely he has failed." Since the focus in the
poem falls on the Christian benevolence of Mary and Warren in ac-
cepting Silas, the world appears largely good.

The scenes involving Mary with the moon and sky convey an al-
most ineffable quality, a sense of direct spiritual contact between her
and heaven which represents a third motif in Frost's poetry, indica-
tive of a basically Christian perspective revealing a satisfying uni-
verse. At one end of the scale this motif appears as fantasy and
superstition; at the other it is intuition, idealism, almost mysticism.

Frost called himself superstitious—and this was evidently no mere
whimsy. Thompson has made it clear that Frost's whole attitude to-

ward life was derived to a significant degree from his mother's Swedenborgianism, and that he consequently believed himself to be mystical even to the extent of having prophetic powers.[6] A recent dissertation, further, argues convincingly that Frost was epistemologically intuitional to a large extent; that is, he believed that knowledge of the external world is to be acquired in large part by intuitive means, as well as empirically or rationally.[7] These tendencies were fostered not only by his mother, but also by his readings of and a general spiritual kinship with Emerson, Thoreau, and William James. Frost's relationship with them will be discussed later; it has, moreover, been explored in detail elsewhere;[8] all we need to note here is that their influence, added to other personal tendencies, helped lead him to approach experience intuitively and in religious terms and, part of the time, to regard the world optimistically and pleasurably as a result.

The degree of immediate contact with the divine that nature sometimes affords, as in "Birches" and "Fragmentary Blue," is one reflection of Frost's "mystical" approach to experience, one which has led some readers to take Frost as an Emersonian. Frost rarely sees as much of the divine in physical things, however, and is seldom as optimistic as Emerson. But in poems like "Sitting by a Bush in Broad Sunlight" and "A Prayer in Spring," we have seen signs that Frost had considerable faith in a beneficent divine plan immediately manifested in our world. In "Sitting by a Bush" the evolutionary process is taken as God's benevolent design on the same kind of intuitional basis employed by William James. The intuitional confidence appears even more strongly in the earlier "Prayer in Spring"; the poet feels no doubt that God will "sanctify" human love and feeling for nature to His "far ends"—and we easily infer that these ends are good.

Poems based on a conventionally hopeful religion are rare in Frost's canon, nevertheless. He was evidently seldom close to sanguine pantheism or to any confidence in the immediate benefits of a divine plan. There are certainly indications of a faith in God's ultimate design, as we shall see, but more normally this faith implied, indeed emphasized, intervening difficulties and uncertainties. When Frost is cheerful, when his poetry shows him to feel at home in the world, it is usually because he is satisfied with it in relatively material, secular, and indeed humanistic terms. He was hardly a thoroughgoing humanist and certainly no atheist, but he derived considerable happiness from the sight and touch of natural things and from the strength, humor, and kindness of man—enough happiness often to color his whole attitude toward experience.

This existential satisfaction rested in a conception of reality and of man's relation to it that was related to the philosophy of William James.[9] Frost, like James, evidently believed that external reality has some kind of independent existence, even though our perception of it may not reflect it directly or accurately. More significantly, James and Frost believed that man's perceptions of reality half create it; such perceptions are therefore highly important in man's life. The implications for man are basically two. Since he knows that his perceptions of reality are incomplete and uncertain, he is bound to search for the "truth" of that reality; "For Once, Then, Something," "Neither Out Far nor In Deep," and "All Revelation" indicate Frost's basic position, suggesting the satisfaction it can afford. In "For Once, Then, Something" the speaker says he has been accused of seeing only the surface reflection of himself in a setting of nature and heaven. He replies that once, however, he may have caught a glimpse in the water of a further reality—"Truth"—independent of man. It was uncertain, but it was there. The tone of the poem is ambiguous and amused, but the impression carried by the images of water, ferns, the summer heaven, cloud puffs, and of leaning over the well-curb to look into the water suggests a pleasant world where man can find quite satisfying occupations, not to mention some kind of dialogue with nature ("Water came to rebuke the too clear water").

"Neither Out Far nor In Deep" is equally ambiguous in tone: the people cannot see much, but there is something to see. Again, what the visible reality signifies is uncertain, but the activity of looking for it is partly satisfying, since the people do see something. Man's general environment, as the poem suggests it, is not unpleasant so much as unclear. We might remember an earlier poem, "The Star-Splitter," where an ex-farmer and the poet spend hours looking at stars through a telescope; they found out little about man's "place among the infinities," but they "said some of the best things they ever said" while they were gazing.

"All Revelation," finally, indicates most specifically Frost's belief in the importance of man's directing his thoughts toward external reality. We cannot tell precisely how much man's mind affects external reality—here represented as penetrating a geode—or just what the results may be, but this "witty" poem suggests in the last two stanzas that the universe responds so that man can comprehend it to some degree at least ("concentrating earth and skies / So none need be afraid of size."). Man's efforts bring out the nature of external reality, helping thereby to produce a universe in which he can feel at home.

On the basis of this attitude and this conception of the world, it is not surprising that a good deal of Frost's most enjoyable time was spent "botanizing," and that his poetry betokens an avid interest in the plants and animals of our world for the sake of the immediate sensuous and emotional pleasure they afford. Indeed, the Frost myth occasionally represents him as a "nature poet" who writes most of his lyrics about the birds and flowers he loved. It is certainly easy to see this aspect of his work in the early poems like "To the Thawing Wind" where he appeals to the "loud Southwester" to

> Run the rattling pages o'er;
> Scatter poems on the floor;
> Turn the poet out of door.

This is very much like Wordsworth's "The Tables Turned" ("Up! up! my Friend, and quit your books"): The vitality of the flowers, birds, and wind make them superior in their own right to the realm of books and the indoors.

This appreciation of external nature continued to run through his poetry the rest of Frost's life, perceptible usually as part of larger poems, but still occasionally as whole poems like "Questioning Faces" (1958):

> The winter owl banked just in time to pass
> And save herself from breaking window glass.
> And her wings straining suddenly aspread
> Caught color from the last of evening red
> In a display of underdown and quill
> To glassed-in children at the windowsill.

This poem shows that Frost was a "painterly poet," as Dorothy Judd Hall observes. He was able to reproduce his observations of natural shape, line, lighting, and color accurately. Here is "an instant in time caught visually: the last flush of sunset, a swift change in flight pattern, a momentary flash of color on outspread wings—all set within the window's frame for the children's view."[10]

This kind of sensuous appreciation of the physical world indicates Frost's basic satisfaction with external reality, which was expressed directly on occasion, as we might expect, in such poems as "Something for Hope." There he suggests that a meadow running to weeds will restore itself naturally: trees will eventually crowd out the weedy bushes, then will be cut for lumber to leave the meadow for grass again. He then concludes with the moral:

> Thus foresight does it and laissez-faire,
> . . . .
> Patience and looking away ahead,
> And leaving some things to take their course.
> Hope may not nourish a cow or horse,
> But *spes alit agricolam* 'tis said.

A basic faith in natural processes underlies the "laissez-faire" agriculture described here. The evidence suggests that, as a similar poem, "Our Hold on the Planet," put it, "nature . . . / Including human nature . . . must be a little more in favor of man." And since man finds his place in the natural order virtually assured, the question of his relationship with the divine world seems practically irrelevant. The emphasis in these poems falls, to begin with, on existential satisfaction, on the pleasures and rewards of life in the natural and human world as man perceives it. If this satisfaction is readily available and assured to man—especially if metaphysical "truth" is uncertain—then man hardly need concern himself with anything else.

The relationship between man and nature is sometimes even closer in Frost's work than this kind of mechanical beneficence, however. Frost is no pantheist, but like Wordsworth he can find a kind of inspiration in external nature, as "To the Thawing Wind" has shown. It is significant that Frost used "The Pasture" as the epigraph to his *Collected Poems,* for the poem suggests the symbolic inspiration he could find in nature. Truth and love, Frost is implying, are the central influences available in nature—and these themes run through much of his work.

A sense of real communion with nature—almost an "I-Thou" relationship on a secular level—is evidenced in certain other poems. In these Frost is not merely a recipient of nature's inspiration, but a participant in its activity, sharing and responding to its harmony. This communion is especially profound in "Iris by Night," in which Frost celebrated his friendship with Edward Thomas by recalling a moment when they were surrounded, indeed embraced, by nature:

> One misty evening, one another's guide,
> We two were groping down a Malvern side
> The last wet fields and dripping hedges home.
> . . . .
> Then a small rainbow like a trellis gate,

> A very small moon-made prismatic bow,
> Stood closely over us through which to go.
> And then . . .
>
> . . . .
>
> It lifted from its dewy pediment
> Its two mote-swimming many-colored ends
> And gathered them together in a ring.
> And we stood in it softly circled round
> From all division time or foe can bring
> In a relation of elected friends.

Even though Thomas was later killed in World War I, Frost remembers the experience in the poem as almost idyllic: The speaker in the poem is so profoundly immersed in human love and the love of nature that the universe is, for the moment, almost miraculously attuned.

Still another theme appears occasionally in Frost's poetry to indicate a link between man and nature. In "The Valley's Singing Day," the poet praises someone—perhaps his wife—for having awakened the birds and started them singing; in "The Aim Was Song" man exerts a beneficial influence on nature by teaching the wind to make music:

> Before man came to blow it right
>   The wind once blew itself untaught,
> And did its loudest day and night
>   In any rough place where it caught.
>
> Man came to tell it what was wrong:
>   It hadn't found the place to blow;
> It blew too hard—the aim was song.
>   And listen—how it ought to go!

The conception of the universe underlying these poems is profoundly satisfying and pleasing, largely because of the closeness of man and nature. This is not to deny the obvious symbolic representation of poetic creativity in these poems; in fact it is one link between humanity and the natural world. Like other poets, such as Wallace Stevens in "The Idea of Order at Key West," Frost suggests that song—that is, poetry—is potential in nature, but that it needs man to bring it out, to shape it. The arrangement is mutually beneficial.

Frost appreciates nature for its own sake, but most often he sees it in relation to man. As he said, almost all of his "nature" poems have people in them,[11] and the poems we have just considered remind us of this. There are also many poems reflecting an interest in humanity independent of nature. The existential satisfaction he felt was based partly on a sense that the natural world is beautiful and on the whole beneficial to man, but more largely on an enjoyment of human activity for its own sake and a confidence in human nature. Consider "Mowing":

> There was never a sound beside the wood but one,
> And that was my long scythe whispering to the ground.
> What was it it whispered? . . .
> . . . .
> Anything more than the truth would have seemed too weak
> To the earnest love that laid the swale in rows,
> Not without feeble-pointed spikes of flowers
> (Pale orchises), and scared a bright green snake.
> The fact is the sweetest dream that labor knows.
> My long scythe whispered and left the hay to make.

The poem reflects a loving relationship between man and nature, as well as suggesting that the mower's work gives meaning to—in a sense, creates—the natural environment. Equally evident is the enjoyment of the physical activity, and the sense of its inherent importance, especially in the last two lines. The same situation obtains in "Two Tramps in Mud Time," where so much of the emphasis falls on the speaker's love of woodchopping as an avocation: "The life of muscles rocking soft / And smooth and moist in vernal heat."

Akin to Frost's enjoyment of physical activity is his even greater pleasure in intellectual activity—and this hardly needs to be illustrated. As a poet who explored and experimented with ideas and words, Frost certainly enjoyed the play of the mind partly for its own sake. "The Mountain" indicates this perhaps most vividly. The conversation between visitor and farmer explores the potentialities of the top of the mountain whose lower slopes the farmer is plowing. Neither man has been to the top, and perhaps for that reason especially, they enjoy speculating about it. The farmer says that there is a spring at the top that is "always cold in summer, warm in winter," but at the end of the poem, he adds:

> "You and I know enough to know it's warm
> Compared with cold, and cold compared with warm.
> But all the fun's in how you say a thing."

The poem is an analogue or symbolic enactment of the poetic pro-cess,[12] like a number of other Frost poems such as "The Oven Bird" and "Directive," and is thus an almost perfect example for him of rewarding play of the mind.

Frost's appreciation of humanity goes deeper than simply enjoying immediate experience, however. Most typically, indeed, it reveals it-self as a kind of humanism. Although he objected strongly to being considered a humanist in an atheistic sense,[13] Frost was in his poetry intensely preoccupied with man, his problems, his potential, and his basic achievements, quite commonly in nonreligious terms. It is true that Frost often represented man as persisting despite the odds against him in a fearful universe, but his faith led him often to a more cheerful, optimistic view of existence. He feels that man has it in him to enjoy his world and his life. Man may not be able to exer-cise complete control over his natural environment, nor to solve the mysteries of the universe—Frost had little faith in technology or sci-ence—but he can maintain the basic values "built into" man for a sat-isfactory way of life.

Another Wordsworthian poem, "The Gum-Gatherer," focuses this humanism. Like Wordsworth's leech-gatherer, the man that Frost meets is resolute and independent; he lives in a simple shack up in the mountains and earns money by gathering spruce gum. He draws on nature for his livelihood, but it is a meager one, and the emphasis in the poem falls most directly on the man himself. Frost testifies to the man's vitality at the beginning, invests him with independence in the course of the poem, and by describing the lumps of gum in al-most glowing terms ("uncut jewels . . . golden brown . . . pink") at-taches a kind of aesthetic value to his occupation. At the end Frost makes plain that the man must find satisfaction in his life, having united vocation and avocation:

> I told him this is a pleasant life,
> To set your breast to the bark of trees
> That all your days are dim beneath,
> And reaching up with a little knife,
> To loose the resin and take it down
> And bring it to market when you please.

The gum-gatherer's resolution appears in many different forms in Frost's humanistic poetry, though not always in quite such a pleasant context. In "Brown's Descent," the farmer sliding down through the fields may be at the mercy of gravity and the glazed snow. Neverthe-less, two aspects of the experience are humanly significant. Brown is not harmed, for he manages to control himself somewhat, even to retaining his lantern and certainly his equanimity; and he recoups the two miles he has lost by bowing "with grace to natural law" and going up around by the road to get home. The poem is a variety of "tall tale," moreover, and the sympathetic amusement invested in it, along with Brown's dignity and perspicacity, reflect Frost's faith in certain basic human values.

In both of these poems we see a significant general aspect of Frost's humanism: he is conscious of man's limitations, as several critics have noted.[14] Man cannot exercise much control over his universe, nor penetrate it very far. This being so, Frost's faith in man could verge on pathos. But neither "The Gum-Gatherer" nor "Brown's Descent" does so, because each protagonist controls his immediate existence and environment satisfactorily, and because each one represents certain positive human values besides the simple quality of resolution. The gum-gatherer represents a kind of aesthetic sense, and Brown embodies human dignity and perspicacity. There are many other poems, as we shall see, which do approach pathos, despite man's resolution and independence, because the odds against man appear so much greater. When Frost emphasizes substantial and positive human values rather than man's persistence in the face of difficulty, however, he usually presents us with a sanguine conception of existence. This is most notably the case in "The Generations of Men" (which, despite the Biblical flavor of the title, is not significantly religious), and in "New Hampshire."

The setting in "The Generations of Men" is the cellar-hole of a house long since deserted, on a rainy day. In other poems the rain could generate despondency, but here it merely reinforces the human warmth of the young man and woman who are evidently falling in love. During their conversation the two distant cousins imaginatively revive their "Grandsir Stark" and "great, great, great, great Granny," bringing themselves closer to each other and to the past, so that the cellar-hole is on its way to becoming a home again. Indeed, the man suggests taking a timber from the cellar-hole and using it

> For a doorsill or other corner piece
> In a new cottage on the ancient spot.
> The life is not yet all gone out of it.

What makes the poem so warmly optimistic is partly the sense of human persistence, but more the emphasis on the vitality, the love, the humor, and the understanding manifested by the two young speakers. This essential humanity makes worldly existence pleasurable and valuable.

"New Hampshire," though in a very different genre, is similarly focused on human activities and values, and finds satisfaction in them. There are references to God and to the Bible in the poem, to be sure, as well as a rather sardonic tone appropriate to the poet's role, here, of a literate farmer-bard. Neither of these motifs influences significantly the general purport of the monologue, however, which is that New Hampshire—and Vermont—are the kinds of places where men can be truly individuals, where basic human characteristics can develop effectively, even to eccentricity, in independence and freedom from commercialism. Frost indicates in one passage that some contact with nature is beneficial: "I'd hate to be a runaway from nature," but he makes clear enough that he is not advocating any kind of pantheism. Human beings are what he is interested in, and as he says in a central passage:

> Where I was living then, New Hampshire offered
> The nearest boundary to escape across.
> I hadn't an illusion in my hand bag
> About the people being better there
> Than those I left behind. I thought they weren't.
> I thought they couldn't be. And yet they were.

People in New Hampshire are better because their basic characters are less likely to be covered over with a veneer of civilization and sophistication.

As a result life is fundamentally satisfactory in places like New Hampshire. Frost says:

> How are we to write
> The Russian novel in America
> As long as life goes so unterribly?

> . . . No state can build
> A literature that shall at once be sound
> And sad on a foundation of well-being.

The notion that great literature emerges only from tragic experience is being played with here, of course, but only half-seriously. Certainly Frost finds life good according to this poem—both in New Hampshire and in the nation as a whole, despite his joking at the expense of other states, because he is satisfied with people. We may think of his later poem, "The Gift Outright," where he crystallizes his love for his country into an assertion that America became a nation only when her people "gave themselves" to her; meaning and validity, even "salvation," reside in humanity.

What made it possible for Frost to believe in and represent man as the foundation of worldly well-being was partly his conservatism. He believed that life and man remained essentially the same, despite minor of superficial changes. Basic human nature is good and competent—the people Frost shows us in much of his poetry prove that—and will remain so since the world they live in is not likely to change radically. Frost's "regionalism," his "pastoral art," provides a constant, unchanging point of reference in human as well as natural terms. The rural world represents the norm; the sophisticated world, with its peculiarities, can be all too mutable.[15]

Frost's world is the pastoral world. Even though he makes excursions into other "dimensions," he retains contact with the simplicities, the fundamental values of what he perceived intuitively as his "normal" environment, natural, human, and spiritual. And since the pastoral world represents what is basic in all life, Frost can find—or invest—his fundamental values in the sophisticated world to some extent. There is a normal basis to be found underneath the veneer. It is this felt normality that provides the key to Frost's optimism. Given Frost's basic conservatism, normality can mean an evident Christian God and a more or less conventional conception of the relationship between man, nature, and the divine. At the same time, normality can mean that external nature is pleasant and beneficent, that human nature is good and effective, and that the two are at least compatible, even mutually rewarding. The evident normality of this world, then, assures man's position in the cosmos, making his life satisfying by rendering his environment comprehensible and manageable. There are, of course, significant differences between the Christian ontology and the more humanistic and secular as reflected in Frost's work. Man is more active, and his satisfactions are more immediate in a humanistic perspective. But either of these positions offers Frost a basis for the geniality we find in his poetry.

Integral to this normal and comprehensible world are the modes in which it is manifested through the themes and images, as well as through the style employed. Sometimes Frost's Christian poetry moves in the high-mimetic or romantic mode, but the principal mode of the optimistic poetry is the low mimetic, as we can see from the domestic animals, the familiar trees and flowers, and the scenes of ordinary pleasant human life and work. And in correlation the style is largely conversational, on a "middle" rather than an elevated level, and is apparently explicit and straightforward rather than obscure. To put it another way, Frost's more optimistic poetry celebrates the normal, the ordinary, the common—by quite conservative standards, to be sure. It seems to be written for the sensible ordinary man that Frost himself often pretended to be; this is part of his pas-

"Acquainted with the Night":
The Fearsome World

It would be difficult for any perceptive or sensitive person to live through the first half of the twentieth century without feeling some misgivings about the state of the world and of man. Frost was no exception. No matter how great his enjoyment of life's simpler pleasures, and whatever the intensity of his religious faith, he evidently most often found the world, nature, the universe, to be uncertain at best, and man to be vulnerable, not to say deficient.

Lawrance Thompson's biography reveals Frost's personal fears, moods of depression, and moments of doubt. In his poetry we can see that these were not merely superficial, but reflected a generally darker conception of life than the popular myth ascribes to him, a sense that external reality is incomprehensible and unmanageable, and sometimes even inimical. Man, therefore, as Frost depicts him, is left in a very uncertain position, and just as important, he suffers from basic deficiencies that make existence especially difficult for him.

Frost sees this fearsome universe and man's plight in several ways, but beneath all of these lie two different ontological perspectives. On the one hand Frost often writes as though the existence of God were irrelevant, indeed virtually as an agnostic existentialist—in the sense of believing that temporal, earthly human life is the primary, even the only valid human frame of reference—to whom external reality is incomprehensible, even meaningless. On the other he writes equally often with the sense that God is harsh and demanding and that the universe and man are fallen. Whether or not Frost was as much of a Puritan as he himself believed, his poetry often reveals a good deal of that perspective. It is equally true, nevertheless, that a more nearly Godless viewpoint manifests itself in Frost's work just as persistently, whether God has temporarily withdrawn, is not perceptible to human beings, or is simply irrelevant to their concerns. Pragmatically speaking, Frost is both Puritan and agnostic existentialist in his darker poems, and in either case, man is virtually helpless, partly because of his situation and partly because of inherent weaknesses and excesses.

There are significant differences between Frost's two basic conceptions of the universe. In general, his religious poems contrast to the existential ones in assuming some degree of purpose in the universe, as one would expect: God is directing—or has directed—the course of events and man's place in them. There is, therefore, some implicit concern with divine and human objectives, if only in Frost's denial of progress. Man's role, if not his nature, also differs according to the poet's ontological perspective. Seen from a Puritan viewpoint, there is little man can accomplish. In an existential framework, he seems less helpless, more active, though he is no more effective in the long run. The general differences in the darker poems parallel those found in Frost's more optimistic works, naturally enough, but they are rather more important here because of this difference in man's role.

External reality—or, as the poet sees it, nature, the world, the universe—is hardly a pleasant or encouraging environment as a great many of Frost's poems represent it, whether he sees it from an agnostic or a Puritan perspective. To begin with, nature is independent of man, *sui generis*. It has its own ways and concerns, to which man is irrelevant. We have seen Frost approach Wordsworth's conception of benevolent nature occasionally, in optimistic poems like "The Pasture" and "The Gum-Gatherer." More typical of Frost, despite the popular myth, is the conception represented by "The Need of Being Versed in Country Things." The burning of the house is an unhappy event in human terms but the birds have their own lives, and man errs if he reads human sympathy into their "murmur." Similarly, "The Most of It" indicates that if there is any response in nature to man's appeal, it is in its own terms, which are essentially alien. Man and external nature are separate and fundamentally different. Nature has its own integrity, which man can hardly understand. There is no suggestion that man has simply lost touch with nature, that all reality is—or was—in any sense united in a spiritual order. The perspective is basically materialistic and existential, for it represents reality as physical, and indicates that man must learn to live in the natural order since it is his only effective context.

Besides those poems where Frost expresses his conception of nature's independence directly, there are many more that assume or imply it. Particularly, several poems indicate that man cannot exercise any real influence on nature for good or ill, much less control it. The destructive forces of human war have little effect on the bird, the butterfly, the spider in "Range-Finding": The passing bullet hardly disturbs the groundbird at her nest, it only momentarily deceives the spider into thinking a fly had shaken his web, and though it breaks the stalk of a flower, the butterfly "its fall had dispossessed . . . stooped to it and fluttering clung." In "The Exposed Nest" the people wish to repair the nest that a mower had exposed, but even though they "cared," they recognize that their efforts to do good might actually do harm, for the mother bird might be frightened by their "meddling" and abandon the nest. In "A Hillside Thaw" the poet imagines himself trying to hold back the rivulets—"ten million silver lizards"—from a melting snowbank, but has to concede that "it takes the moon for this," that only the chill of night can stop them, and he ends by saying, "The thought of my attempting such a stay!" When we contrast this attitude with that of poems like "The Aim Was Song," wherein man teaches the wind to make music, we see how divided Frost's mind was.

The universe appears just as inaccessible to man in those poems Frost wrote from a dark religious perspective. Indeed, it seems more so because the focus is not simply on the trees, flowers, and animals we can see around us, but on a spiritual order. Frost indicates in "The Trial by Existence" and "A Passing Glimpse," for instance, that it is not merely external reality, material things, that man is out of touch with, but a more fundamental and significant order of being. The motif found so early in "The Trial by Existence" runs throughout his poetry. Man has no memory of heaven or of his choosing life on earth to make his "earthly woe" more bearable.[1] He cannot, in other words, comprehend nor even perceive clearly the real context in which he exists. He may believe that heaven exists, but he has only "passing glimpses" of it, as a passenger on a train briefly catches sight of flowers in a meadow: "Heaven gives its glimpses only to those / Not in a position to look too close."[2] Thus the universe, indeed all reality or experience outside the individual's own mind, or at its widest, his life as finite man, must remain largely mysterious.

But man's environment is not merely incomprehensible and inaccessible; it also embodies great power which, because its sources are mysterious, can be perilous to man. Whether Frost represents this power in materialistic or religious terms, it is a striking feature of many poems. From early works like "The Draft Horse" (c. 1920) and "Storm Fear" (1923) to "Peril of Hope," which appeared in 1961, the sense that the universe and its general conditions are at once powerful, mutable, and uncertain is never very far in the background. Sometimes Frost emphasizes the power of natural or divine forces, especially their uncontrollable destructiveness. Sometimes he makes us conscious of their treacherousness, their arbitrariness. And he often stresses the consequent changeableness of the conditions in which man exists.

In "Storm Fear" Frost represents natural forces partly as a kind of wolf, partly as something insidious ("the cold creeps") and harder to visualize, but even more dangerous:

> When the wind works against us in the dark,
> And pelts with snow
> The lower-chamber window on the east . . .
>
> I count our strength,
> Two and a child . . .
>
> And my heart owns a doubt
> Whether 'tis in us to arise with day
> And save ourselves unaided.

The emphasis here falls on the power of nature that threatens to destroy the small family. And since the "beast's" appeal to come out is difficult to resist ("costs no inward struggle not to go"), the treacherousness of that threat is also brought out. Occasionally Frost represents the natural world more impersonally, with less emphasis on its connection with mankind but with an equally strong sense that it is destructively mutable. In "Spring Pools," for example, the pools and the flowers beside them in the spring will disappear in the course of the season, consumed by the trees as they nourish themselves.

As Lynen says, this is a "sinister" poem.[3] The trees here have none of the pleasant connotations that they often have in Frost, but are about to destroy—"blot out and drink up and sweep away"—the innocence and purity of the spring pools and flowers. Natural conditions are much the same here as in "In Hardwood Groves." The emphasis in that earlier poem falls even more on the cycle of nature, but the same sense of an underlying ruthlessness is there:

> Before the leaves can mount again
> To fill the trees with another shade,
> They must go down past things coming up.
> They must go down into the dark decayed.
>
> They *must* be pierced by flowers and put
> Beneath the feet of dancing flowers.
> However it is in some other world
> I know that this is the way in ours.

These poems have certain implications for man which we will have to examine later, but the general destructiveness, treacherousness, and changeableness of the material universe man inhabits is made explicit in the brief late poem, "Peril of Hope":

> It is right in there
> Betwixt and between
> The orchard bare
> And the orchard green,
>
> When the boughs are right
> In a flowery burst
> of pink and white,
> That we fear the worst.

"Storm Fear" approaches Frost's Puritan poems on the same subject by making natural forces animate—as a "beast," and as the cold that "creeps." In "The Draft Horse" external conditions are not impersonal nor even, strictly speaking, natural forces at all. They are embodied in the actions of a sinister priestlike figure who evidently acts for some greater power, suddenly appearing in the dark woods to stab to death the ponderous horse pulling the hapless couple's wagon.[4] The horse-slayer represents both some divinity, "someone he had to obey," and also certain natural forces, since he came "out of the trees" of the "pitch-dark limitless grove." These natural forces are evidently part of the divine order of the ruling God, and as a result, the forces enveloping the human pair seem more than doubled. The main emphasis of the poem falls on man, but behind this lies the assumption that God exercises an arbitrary power over man. A later poem, "Fear of God," spells this out clearly, adjuring us to "stay unassuming," because any license to become "someone" is owed to "an arbitrary god / Whose mercy to you rather than to others / Won't bear too critical examination."

The best known, perhaps, of the poems stressing God's destructive power is "Once by the Pacific." The storm is just as bestial here as in "Storm Fear," and more frightening for several reasons. Its power and potential destructiveness are described more forcefully and at greater length, for one thing—the "rage" is built up intensively in the course of the poem. In addition, the brutality of the demonic power is easy to visualize in the "locks blown forward in the gleam of eyes." From this figure, linked with the "dark intent," the "rage," and especially with the concluding line, we receive the impression that this is no fortuitous or "natural" occurrence, but a very deliberate action. This vision of the end of the world, moreover, is made worse because there is no mention of any reason for it; the violence of the storm thus becomes willful and arbitrary.

Frost sees our universe, then, as a most problematic environment. The conditions man is subject to may be mechanical and material, the function of natural laws, or they may embody the will of a deity. In either case, man confronts inscrutable power. It is not merely the power itself that makes this confrontation difficult, however, but certain characteristics of the source of these powers. Usually, Frost is inclined to look at man pragmatically—what counts is how one behaves or, ultimately, how one deals, if at all, with the powers that oppress us, be they natural or divine. But there are various images and motifs in Frost's poetry that point beyond the merely practical and suggest the basic nature of the universe. He is never a systematic philosopher, but some of his ontological notions are clear.

The most radical conception one can infer from Frost's poetry is that the universe is fundamentally meaningless. Behind the self-satisfying activities of birds and beasts, behind the surface appearances of mountains and streams that we often find so attractive, and behind the cycle of the seasons and natural growth, lies nothing identifiable. This is the reason why natural forces seem alien and incomprehensible in so much of Frost's work: there is nothing to comprehend beyond the observable facts and phenomena. The universe is simply a place, not a manifestation of anything higher or spiritually more significant. This is no doubt the reason why so many critics have considered Frost a skeptic much of the time. Recent analyses of his poetic and philosophic stance have led to observations that in his poetry he occupied the position of a "pragmatic agnostic," and that some of his poems reflect "a vision of the substratum of nothingness that underlies all human endeavour."[5] The lines that most overtly suggest this skepticism may be those from "West-Running Brook" which tells how "existence" "seriously, sadly, runs away / To fill the abyss's void with emptiness."

Several poems already considered, such as "The Most of It," also seem to imply that what we perceive—or half perceive—in nature is virtually all there is. Further, poems like "Into My Own," "Acquainted with the Night," and "Desert Places" suggest more directly this kind of existential nothingness, particularly as an element in the poet's depression. "Desert Places," especially, makes an analogy between the speaker's feeling of desolation and nature's emptiness:

> I am too absent-spirited to count;
> The loneliness includes me unawares.
>
> And lonely as it is, that loneliness
> Will be more lonely ere it will be less—
> A blanker whiteness of benighted snow
> With no expression, nothing to express.

Snow, night, and woods are common symbols for Frost of the imper-
sonal, deathly void that surrounds the clear area of man's existence.
Here this void is further represented by the "empty spaces / Between
stars—on stars where no human race is." As usual, Frost is more con-
cerned with his own—that is, man's—feelings, but we realize that in
discounting the emptiness of interstellar space in favor of the earth's,
he is saying taht all of man's environment is "blank" and "benighted,"
even the most familiar.

These poems which reveal an implicit sense of "nothingness" are
relatively uncommon for Frost, however. More typically, he expres-
ses a religious conception of the nature of the universe, which man-
ifests itself in his darker poems especially in two ways. First, he often
sees reality—including man—as a "diminished thing," as a falling off
from Eden; and second, he exaggerates the Puritan notion of a
harsh God into a feeling that the universe is governed by an almost
evil deity, by "darkness."

The central position of the Eden myth has been indicated by sev-
eral critics.[6] The keynotes are sounded in "Nothing Gold Can Stay."
The focus in this poem is primarily on external nature, but the con-
nection with man's career appears in the line "So Eden sank to
grief." The emphasis falls on the process of loss which seems to Frost
to be built into existence, the loss of Eden being paralleled and re-
peated in the seasonal changes every year. The same theme appears
in "The Oven Bird," which raises in addition the question of "what
to make of a diminished thing"—how man is to behave, having lost
Eden. Similarly, "Spring Pools" embodies the theme of loss in a
natural context, but puts more emphasis on what is lost—the fragile
beauty of the flowers (analogues of Eve in the Garden) and the pu-
rity of the pools that "reflect / The total sky almost without defect."

In many poems, Frost focuses particularly on what is left to man
and nature since the Fall. The innocent beauty and the direct contact
with heaven have been lost; what remains, besides the continual rep-
etition of the Fall in the course of the seasons and elsewhere? We
can see something of the state of nature now that it has been "di-
minished" in "The Oven Bird" and "Spring Pools," in the symbolic
"old" and "dark" foliage of summer woods, but one of the most strik-
ing representations of this subject is "A Winter Eden":

> A winter garden in an alder swamp,
> Where conies now come out to sun and romp,
> As near a paradise as it can be
> And not melt snow or start a dormant tree.

It lifts existence on a plane of snow
One level higher than the earth below,
One level nearer heaven overhead . . .
. . . .
This Eden day is done at two o'clock.
An hour of winter day might seem too short
To make it worth life's while to wake up and sport.

The most remarkable feature of this poem is the combination of the poignantly ironic argument with a straightforward, restrained tone. It is sharply ironic to suggest that the cold, the heaped-up snow, and the consequent restraint of love and vitality should raise nature closer to heaven, yet the tone of the poem is not bitter nor really even resigned. The last sentence seems to raise the question of whether this too brief and too distant approximation of paradise is worth the effort, but the answer is clearly that it is—with reservations—as the activity of the birds and beasts have indicated. The poem offers one answer to the question of "what to make of a diminished thing."

The irony in "A Winter Eden" leads us close to a vision of reality in which the universe is ruled by an oppressive and vengeful deity, if not an evil one. If this winter scene, with its "gaunt . . . beast" and "loveless birds," represents Eden, the God who created it must be harsh indeed. "Design" suggests this most impressively. Despite Frost's original intentions, the sonnet may validly be taken—and usually is—to be more of a statement than a question, to indicate what Frost often took the nature of God to be. This vision of darkness correlates with many of his other poems, some of which we have already noted. The storm in "Once by the Pacific" seems to be the instrument with which an angry and brutal God intends to destroy the world; similarly, the the horse-killer in "The Draft Horse" evidently obeys an incomprehensibly hostile tyrant-deity. The same vision of supreme power lies behind "The Lovely Shall Be Choosers," which describe how the seven "joys" in the life of the poet's mother were twisted into sorrows at the behest of "The Voice," whose command, "Hurl her down!" opens the poem.[7]

Such a deity, derived from the Puritan conception of a demanding God, is clearly indifferent to man's happiness and welfare at best, and very often appears deliberately hostile. Even when Frost takes a more agnostic view, the attitude of the universe toward man seems equally dubious. An early lyric, "Stars," is commonly cited to illustrate the indifference to man that Frost often found in an apparently Godless universe; it concludes:

And yet with neither love nor hate,
Those stars like some snow-white
Minerva's snow-white marble eyes
Without the gift of sight.

Later poems also manifest this indifference: "The Wood-Pile," for instance, suggests that man can be in nature, but will lack real contact with it. There is nothing inspiring or sympathetic in the natural setting described in the opening lines—it is a "frozen swamp," on a "gray day," and the trees seem like prison bars, "all in lines / Straight up and down." What is more, the speaker is "far from home." Then, the small bird and the poet have no real contact, although the man pretends momentarily that they do. Finally, the wood-pile itself, evidence of man's energy and expectancy, is being reabsorbed dispassionately by natural forces.

Nature's attitude in "The Wood-Pile" is mild compared to that manifested in "Storm Fear." In that poem, in the later long narrative "Snow," and in others like them, nature seems deliberately maleficent. But on the whole Frost ascribes to nature only a relatively mild perversity, like that embodied in "Peril of Hope" and in the uncertain weather in "Two Tramps in Mud Time," where "winter is only playing possum." This dubious situation still allows man some tenuous happiness—the kind of immediate satisfaction with external nature and human activities which "makes up in height for what it lacks in length."[8]

When Frost feels that the universe is really inimical to man, he usually sees it as the instrument of a harsh God, or worse, an evil one, as in "Design," and "The Lovely Shall Be Choosers." Occasionally, he will try to take our situation lightly, as in "The Lesson for Today" and "Not All There"; toward the end of his life he wrote,

Forgive, O Lord, my little jokes on Thee
And I'll forgive Thy great big one on me.

The epigram has an undertone of uncertainty, however, for anyone who knows Frost's work well; it is hard to conceive of "The Draft Horse" or "The Lovely Shall Be Choosers" as "little jokes." What is more, God's "great big joke" betrays a strongly sardonic sense of humor, if we judge from Frost's poetry. At best—according to "The Trial by Existence" and "The Fear of God"—He is continually testing man's humility and courage; at worst, He is maliciously making it hard for man to survive at all.

Frost's main concern is with man. The focus in his poetry is almost always on man's position and attitude and especially on his feelings. Frost reveals a great deal about his conception of the universe and external reality in his poetry, but what is most important to him is man's thoughts, emotions, and behavior as they determine or reflect his relationship with the universe. What does man do, and how does he feel in a universe as dark as this?—that is a central question for Frost. The answer is determined largely by the fact that man is sharply limited as Frost sees him, in both his intellectual powers and his perceptions. A few poems suggest beneficial—or at least not unpleasant—aspects of these limitations, and some critics have argued that Frost maintained a humanistic faith in man's other resources such as love, courage, and humor despite the seriousness of his deficiencies.[9] But we find many indications, direct and indirect, in both the agnostic and the Puritanical poetry that Frost considers man very limited.

In several poems Frost indicates that man fails to understand nature and its relationship to him. He says we "cannot look out far" nor "in deep," so that after we have looked, "Do we know any better where we are?"[10] He writes,

> We dance around in a ring and suppose,
> But the Secret sits in the middle and knows.

In more clearly religious poems, Frost points out man's intellectual limitations equally emphatically. "The Trial by Existence," as we have seen, describes individual men's coming to earth in ignorance of both their heavenly provenance and their choice of life. In "I Will Sing You One-O" he puts this ignorance in terms of the restrictions on man's intellection, referring to the farthest constellations, "to which man sends his / Speculation, / Beyond which God is." Most significantly, Frost considers man's rational limitations at length in *A Masque of Reason*. Although he says, "I will take my incompleteness with the rest" in a fairly resolute—or at least resigned—tone in "The Lesson for Today," he voices what amounts to a complaint in the *Masque of Reason*: "There's no connection man can reason out / Between his just deserts and what he gets." Job, representing man, has such great—and, it seems, obtuse—faith in reason that he can hardly understand that he must submit to "unreason."

Frost's belief in the limitations of man's perceptions and rationality has profound implications for man which are revealed in many ways in the poetry.[11] Generally these limitations help explain why the universe seems incomprehensible and uncontrollable. The trouble is not only with the problematic nature of the universe—time and motion, or mutability, being perhaps the most difficult inherent problems —but also with man's finite mind.[12] The general result is that according to Frost's vision man finds himself amid a confusion that he cannot very well dispel or control.

Man's position thus is inherently difficult, whether Frost looks on the universe as an agnostic or as a Puritan. The universe may be "empty" or meaningless, as poems like "Desert Places" suggest; it may be "diminished," according to "Nothing Gold Can Stay," or worse as in "Design." In any case, man finds himself isolated, alienated, and cut off even from other men by barriers of one kind or another. And because he is isolated in the face of the power of the universe, he is vulnerable, especially when that power is wielded treacherously and inimically.

"An Old Man's Winter Night" manifests the vulnerability of man in an empty universe most poignantly. The protagonist has lost what perceptiveness he may once have had and he can no longer think clearly. He cannot remember what brought him to the empty room —he is "at a loss." He is not conscious of any threat when "all out-of-doors looked darkly in at him," nor does he feel any necessity to resist the darkness. To say that he "scared the outer night" seems patently ironic, since he hardly knows what he is doing. This "aged man—one man—can't keep a house," isolated as he is, but he does not feel the vulnerability we see in him, because of his depersonalization through age and weariness. And because he does not realize how helpless he is, he seems that much more pitiable.

The human insecurity that is only suggested in "An Old Man's Winter Night" is manifested clearly, along with a continued emphasis on man's isolation, in many other poems. We have noted that the protagonist in "Storm Fear" feels his isolation and his insecurity keenly, as the original gloss to the poem indicates: "He is afraid of his own isolation." In this poem man confronts natural forces directly, but often man's plight is not so simple. The five-poem series entitled "The Hill Wife," for example, shows the gradual destruction of a young wife, isolated with her husband on a hill farm in New England and vulnerable to the loneliness and the fears that the isolation engenders. Lacking the necessary strength of mind, she is at the mercy of external nature through her affection for the indifferent birds (as in "The Need of Being Versed . . ."), and through her fears of the night and of the "dark pine that kept / Forever trying the window latch." She is also insecure in her relationship with other people, however; she fears—neurotically—a passing tramp, and eventually loses touch even with her busy husband, and runs away to disappear. "The Impulse," the last poem in the series, ends:

> Sudden and swift and light as that
>   The ties gave,
> And he learned of finalities
>   Besides the grave.

One can imagine similar loneliness in the situation of the logging camp described in "The Census-Taker":

> The only dwelling in a waste cut over
> A hundred square miles round it in the mountains:
> And that not dwelt in now by men or women.

The poem concludes with the words of the poet-census-taker, "It must be I want life to go on living," and it is this assumption that makes the vulnerability of insufficient man especially poignant.

"A Servant to Servants" is the most powerful of Frost's accounts of human alienation in an impersonal universe. Its power comes from its immediacy, for it is a dramatic monologue, and from the speaker's lack of sentimentality: She is quite matter-of-fact about her deterioration. Without self-pity she observes that she can no longer respond to the fresh air and the view of the lake—nor, indeed, feel much of anything—and she recognizes the futility of trying to escape the isolated, drudging existence that is destroying her. She needs rest from "doing / Things over and over that just won't stay done." The hired men she serves hardly notice her presence, and her husband "undertakes too much" to have any real understanding of her: "He thinks I'll be all right with doctoring," she says. But insanity runs in her family, and she knows she will end in the asylum, where she has been once already. Her position, fundamentally, is that of all men in an unfeeling universe as Frost sees it—doomed to continual labor, in very tenuous contact with the surface of nature and unable to penetrate beneath it, and separated from other men by lack of understanding.

"A Servant to Servants" is ambiguous. We can read it both as the epitome of Godless existential man, and as the embodiment of fallen man condemned to labor, with original sin—the prime instance of human insanity in the Puritan context—always hanging over his head. The poem indicates, in this ambiguity, that Frost sees man's position in the same way, no matter whether he looks at the universe temporally or spiritually. In either case, man has alienated himself and made his position insecure; this is the vision reflected in so many of Frost's more pessimistic poems, with varying focal concerns. In "Once by the Pacific," the emphasis falls on God's wrath over fallen man, as it does in "The Fear of God." "The Draft Horse" emphasizes a tyrannical God's insisting on man's humble labor ("Wanted us to get down / And walk the rest of the way"), with the preliminary assumption that man suffers from the consequences of the original sin ("With a lantern that wouldn't burn / In too frail a buggy"). "A Cabin in the Clearing" brings out particularly man's postlapsarian inability to achieve contact with God or to obtain direction from Him: Men "ask philosophers / Who come to look in on them from the pulpit" where they are. Man's isolation from God and from other men is also found in "The Draft Horse," where the couple are traveling alone "through a pitch-dark limitless grove." In most of the Puritanical poems, however, a more important keynote is the insecurity of man's position. His frailty and the uncertainty of his labor in response to the demands of a harsh God leave him in an uncertain position indeed.

This insecurity is most clearly indicated in *A Masque of Mercy.* The God that appears in *A Masque of Reason* and is discussed in *A Masque of Mercy* does not seem as harsh as He does elsewhere, but He is certainly unreasonable, hence incomprehensible, as man perceives Him. *A Masque of Reason* emphasizes Job's confusion and uncertainty in the face of God's freedom from human rationality. Similarly, in *A Masque of Mercy,* the Sermon on the Mount is described as an "irresistible impossibility. / A lofty beauty no one can live up to, / Yet no one turn from trying to live up to." God holds man up to standards no one is capable of fulfilling—"Failure is failure, but success is failure," says the apostle Paul—so that there is no remedy except in God's mercy. The emphasis falls not on the assurance of God's mercy, however, but on the severity of His standards. As the Keeper ("My Brother's") puts it:

> . . . I can see that the uncertainty
> In which we act is a severity,
> A cruelty, amounting to injustice
> That nothing but God's mercy can assuage.

The Keeper calls himself a poet and is somewhat skeptical of Paul's dogma until the end of the play; he represents the very real question of why we should make such an effort if God treats success and failure the same. The emphasis in the *Masques,* as in much of Frost's darker religious poetry, is on the uncertainty and difficulty of the position God has put man in. Moreover, this God may resemble either a God of Wrath (as in "Once by the Pacific") or a merciful Christian God, but man's position is, in effect, the same in either case because of his inherent deficiencies.

Man is commonly in difficult straits, then. Since his capabilities are limited, the universe is largely incomprehensible and uncontrollable whether seen existentially or puritanically, and man's position, in either case, is equally unfortunate as a result. How does man then behave, according to Frost; what stance does he take, what attitudes does he adopt, and how does he feel? What kind of an impression does Frost present of man and his responses to his situation?

The picture Frost creates in much of his poetry is certainly discouraging. Sometimes he finds grounds for hope, but often he shows men to be pitiable at best, and at worst, self-centered, unrealistic, and even destructive. They are not the "odious little vermin" that Swift took them to be in *Gulliver's Travels,* but they often seem unable to exercise the intelligence and the restraint that could make their existence more bearable.

When Frost depicts men and women in an apparently Godless universe, he often shows them trying to be so independent of their surroundings and of other people that they lose their human understanding and sympathy, and even verge on escapism. They often deny, or fail to achieve, real contact with others or with the natural world. Their behavior reflects a pride that inevitably, given an indifferent universe, makes them lonely and fearful. This is the picture we find particularly in the "dialogue of contraries" between man and wife, as Robert H. Swennes describes it.[13] "Home Burial," for instance, presents clearly and tragically a couple who cannot understand each other's emotions and modes of thinking. Each of the two speakers believes that only his or her own attitude and behavior is valid, thereby revealing a failure to understand oneself as well as the other. The wife considers the husband unfeeling and brutal because he can speak so casually about his dead child and indeed could actually dig the "little grave." Consequently, she feels he can never understand her emotions, not having any of his own: she is "sure that he wouldn't see." The man, on his part, although he professes to want to understand her feelings, reveals that he considers it overly feminine to be as grief-stricken as his wife. He asks to be "let . . . into" her grief, a sexual metaphor that suggests his need to dominate her. We may infer that he has deep feelings about the death of his child, but his insensitive account of burying the child in lines 91–93, which imply that the child, too, will rot in the grave, shows that the practical and physical terms in which he deals with life make it impossible for him fully to comprehend his wife's despair. This is a common male reaction in Frost's work;[14] like many others, this man feels too much pride in his own nature as a man to accord any real validity to a more "feminine" attitude toward experience. The husband here says, "A man must partly give up being a man / With womenfolk."

In other dialogues between man and wife this lack of understanding is revealed in somewhat more pitiable terms, as in "The Hill Wife" and "A Servant to Servants." Further, many other poems focusing on man as an individual represent this human egoism in a number of ways. "Acquainted with the Night" shows the poet himself walking alone and lonely, cut off from other human beings and from the universe as a whole:

> I have been one acquainted with the night.
> I have walked out in rain—and back in rain.
> I have outwalked the furthest city light.
> . . . .
>
> I have stood still and stopped the sound of feet
> When far away an interrupted cry
> Came over houses from another street,
>
> But not to call me back or say good-by;
> And further still at an unearthly height
> One luminary clock against the sky
>
> Proclaimed the time was neither wrong nor right.
> I have been one acquainted with the night.

The speaker is almost entirely self-centered and detached. He does not seem to be impelled by pride, but he certainly denies any contact with other human beings. The "one luminary clock against the sky" suggests because of its "unearthly height" the isolation of the speaker and therefore of man in general in the universe. Night in the poem seems to symbolize the void in which man exists, as it and the snow do in "Desert Places."

A different manifestation of man's self-centeredness appears in "The Bear," where man is represented as caged in the universe, alone, and almost completely absorbed with himself. He is a ridiculous figure, trapped within the limits of his metaphysical perceptions,

> The telescope at one end of his beat,
> And at the other end the microscope,
> Two instruments of nearly equal hope,
> And in conjunction giving quite a spread.
> Or if he rests from scientific tread,
> 'Tis only to sit back and sway his head
> Through ninety-odd degrees of arc, it seems,
> Between two metaphysical extremes.

Because of his pointless busy-ness, he is a figure of fun, like the ants in "Departmental"—"A baggy figure, equally pathetic / When sedentary and when peripatetic."

Frost suggests one solution to man's isolation in the world in "Provide, Provide":

> Make the whole stock exchange your own!
> If need be occupy a throne,
> Where nobody can call *you* crone.
> . . . .
> Better to go down dignified
> With boughten friendship at your side
> Than none at all. Provide, provide!

Judging from the rest of Frost's work, as well as the events of his life, we can hardly take seriously his suggestion that one should make money and buy friendship to reinforce one's pride. He is more serious in lines 13 and 14, where he says that being true to oneself is a possible solution, but the poem is primarily an ironic argument against artificial human pride as a remedy for man's loneliness.

This human self-centeredness and the consequent pride, fear, and loneliness are reflections of man's basic failure to be realistic about his position in the universe and his relationship with other people. In many poems we find Frost suggesting other consequences of man's failure to accommodate himself to his limitations. He shows man to be dissatisfied, to complain, on the one hand, and to undertake futile activities on the other because he is unable to understand or to achieve as much as he would like. In the relatively early poem, "The Star-Splitter," the farmer hopes to find out more about "man's place among the infinities" with his telescope. The narrator of the poem, however, who seems to be fairly close to Frost himself, considers the activity futile—entertaining but doomed to failure as metaphysical inquiry. In "Neither Out Far nor In Deep," somewhat the same attitude is expressed. The conclusion of this poem is ambiguous, of course, but since the perceptions of the watchers are limited, their activity is practically as futile as that of the farmer with his telescope.

The foolishness of trying to achieve more than possible for a human being is presented in several poems such as "The Road Not Taken" and "The Wood-Pile." Frost mocked Edward Thomas gently in the first of these for hesitating over choices, the implication being that man must make them, and since events will take their course almost fatally, many times the choice is in effect unimportant. If man cannot effectively control his destiny, he may as well accept it in a practical fashion as it comes. Similarly, in "The Wood-Pile" Frost presents in symbolic terms the futility of many of man's achievements, while conceding an admiration for the impulse that prompts them. It seems foolish as well as pitiable for man to expend himself on labor that will come to naught, an attitude which has something in common with Frost's scorn for social planning, given his faith in individual initiative.

Frost does not always represent men as quite so foolishly unrealistic, nor, on the other hand, as proud and self-centered. He often feels that men can be happy in the universe, but there are moments and occasions when he depicts them not only as unrealistic and self-centered, but also as destructive and even cruel. The universe is indifferent, or perhaps even hostile to man; men, too, at times appear to Frost indifferent to others, even malevolent. Few of his poems directly present men thus, but the ambiguity of much of his poetry reveals that he was conscious of man's bad side as well as the good. A few of his best-known poems, though, as well as some of his less familiar ones, are aimed at the resentfulness, the greediness, the anger of men, and at their violence in an apparently Godless universe. Very rare are the poems in which Frost takes men to task for attacking nature. Usually nature has the upper hand and men as a result feel the fear and loneliness that we see so often. In "A Brook in the City," however, Frost illustrates what can happen when man does get the upper hand:

> ... The brook was thrown
> Deep in a sewer dungeon under stone
> In fetid darkness still to live and run —
> And all for nothing it had ever done,
> Except forget to go in fear perhaps.
> ....
> ... But I wonder
> If from its being kept forever under,
> The thoughts may not have risen that so keep
> This new-built city from both work and sleep.

In this poem we are struck by the contrast with other works depicting a direct response to nature, like "The Pasture" and "Hyla Brook." Here man appears deliberately cruel and repressive. The brook, moreover, is "an immortal force"; it is personified "thrown / Deep in a sewer dungeon under stone," and in conclusion is given the power to influence almost mystically the activities of the people in the city built over it. To offend it is thus almost sacrilegious.

Much more common are the poems that take man to task for his destructive passions toward his own kind. Frost was familiar with these passions and some of these poems derive from his own experience, "Beyond Words" and "Fire and Ice" being obvious cases in point. The first is an almost direct expression of animosity by the poet himself, while the latter testifies clearly to his familiarity with the destructive power of hatred.

This malevolence in man seems to exist on a basic personal level, but in some poems, such as "Build Soil," Frost makes it clear that if men are not careful, these natural personal reactions within an unfeeling universe can become systematized in social, economic, and political terms.

> In your sense of the word ambition has
> Been socialized—the first propensity
> To be attempted. Greed may well come next.
> But the worst one of all to leave uncurbed,
> Unsocialized, is ingenuity:
> Which for no sordid self-aggrandizement,
> For nothing but its own blind satisfaction
> (In this it is as much like hate as love),
> Works in the dark as much against as for us.
> Even while we talk some chemist at Columbia
> Is stealthily contriving wool from jute
> That when let loose upon the grazing world
> Will put ten thousand farmers out of sheep.
> Everyone asks for freedom for himself,
> The man free love, the businessman free trade,
> The writer and talker free speech and free press.
> Political ambition has been taught,
> By being punished back, it is not free:
> It must at some point gracefully refrain.
> Greed has been taught a little abnegation
> And shall be more before we're done with it.
> It is just fool enough to think itself
> Self-taught. But our brute snarling and lashing taught it.
> None shall be as ambitious as he can.
> None should be as ingenious as he could,
> Not if I had my say. Bounds should be set
> To ingenuity for being so cruel
> In bringing change unheralded on the unready.

The emphasis here is on the greed that is potential in human nature and which Frost believed socialization or social planning of any kind would be likely to encourage. We may be struck by the similarity between the greed suggested here and the cruelty evinced in "A Brook in the City," for the life of the brook was sacrificed to man's commercial desires. Both poems represent—as do many others—what can happen when man stands alone, independent of his environment: He feels that there is nothing meaningful to him in the universe to which he can respond directly.

The most violent of Frost's poems, at least implicitly, is "The Vanishing Red," where it is clear that the miller has pushed John, the Indian, into the wheel pit and killed him quite callously. What is not so clear is his motive. It seems to be something of a general antipathy: he feels that the Indian is "one who had no right to be heard from," perhaps simply because he was "the last Red Man / In Acton." The miller may feel that Indians are an inferior race that have been superseded, and since he holds " 'with getting a thing done with,' " he takes it onto himself to eliminate this grunting savage. There is no sympathy for the miller, but since Frost was sometimes guilty of the prejudice the miller felt, he indicates in lines 9–13 how our attitude toward the miller should be modified by our inability to appreciate the context of the event. Further, Frost was no stranger to the notion of violence in general. He was not intrinsically opposed to war; he felt that the United States should remain strong militarily even long after World War II was over, and despite the loss of friends such as Edward Thomas in World War I, he acknowledged that he found a certain amount of enjoyment in the excitement of that war.[15]

If man is self-centered when Frost sees him agnostically, he is no less so when Frost sees him in a dark religious light in a diminished or apparently evil universe. Such a universe is almost as incomprehensible and certainly as uncontrollable as the agnostic's, and man's position is just as isolated and insecure. In this universe man's reactions are somewhat different from those we have just observed, however. There is a God governing the universe with whom man must contend. This God may be demanding, or he may seem to be malevolent, but in either case, man alternately tries to be independent and carry on his existence simply in personal terms, or in terms of a more generally socialized human life. Alternately, failing to achieve independence, he retreats, defeated or inert, giving in to despair. Sometimes, as a result either of the frustration and the egotism stemming from his attempt to be independent, or from the despair and fear created by his sense of defeat, man becomes destructive.

Occasionally, men act as though God were simply not there:

Not All There

I turned to speak to God
About the world's despair;
But to make bad matters worse
I found God wasn't there.

God turned to speak to me
(Don't anybody laugh);
God found I wasn't there—
At least not over half.

Even in this weak position man reacts by trying to organize his life
and experience in social terms, the assumption evidently being that
if the personal strength is lacking, there is safety in numbers. Frost
sees this attempt, however, as futile and ridiculous. "Departmental"
presents us with a clear picture of this societal organization. Any so-
ciety which is organized mechanically, relegating a concern with God
to a committee, is intellectually and emotionally dead, and when con-
sidered at a sufficient distance, ridiculous. The same basic human
situation is described and attacked more intensely in "Build Soil."
There Frost says, "long before I'm interpersonal, / Away 'way down
inside I'm personal." The burden of the long poem is that social
oranization is artificial and is inclined to accentuate the bad in man,
such as his greediness. Frost argues for unsociability, for individ-
ualism; he says one must build one's own intellectual and spiritual
soil rather than dissipate it by collaborating weakly with human soci-
ety.

Not surprisingly, this individualism is one form of man's reaction
to the diminished or evil world that Frost castigates in other con-
texts. When men become too thoroughly self-centered, absorbed in
themselves, they can become what Nitchie called "prudential."[16] In
this position, as Frost depicts it, men play it safe, cultivate their own
gardens and ignore any wider responsibilities, including those of
metaphysical speculation. Frost himself takes this stance not only in
"Build Soil" in some sense, and similar poems, but also in the very
act of writing about his religious preoccupations, by enacting his re-
ligious doubts.[17] He distances them, rationalizing his fears and con-
victions. On many occasions Frost denied that he was a skeptic,[18] but
he seems to be trying to tell himself over and over again in the
Masques and in earlier poems like "The Trial by Existence," as well as
in some of the more optimistic religious poems like "Innate Helium"
and "A Steeple on the House," that there *is* a God who is concerned
with human affairs. The persistent reiteration suggests that he tends

equally strongly to doubt that belief, as many of the characters in his monologues and dialogues do. Typically, he tries to stick to his own personal sphere, organizing his life as best he can; in his well-known phrase, he tries to make "momentary stays" against the confusion that surrounds him.

It is a surprisingly short step from this "prudential" stance of trying to govern one's life quietly and safely to Nitchie's "anthropocentric" man.[19] In this role, man tries to create his world. God has allowed the universe to decline, and man is dissatisfied with the world as God has left it. Many men in Frost's poems seem to feel that the deterioration, indeed the cruelty of the world, which we see in a poem like "Design," could be at least mitigated, and they—or mankind as a whole—set themselves up as the standard for organizing and maintaining experiences, making demands on God, expecting Him to conform to human expectations. Frost has little sympathy with this behavior. On many occasions he argues for the necessity of at least a tentative faith in God; "something has to be left to God," as he says at the end of "Good-By and Keep Cold." "The Fear of God" and the *Masques* are the most direct arguments against this too-demanding stance:

The Fear of God

If you should rise from Nowhere up to Somewhere,
From being No one up to being Someone,
Be sure to keep repeating to yourself
You owe it to an arbitrary god
Whose mercy to you rather than to others
Won't bear too critical examination.
Stay unassuming . . .

Human pride and ambition tend to take too much credit—man should rather consider himself fortunate to have achieved whatever he has because the God he serves is arbitrary and incomprehensible. In the *Masque of Reason* God cannot be rationalized in human terms, so that His actions are in the last analysis incomprehensible. Job, in requesting an explanation for what God had done, represents all men who make demands on the Deity that He will not or cannot satisfy because He does not operate in the same terms as man. In the *Masque of Mercy* Jonah acts much the same way.[20] He expects God to behave the way a man would, wreaking vengeance when Jonah would. He can hardly understand God's mercy. Even when he is clearly conscious of the existence of God in the universe, therefore, man tends to be self-centered and tries to be independent. Sometimes this independence is restrained, or circumspect, though it leads to feelings of frustration, like Job's, but very often it is a more aggressive independence. In Frost's darker religious poems, the characters often seem to resent the power of God, even to the point of trying to disregard it.

In addition to these semipositive reactions to the power of God, Frost also finds a negative reaction. Instead of adopting a partly active posture, men often just give up in the face of a harsh God and a diminished or evil universe. This retreat may appear as a desire to escape, to try to avoid the situation and its emotional and intellectual implications, while in a more severe form it appears as inertia, a giving in to a sense of defeat. In "Escapist Never," apparently speaking of himself, Frost insists that he behaves positively:

> He is no fugitive . . .
> . . . .
> . . . He is a pursuer.
> He seeks a seeker who in his turn seeks
> Another still, lost far into the distance.
> . . . .
> His life is a pursuit of a pursuit forever.

The inference, of course, is that many people are escapists, reacting negatively to their plight. In "The Runaway," the terrified colt is analogous to human beings in the uncertain universe of the Puritans. Abandoned by the authority figure, he is trying to escape the snow, a condition of his existence he cannot understand. Because the attempt is futile, it is of course that much more pitiable.

Frost presents a somewhat less pitiful human performance in "A Boundless Moment." By suggesting that the vision far off in the maples is "Paradise-in-Bloom" the speaker is trying to pretend that the decline of nature since the Fall has not occurred. This poem, like "The Oven Bird," represents an attempt to deal with a "diminished thing." Here, the speaker tries to deceive himself momentarily into escaping the diminishment, but the tone of resignation of the last two lines suggests that he knows this is impossible.

This resignation shades in a number of poems into a feeling of passive desolation. Even in the relatively idealistic "Trial by Existence," the last stanza makes it clear that life on earth is difficult and painful, and that man finds it hard to bear:

> 'Tis of the essence of life here,
>   Though we choose greatly, still to lack
> The lasting memory at all clear,

>   The lasting memory at all clear,
>   That life has for us on the wrack
>   Nothing but what we somehow chose;
>   Thus are we wholly stripped of pride
>   In the pain that has but one close,
>   Bearing it crushed and mystified.

This near-despair is one extreme of the defeated stance that Frost sometimes finds in man confronted by a demanding God. It appears again, and more potently, in "Bereft":

>   Where had I heard this wind before
>   Change like this to a deeper roar?
>   What would it take my standing there for,
>   Holding open a restive door,
>   Looking downhill to a frothy shore?
>   Summer was past and day was past.
>   Somber clouds in the west were massed.
>   . . . .
>   Something sinister in the tone
>   Told me my secret must be known:
>   Word I was in the house alone
>   Somehow must have gotten abroad,
>   Word I was in my life alone,
>   Word I had no one left but God.

It is possible to read the last line here as a kind of consolation, to take God as a last reassurance and support in a time of sadness. The weight of the poem falls so heavily on despair, however, that Frost seems rather to elicit a sense of abandonment. It is as if he had in mind the same kind of God hinted at in "Design," a God who would reduce a human being to isolation and vulnerability. If Frost felt this sense of defeat or near-despair himself at times, he also recognized it as an invalid and cowardly reaction to man's position, as we can see from the *Masque of Mercy* and other poems. The *Masque of Mercy* is a call for courage and persistence, as was the very early "Trial by Existence"; it rejects the defeatism that the Keeper manifests early in the *Masque*. He is so conscious of the impossibility of meeting God's standards, feeling so strongly that man is doomed to failure, that it hardly seems worthwhile to try to meet those standards at all.

In such a dark universe both this near-despair on the one hand and the self-centered pride on the other can lead to destructiveness and cruelty in man. Sometimes Frost describes this destructiveness as an aberration, an abnormal human reaction to a universe that could be perfectly satisfactory. In "I Will Sing You One-O," for example, Frost writes that long ago, "man began / To drag down man / And nation nation," but these lines are set off clearly against the confidence in God that the body of the poem testifies to. Similarly, in many of the poems representing disputes between man and wife the relationship is analogous to the postlapsarian disputes between Adam and Eve in *Paradise Lost*. This is certainly the case in "Home Burial"; the man and wife in that poem have lost all sense of real understanding and communion with each other. It is possible for man and wife to communicate effectively and to understand each other, as we know from other Frost poems like "West-Running Brook" and "The Death of the Hired Man." The anger and the lack of contact in "Home Burial" seem abnormal.

In certain other poems, nevertheless, destructiveness and cruelty seem to be inherent in the universe, and therefore by implication in man. In "The Peaceful Shepherd" Frost indicates that religion, as well as trade and government, is a source of human contentiousness: "The Cross, the Crown, the Scales may all / As well have been the Sword." Because these have ruled our lives, that is, men have warred. "The Flood" presents us with a similar picture; that his context there is religious is evident from the echo in the poem of Isaiah 34, where the fury of the Lord is manifested in a kind of universal bloodbath.

In Frost's more pessimistic moods, he both derogates and pities man for the stance he adopts and the feelings he suffers in his isolated and vulnerable position in the universe. He condemns man for his egotism, his pride, his lack of realism, and his occasional defeatism; he pities man for the fear and loneliness that he has to endure. Sometimes he laughs at man, as in "Departmental"; at other times he sympathizes with him because he shares the same experiences and feelings. As one would expect, his position is primarily conservative in this context—conservative and classical. It is classical in its implicit faith in the absolute values of religion, in regular patterns of experience, and in a consequent insistence on normality and restraint in human behavior. Richard P. Adams argues that Frost is predominantly romantic,[21] and in the widest terms this may be the case, but he has strong conservative tendencies which lead him to condemn man's pride, his romantic independence and ambition, and his violence.

Particularly, Frost opposes romanticism in terms of what Nitchie calls anthropocentrism, more nearly approving instead the behavior of the prudential man. Anthropocentric man, according to Nitchie, defines his existence and organizes his experience in humanistic terms. This tendency can lead to certain extremes, as we have just seen. In a materialistic universe, man becomes overly self-centered, denies contact with his environment, and sometimes with other people. He can become dissatisfied even with his own achievements and perceptions, and can develop overweening ambition. These tendencies can result in the violence and cruelty that we have seen in poems like "A Brook in the City" and "The Vanishing Red." In the Puritan's universe, diminished or close to evil as it may seem, anthropocentric man can become too satisfied with the societies he has created himself, or can demand of God that He conform to "reasonable" human standards. Frost's approval of a more prudential stance appears in this context mainly in his distancing of his religious doubts in the act of writing about them. However, if prudential man goes so far along the road he has chosen that he feels a sense of defeat or manifests a desire to escape, he is to be condemned. He is pitiable in many cases, of course, but Frost usually indicates that a state of despair and inertia is not a valid human response.

In recent years the darkness in Frost has received considerably more emphasis than the qualities on which the Frost myth is based. The myth is still with us, but critics and scholars have focused more intently on the pessimism in Frost's work than on the optimism, with considerable justification. Frost's work has never been considered totally dark, although when *North of Boston* first came out, some critics felt that it offered a very bleak picture indeed of northern New England life. Usually, now, his work is taken as essentiall dark, with some glimmers of relief, or as consisting of a dark side and a light side, often mixed. This seems to me the most accurate assessment, though Frost is more fundamentally somber than otherwise. No matter whether Frost sees the world from an agnostic or a religious point of view, he more commonly finds man limited in his competence and unfortunately situated in a difficult universe. The ironic mode and the demonic imagery are somewhat more typical of Frost, despite the everyday or ordinary level of imagery that we remarked in his more optimistic poetry.

It is difficult to say whether Frost's agnostic view of the world presents a darker picture than the religious view. In his agnostic view the universe seems meaningless and virtually empty, a "void," as many critics have called it. In this void man tries to create, to generate a purpose, acting on his own initiative and following the dictates of his own perceptions and inclinations. Frost commonly presents this kind of activity as futile and often ridiculous; it seems to be unrealistic, to lack common sense, aiming at achieving more than is possible for a human being. As a Puritan, on the other hand, Frost sees the universe as controlled, but diminished, almost evil in pragmatic terms. In this situation man tries to avoid control or to shift it

[8]

"The Middleness of the Road": Resolutions

The antitheses in the world view embodied in Frost's poetry would seem to be irreconcilable. How can the humanism apparent in such poems as "Mowing" and "An Old Man's Winter Night" correlate with the religious attitudes of "A Steeple on the House" or the *Masques*? How can the optimistic "Birches" and "Two Look at Two" stem from the same ground as "Design" and "Home Burial"? It is possible in some cases to attribute these differences to changes in mood or perspective, but, as we have seen, they are for the most part more fundamental, for they reflect different perceptions of the nature of the cosmos and of man's relationship to it. The dualism in Frost's views and his work has been explored and described from various points of view. In regard to the relationship between physical reality and the observer's perceptions, it has been argued that "Frost's theory of perception is epistemologically dualistic in that he recognizes that reality in nature, whether cosmic or human, is the result of the interaction of sense data and independently existing physical objects."[1] Another kind of epistemological dualism has been found in Frost's very means of perceiving reality: "Frost's source of knowledge is ... both intuitional and rational-empirical; his 'theme' of knowledge thus lies in a state of tension that is dualistic in nature."[2] Further, Frost's poetry has been described as basically Gnostic, that is, founded on a dual conception of God, consisting of a higher, more spiritual and good entity and a second, antithetical entity, both of which correspond to manifestations in man's nature.[3] In addition to these we can recall discussions of classicism and romanticism in Frost, of the relationship between man and nature, and between the confusion of existence and the opposing impulse toward form, and of many other polar oppositions. Tension between these various poles is most characteristic of Frost's work.

This conflict could be destructive or at least enervating were it not mitigated by a sense of balance, and this balance is Frost's solution to the polar oppositions. He either found it impossible, or simply refused, to try to reconcile the antitheses or to resolve the oppositions in favor of one pole or another. Instead he preferred to maintain them in a state of suspension, recognizing or acceding unconsciously to the validity of both poles. This balance, uncertain though it may be, is as characteristic of Frost's work as the tension which it resolves and at the same time maintains. The balance is sometimes evident as a feature of Frost's poetic technique and sometimes as idea or theme implied or expressed, that is, as the "wisdom" the poetry is designed to attain.

The reflection of the balance in Frost's poetic technique we considered briefly in Chapter 5; there we noted the characteristic ambiguity, the use of paradox, and the persistent irony, which is dualistic in its opposition of an apparent situation or perspective to a real, valid one. Frost's style and tone, according to William H. Pritchard, also generally reflect the balance the poet found necessary in his poetic voice. Pritchard calls this a "middle style" which, by a "decorum of presentation," fits the meaning of such poems as "The Oven Bird" and "Mowing" perfectly.[4] Another study of Frost's imagery identifies certain images which characteristically must be taken in at least two ways that counter one another, thus offering "a compact means of seeing more than one dimension to the meaning of the poem," achieving a balance between different interpretations.[5] The structure of Frost's poems, metrical, syntactic, metaphorical, and otherwise, is similarly described as balanced in an almost mathematical sense by Norman Weinstein.[6]

These technical features of Frost's poetry amount to his form, and this form—especially in its balance—is one means of resisting the confusion of existence. In this sense the form is not simply technique but meaning, just as much as the ideas and themes implied or expressed directly. These themes and the balanced antitheses embodied in them have been studied persistently in Radcliffe Squires's *The Major Themes of Robert Frost*, George W. Nitchie's *Human Values in the Poetry of Robert Frost*, and in various articles by other scholars. Donald J. Greiner, for example, in a 1968 study, indicated Frost's belief that "an honest appraisal of reality permits a conception of nature which accepts both confusion and form."[7] The personae in Frost's poems are often torn between the two. As Greiner says, "Creation of form . . . is useless unless a balance between too much resistance to confusion and too little accompanies it."[8] By "form" in this context Greiner means not so much poetic form but more nearly personal control or a sense of direction in life; he cites the woman in "A Servant to Servants" as one who has too little resistance to confusion, while he points out that in "The Need of Being Versed in Country Things" Frost stresses the necessity of accepting external reality, unpleasant though it is sometimes.

One must be familiar with much of Frost's canon to perceive this balance clearly, for it generally emerges only between poems, some representing one pole or a combination of poles, others representing opposing poles. Occasionally one finds a poem that argues specifically for the concept of balance as an ideal or at least as a normal state of affairs. Usually this argument is expressed in terms of a specific set of poles, but the focus is particularly on balance itself. "Two Tramps in Mud Time" comes to mind as an example; there Frost writes in the last stanza,

> My object in living is to unite
> My avocation and my vocation
> As my two eyes make one in sight.
> Only where love and need are one,
> And the work is play for mortal stakes,
> Is the deed ever really done
> For Heaven and the future's sakes.

This praise of balance states explicitly the point of the poem as a whole, both in the work of the speaker and in the delicate seasonal balance between the warmth of the sun and the chill of the wind. In "The Vantage Point," a much earlier poem, Frost describes himself lying where he can see man's world at a distance on one side and on the other side, close up, the world of nature in the grass. And there is, of course, "Birches," in which Frost says, "I'd like to get away from earth awhile / And then come back to it and begin over . . . / That would be good both going and coming back"; this poem anticipates the images in "A Silken Tent" of the central tent pole "that is its pinnacle to heavenward" and the cords, "countless silken ties of love and thought," that hold the tent to earth.

Frost was quite conscious that his conception of existence depended on balanced oppositions between poles. In his preface to Sarah Cleghorn's biography, he speaks of the "strain" of deciding "between endless . . . things in pairs ordained to everlasting opposition"; in a letter to Sidney Cox he had written "Get up there high enough and the differences that make controversy become only the two legs of a body the weight of which is on one in one period, on the other in the next. Democracy monarchy; puritanism paganism; form content; conservatism radicalism; systole diastole; rustic urbane; literary colloquial; work play."[9] This pervasive dualism, with the resulting tension and the balancing between opposites, was basic to Frost's thinking and therefore to his poetry during his whole career.

The most fundamental oppositions in Frost's world view were those we observed in Chapters 6 and 7, between secularism or agnosticism and Christianity, and between pessimism and optimism. These two antitheses are as doubtfully balanced as other opposed poles in Frost's work, and typically, the balance is achieved in the context of the work as a whole, some poems embodying one side of the antithesis, other poems the other. For the most part Frost did not like to make the confrontation between the poles direct or explicit, preferring instead to represent one position or another. That the choice is not a final one but merely momentary is evident from the appearance of other poems representing the opposite position, as well as from the fact that there are certain poems in which a more or less direct confrontation does take place and a balance between the opposing poles is maintained.

The antithesis between optimism and pessimism in Frost is probably most basic, or at least most prominent. As we have seen, he felt on the one hand that the universe and man's relationship to it are viable or manageable, while on the other hand he often felt pessimistic, believing that the universe and man's position were uncontrollable and difficult at best. We can expect changes in mood in any poet, but what we are considering here is different perceptions of the nature of the cosmos. To illustrate some of the ways that the antithesis between optimism and pessimism is represented in single Frost poems, let us consider "The Tuft of Flowers," "The Onset," "Neither Out Far nor In Deep," and "The Death of the Hired Man."

"The Tuft of Flowers" is the simplest and most explicit case, but it has its own peculiar difficulties from our point of view. The central conflict in the poem is between the sense that human beings work together and that they work apart, between the idea that mankind is unified and that all men are isolated. Early in the poem the speaker comes to feel that men are always "alone . . . / 'Whether they work together or apart.' " In the course of the poem the speaker becomes conscious that a mower before him had had the same appreciation of a tuft of flowers and had spared it just as the speaker himself might have done. He ends the poem in the belief that " 'men work together . . . / Whether they work together or apart.' " The emphasis naturally falls on the more optimistic belief because most of the poem seems to lead up to it. At the same time, however, the tone of the poem maintains a wistful note, implying that men are isolated almost as effectively as they are unified. The balance between the two poles of the antithesis is not perfect, but the pessimistic note is strong enough to mitigate the conclusion and make its optimism sound rather like wishful thinking. "The Tuft of Flowers" provides a tentative confrontation between the humane love of "Iris by Night" and "A Missive Missile" on the one hand and the sense of individual isolation of "Bereft" and "Acquainted with the Night."

"The Onset" is a denser, richer, and more problematic poem. Its structure is somewhat similar to that of "The Tuft of Flowers" in that the first stanza presents the onset of winter, the first snowfall, which suggests to the speaker the coming of death, while the second stanza indicates that eventually the spring will come and with it rebirth. The darkness of the first stanza is much more intense than the pessimism at the beginning of "The Tuft of Flowers." The onset of winter takes place on "a fated night," "in dark woods," with the sound of "hissing," and the speaker feels like someone who "lets death descend / Upon him" without having achieved anything significant, "with nothing done / To evil." The second stanza makes the explicit point that, as the speaker puts it, "winter death has never tried / The earth but it has failed," and eventually he expects to "see the snow all go downhill / In water of a slender April rill," and "Nothing will be left white but here a birch, / And there a clump of houses with a church." The conclusion is thus overtly optimistic, but it is balanced by two other aspects of the poem. First, the intensity of the first stanza is so great that it tends to overshadow the optimism of the final stanza, and second, the imagery in the last stanza is much more pervasively dark than the explicit statement—the heaped-up snow, the withered brake and dead leaves, and the snakelike rill set the tone. The poetic "stuff" of the stanza, in contrast to the discursive point made, is almost as pessimistic as the first stanza, and helps maintain and in fact reinforce the world view. We have a contrast, therefore, within this poem between the pessimism expressed overtly in the first stanza and implicitly in the second, and the explicit message, which is optimistic. One cannot easily say whether the poem represents a friendly or an unfriendly, a manageable or a difficult cosmos as its basic meaning; it suggests both simultaneously as if the threats of nature in "Once by the Pacific" and "The Peril of Hope" were combined with the optimism of "A Hillside Thaw" and "A Prayer in Spring."

In "Neither Out Far nor In Deep" the ambiguity is even more difficult to resolve. Mankind is pictured turning its back on its normal or ordinary life, the land, and persistently looking out to sea, as if it were the source of knowledge. But the sea is obscure; man can neither look out far nor in deep. Still, he persists in looking. The problem is partly tonal here. Since the universe by implication is opaque to man's vision, his position in the cosmos would seem to be uncertain at best. At the same time, he persists in attempting to probe its secrets. Is man to be scorned for spending his time on a futile task, or admired and sympathized with for his courage and determination? The answer is both. This ambiguity we can see also in "For Once, Then, Something" and "The Star-Splitter"; it represents a balance between the concept of man as limited both because of his own deficiencies and because of the opacity of the universe that we find in *A Masque of Reason* and "An Old Man's Winter Night," and the sense that man deserves credit for resolution within his limitations, as "Brown's Descent" and other poems suggest—in "The Lesson for To-Day" Frost resolutely says, "I take my incompleteness with the rest."

There are a number of opposing elements in the antithesis between optimism and pessimism in "The Death of the Hired Man," and because the poem is dramatic, providing little direct help from a narrator, the difficulty in assigning greater importance to one side or another is increased. There is certainly a dark side to the poem. Warren, to begin with, is rather impatient with and unsympathetic to Silas. He is like the world outside the farm, in which Silas's wealthy brother shows no charity and where there are always economic factors that put pressure on farmers like Warren and hired men like Silas. The darkest aspects of the poem lie in Silas himself. He is almost the epitome of vulnerable and helpless man. He is lonely, "worthless," and uncomprehending. His "one accomplishment" —building a load of hay efficiently—is insignificant in a cosmic context, and the poem ends with his death. On the other hand, there are positive features of the world and its inhabitants embodied in the poem. Mary is an agent of mercy and love. What is more, she has some kind of almost mystical contact with the heavens, as the descriptive passages in the poem suggest, while her reception of Silas manifests the charity that his own brother lacks. Most important is the fact that Mary and Warren understand and respond to each other lovingly. In contrast to the couple in "Home Burial," Mary and Warren are at one with each other. Thus the poem seems to be saying that man is helpless and vulnerable and the world is difficult for him, but that with love he can help himself to make his position easier. The poem balances the human loneliness and hopelessness of "The Hill Wife" and "A Servant to Servants" against the compassion and the sense of hope despite discouragement found in "A Prayer in Spring," "Generations of Men," and "Never Again Would Birds' Song Be the Same."

The other basic antithesis we have considered, between Christianity and agnosticism or humanism, is found balanced in "The Star-Splitter," "For Once, Then, Something," "A Servant to Servants," and "The Grindstone," among others. Christianity, or conventional religiousness as we have sometimes referred to it, entails a cosmos controlled by God, either harsh or benevolent, and envisages man as fallen, perhaps, but open to salvation. Agnosticism, in contrast, as we have used the term, implies an uncertainty about the existence of a God, and consequently sees the world as either good or bad, but as man's only certain context.

"The Star-Splitter" tells of how Brad McLaughlin, who failed at "hugger-mugger farming,"

> . . . burned his house down for the fire insurance
> And spent the proceeds on a telescope
> To satisfy a lifelong curiosity
> About our place among the infinities.

Brad was frustrated, that is, in a normal, worldly occupation and was led therefore to attempt metaphysical exploration, even spiritual enlargement, through a sacrifice of his worldly goods—and perhaps of conventional morality as well. The poem implies that "our place among the infinities" is more important than ordinary human affairs, especially second-rate farming, that man has a place among the infinities and that it is desirable, at least, to try to find out what it is. But Brad's attempt leads nowhere. All that happens is that he and the narrator look through the telescope at an ambiguous image of a star and spend the time in entertaining talk. As the narrator says at the end, "Do we know any better where we are, / And how it stands between the night tonight / And a man with a smoky lantern chimney?" Perhaps there is nothing to be seen in the heavens; or perhaps man is incapable of seeing anything there. Most probably, what is there is hidden by remoteness, so that man's only possible solution is some kind of worldly but limited satisfaction. The poet balances off the suggestion that it is important to try to find one's metaphysical position against the necessity of man's limiting himself to his own worldly realm.

We find a similar though more deliberate balance in "For Once, Then, Something." The antithesis in this poem, too, is between limited human preoccupations in an earthly environment, and the possibility of seeing beyond those limits into a supernatural or spiritual order. The speaker says he had been accused of seeing in the well-water only a reflection of himself, "in the summer heaven, godlike, / Looking out of a wreath of fern and cloud puffs." In other words, a man should not be so preoccupied with his own importance as to elevate himself to the status of a god; he might well look beyond his own concerns, beyond the order of nature. When the speaker does manage, once, to see through the surface picture, however, he cannot tell what he has seen: "Truth? A pebble of quartz?" Is there anything beyond the physical to see? If there is, can man see it? The fact that the water, as the speaker says, "came to rebuke the too clear water" suggests that nature is preventing any insight because it has a will as an instrument of God, or as an indifferent power. The fact that it is rather improbable in realistic terms that one could see Truth at the bottom of a well may suggest that man is limited to earthly reality, but otherwise the poem is almost perfectly ambiguous. Frost has very carefully balanced a spiritual and a humanistic view of the universe here and in "The Star-Splitter." In neither does he refer specifically to God, but both imply that there may be a larger, supernatural dimension to man's existence which he should know more about, while at the same time suggesting that this further dimension may be nothing but an illusion, that physical reality may be all there is, or that man is by nature limited to a restricted realm.

In "A Servant to Servants" the antithesis between Christianity and agnosticism is manifested somewhat differently. On one level, the woman tells a story of her overinvolvement with human activity, of her susceptibility to the confusion of existence in a purely physical context. She has too much work to do, her husband does not understand her, she finds no satisfaction in her existence. All these things aggravate the hereditary strain of insanity to which she knows she is succumbing. At the same time, however, she can be considered an archetypal postlapsarian Eve, suffering under God's curse of labor which is aggravating her inheritance of original sin, the madness that runs in her family. She is analogous to Job, and to the speaker in "Bereft," especially since her last words imply that she exists in a spiritual order as well as her immediate physical one: "There's work enough to do . . . / I shan't catch up in this world, anyway." She is also like "The Hill Wife" in her loneliness and isolation in a purely physical context. Again, the balance between the spiritual and the secular is evident.

"The Grindstone" is one of Frost's more complex poems, equivalent in some degree to "West-Running Brook" and "Directive," which we shall consider later. The antithesis between a conventional religious view and an agnostic one appears first in terms of the contrast between a literal interpretation of the poem and a symbolic one, and secondly in terms of different symbolic interpretations. If we take the poem literally it describes how an old man and a boy (the narrator when younger) sharpened a scythe on a grindstone. Even in closer readings we remain conscious of this earthly, human and secular level of meaning. But man is not to be restricted to a material context, as the symbolic intent of the poem indicates. Frost suggests thus that common sense is limited, for he invests the poem with a higher, more nearly spiritual significance as well.

There are various symbolic implications, however. Lynen takes the sharpening to be concerned with the "creative process."[10] The created work is achieved in a worldly context, that is, by the operation of the "oblate spheroid" of the grindstone—the world. With the world as agent, the process is governed by the Apollonian "Father-Time-like" figure who evidently represents the intellectual and judgmental functions of man, while the dynamic impulse toward creativity is represented by the boy, perhaps the Dionysian and physical side of man. Whatever else it is, the poem can certainly be taken as one of many in which Frost is concerned implicitly with the writing of poetry.[11] In this sense the poem pertains to a peculiarly human process and with the faculties in man that make it possible. At the same time other dimensions suggest themselves, partly through the image of the "ruinous live apple tree" which figures in several lines and suggests that the laboriousness of the creative process is due partly to the fallen state of the world. A further dimension is also suggested by the conclusion of the poem where the speaker says, "Wasn't there danger of a turn too much? / . . . I was for leaving something for the whetter," which resembles the end of "Good-By and Keep Cold": "something has to be left to God." Furthermore, if we look at the characters in "The Grindstone" slightly differently, we can see that the old man fulfills an almost Godlike function; for one thing, he is the judge of when the job is done. The boy, "who gave his life to keep [the wheel] going round," feels he too should have some say in the matter, but in essence does nothing but provide the impulse, the power for the grinding. The relationship between the two seen from this perspective suggests that between God and man in *A Masque of Mercy* and "The Fear of God." Man must do his very best, though he can never know if it will be acceptable. The conjunction of the Christian view and a more secular one in "The Grindstone" makes almost for a fusion of the two perspectives. On the one hand, we find primary emphasis on a physical activity and symbolically on an immediately human creative effort, while at the same time we find a strong suggestion of a context in which the final judgment on a created work is not man's but God's.

The effect of the various antitheses, especially those balancing an optimistic conception of the cosmos with a pessimistic one, and a secular or agnostic view with a more conventionally religious one, is to establish for Frost a poetic stance that has pleased most of his readers, annoyed some, and puzzled a good many who have considered it carefully. By poetic stance I mean an attitude toward experience and toward other people, a mental set embodied in the poetry by many means—the tone, the way the imagery and metaphor are handled, the style and the kinds of structure. The stance, any stance, is largely a matter of technique and method, but it is also partly reflected substantively in expressed or implied assertions. Sometimes it is manifested passively, and sometimes actively, the difference being much like that between Nitchie's prudential man and anthropocentric man.[12]

Frost's poetic attitude is often passive in demanding that man accomodate himself to the conditions of his existence or at least accept them. There is often considerable courage as well as simply patience and forebearance in this, but it is basically a "mediating" mode in which man takes into account but does not commit himself to the poles of the antitheses that confront him.[13] He insists on being able to look both ways and adopts a defensive posture in order to do so. Many people have found in Frost a spiritual strength in this posture, although Sampley suggests that there are some poems that show him "in retreat from the responsibilities of life."[14] The kind of retreat that takes place, however, is always temporary. Sampley cites "A Drumlin Woodchuck" and "One Step Backward Taken"; the point in these poems is specifically that in order to survive, to preserve one's strength for continued resistance to confusion, one must make minor temporary concessions. Frost did not equate retreat with defeat; in his last poem ("In Winter in the Woods . . . "), he tells of how he chopped down a maple and then shouldered his ax and went home, concluding,

> I see for Nature no defeat
> In one tree's overthrow
> Or for myself in my retreat
> For yet another blow.

The poem "Acceptance" seems to offer the clearest picture of this defensive posture in the words of the bird who has just managed to get back to his nest, thinking,

> . . . "Safe!
> Now let the night be dark for all of me.
> Let the night be too dark for me to see
> Into the future. Let what will be, be."

In other poems, especially those in which man is directly confronted either by diminished nature, the fallen world, or a threatening universe, the stance is not quite so defensive. "A Winter Eden" shows the animals—surrogates for man—making the best of and actually enjoying their considerably diminished Eden. "The Oven Bird" has perhaps made the most of a diminished thing; he seems to have recognized that although the summer is diminished from the spring it can be accepted on certain conditions. Although it does not sing melodically, the oven bird has not turned silent like the other birds. In fact he makes a loud and defiant sound.

It often takes courage to accept the inevitable, however, and this too is part of Frost's defensive attitude. This stoicism Peter Viereck called a "Greek cheerfulness";[15] it is the state of mind manifested in one way by the woman in "A Servant to Servants," and the contentment and determination of the speaker who resists the temptation of death in "Stopping by Woods on a Snowy Evening." It is, in other words, the mental set of one who has accepted the "trial by existence" on its own terms and is making the best of it. This kind of courage is found particularly in the deceptiveness and the humor so typical of Frost. This humor is both a defensive gesture to prevent his becoming too vulnerable and also something of a positive achievement, a way of enjoying what otherwise might be devastating. This, I believe, is the case with the *Masques* as well as with minor poems like "Departmental," "Provide, Provide," and "The Bear."

The more active manifestation of Frost's poetic stance perhaps has its roots in this courage. It goes well beyond the retreat, the husbanding of one's resources characteristic of the prudential man, and becomes a genuine achievement. This active attitude reflects a determination to accomplish something, not merely to save oneself or to endure. One specific kind of achievement familiar to all readers of Frost is that of form. An impulsion toward the achievement of form is embodied in "The Grindstone," for example. There the narrator specifies that he is worried about the precise state of the edge that the two of them are sharpening: he does not want it ruined. The wood-pile, in the poem of that name, manifests the same kind of impulsion, as does the harvesting in "After Apple-Picking." Most clearly, the ax-helve represents the epitome of perfect form as the narrator describes it in that poem. The form is shaped organically with the wood rather than imposed artificially; it will endure, it is useful, and it is beautiful. Form is certainly one particular way of resisting confusion that was close to Frost's heart.

The most basic and pervading element of Frost's active posture is his determination to maintain a faith, to act on the assumption "as if" in various contexts. This faith can appear as a saving illusion as it does in "A Boundless Moment," where the speaker enjoys pretending briefly that "A young beech clinging to its last year's leaves" is " 'the Paradise-in-Bloom.' "

This "as if" assumption is considerably more significant, however. It is a religious faith to begin with, deliberately maintained. In many of his works, as we have seen, Frost reveals a skepticism, or at least an uncertainty about the existence or the benevolence of God, but he very often insisted on making the assumption that God exists and that there is a purpose to man's existence. This is evident not only in "The Trial by Existence," an early myth-poem, but also in the later *Masques*. This "as if" attitude also has its secular manifestation as a reflection of a Jamesian conception of the relation between man and reality. Frost often reveals considerable doubt about the nature of reality and about man's ability to perceive it accurately;[16] in "All Revelation" he assumes that the nature of reality depends somewhat on man's own perceptions. In other words, Frost behaves as if reality had a partly independent existence, but that it is partly created by our own conception of it. The appearance of things may be one of confusion, but he assumes that it is possible to make some sense out of it. This Jamesian version of his "as if" principle is illustrated in "The Mountain" and in "Two Look at Two." In "The Mountain" the farmer and the narrator discuss the spring at the top of the mountain as if it really existed and as if it really were cold in summer and warm in winter, although neither quite believes this. In "Two Look at Two" Frost says specifically that the human pair feel "as if" the earth and the deer returned their love.

This "as if " principle attains the stature of a myth to rationalize and make valid Frost's experience. The main features of this myth and of the quest that springs from it are especially well summarized by Arthur M. Sampley.[17] Although I would describe the myth slightly differently, I agree with his observation that for Frost it has the same validity as Yeats's, and Eliot's visions have for them. Frost's myth is less systematic but just as effective. The main outlines of the myth are most clearly seen in "West-Running Brook" and "Directive," where the quest is described most explicitly. These two poems will indicate how effective the myth is in fostering an active stance as well as a passive one against the confusion of existence.

"West-Running Brook" represents a Heraclitan conception of the universe,[18] in the first place because of the operation of entropy. As Fred, the man in the poem, says, "Existence . . . runs away / To fill the abyss's void with emptiness." As the wave over the rock in the stream curls back against the flow of the water, however, so there is something in existence that constitutes a general "backward motion toward the source," a perpetual resistance, to be deliberately fostered at times, back toward God or toward some nontheistic source of energy. The desire for permanence which this resistance to the downward flow betokens is inevitably frustrated, except in the actual contrariety itself, not only of the wave to the stream but also in many other kinds of similar contraries manifested in the poem. These contraries really exist in their own right, as Fred indicates, but also exist in our perceptions of them. He points out, for example, that the backward motion of the wave against the stream is what "most we see ourselves in," while his wife has already suggested, symbolically and fancifully, that the wave had waved to them.

The poem is in fact a tissue of contraries, all of them connected and interwoven.[19] The most obvious antitheses are those of resistance and decline, man and woman, reason (in Fred) and romance (in his wife), and permanence and change. The poem is a kind of emblem of the world and all existence, which consists, as the poem makes clear symbolically, of a similar tissue of contraries.

According to Heraclitus, the conflict between these contraries resulted in harmony, but this poem does not seem to suggest this. Rather, the opposing poles of all of these antitheses are maintained simultaneously in a balance sustained by the assumption that both are valid. Frost's half-created myth of unresolved antitheses reflects what Kenneth Burke calls an "and / also" perception.

The stance implied and fostered by this myth is passive in the sense that it demands of man a suspended state of mind, an ability to tolerate opposed values, conflicting alternatives. The myth also fosters an active attitude in demanding of man that he transcend the opposition between antithetical poles by working with both and deriving from their opposition some satisfactory mode of experience especially by working from his own personal experience, his particular situation, rather than with abstractions derived from others.[20]

This active search for a satisfactory mode of existence is symbolized as a quest in a number of poems. In general the quest is for some kind of significance to human life, some validating principle. In religious terms we can find this quest in the *Masques*, but it is also reflected in Frost's greatest poem, "Directive," although there it is embodied in somewhat more secular terms. The poem first appears as a retreat back in time out of the confusion of the modern world. The trip goes back past things that have been destroyed in the course of creating the present civilization—that is, the road that is no more a road, the two village cultures that are lost, and the deserted farm, not to mention the obviously symbolic old apple trees that have been "shaded out" by the new woods. The retreat seems to be to a time of simplicity, a place where isolation and quiet are available; it is easy to see analogies to Thoreau's *Walden*.[21] This retreat to childlike simplicity and safety is a kind of "one step backward" that makes it possible to endure the modern confusion.

This is not merely an escape from something, however; it is also a search for something, a quest aimed at a goal. The speaker sets himself up as a guide who wants to help the reader find himself, to attain wholeness from the renewing waters of the spring. In Christian terms it is explicitly a Grail quest. The searchers endure certain ordeals, as represented by the watching eyes from the cellar holes and the half-sinister rustling of the new woods. They penetrate into a dead land where they find an equivalent of the Chapel Perilous, the deserted farm, and ultimately a goblet like the Grail from which they drink the sacramental waters. The result is a renewal of the spirit, a kind of rebirth, not merely a restoration.[22]

The quest has also a secular dimension in symbolic terms. It is an archetypal search for the source of life and energy. Water has always had that value, which has been reflected in literature for thousands of years, as it is here, as well as in "West-Running Brook," "The Pasture," and many of Frost's other poems. Here the search leaves behind modern society and penetrates back into a more elemental one. Village cultures are left behind, and we arrive at a single farm and even a children's playhouse, which epitomize society. We also go past cold and unfriendly nature indicated by the marks of the glacier and its residual coolness, and past natural violence hinted at in the reference to raging valley streams. Behind or beneath these manifestations of nature lies the pure and beneficent spring, the natural source of all life. This quest is also expressed implicitly in terms of art and specifically poetry, as we shall see.

As one would expect in a central poem in Frost's canon, "Directive" has its dark side and its more optimistic one set nearly in balance. The sense of modern confusion and the consequent destruction of human cultures is certainly to be lamented, and the sense of threatening nature is not encouraging. Against these evidences of darkness stands the achievement of the quest as a whole; the life-giving spring, the source, and the sacrament that it offers in Christian terms, is still there, still available. This myth—a pretense, an "as if"—provides for a resolute posture and symbolically suggests the attainment of knowledge that will validate man's experience. "West-Running Brook" and "Directive" are obviously key poems in Frost's canon, not only because they present the basis for both a passive and an active poetic stance, but also because they indicate a balance in his work between a darker and a more optimistic perception of the universe, and between a Christian world view and a more secular one. They are also central works, indeed climactic, because of the images and motifs embodied in them, which reflect and pull together those in a great deal of the rest of his work.[23]

Frost's poetic stance was intended to enable man, as Frost's personae represent him, to resist the confusion of existence. Very rarely did Frost ever suggest that one viable solution would be to escape, to back down in the face of the confusion. "An Empty Threat" suggests briefly and not very seriously—witness the title—that he would be willing to concede defeat and take refuge in the isolation of Hudson's Bay, and in "New Hampshire" he expresses anger and frustration at attempts to involve him in the kinds of choices typical of modern life. Instead of being either "prude or puke" he says, " 'Me for the hills where I don't have to choose.' " It is clear, nevertheless, that Frost did not generally accept the idea of evading experience. In "Escapist–Never" he is speaking about himself–and man–when he says,

> He is no fugitive . . .
> His life is a pursuit of a pursuit forever.
> It is the future that creates his present.
> All is an interminable chain of longing.

Frost is always seeking solutions to the problems confronting mankind, to the difficulty of facing the confusion of modern existence and therefore of resolving the opposition between various poles that produces the confusion.

Aside from the basic myth embodied in "West-Running Brook" and "Directive," there are two particular means of dealing with the antitheses of modern life that serve throughout Frost's work to help him establish a viable poetic stance. The first lies in the relationship between man and woman as Frost presents it in so many of his poems. Scores of his poems throughout his career focus specifically on the relationship between man and woman either directly, as in "Home Burial" and "The Death of the Hired Man," or by presenting one or another of the partners, as in "The Housekeeper" and "The Thatch."

Man and woman seem to Frost to represent alternative approaches to life, potentially in conflict but capable of complementing each other. Man seems to Frost to embody rationality, destructiveness, and a certain insensitivity, while woman seems to embody imaginativeness, creativity, and sensitiveness and therefore vulnerability. These differences we have seen clearly in "The Death of the Hired Man," "Home Burial," and certainly "West-Running Brook." A main problem for Frost is resolving the differences or achieving between them a balance that will render the relationship, usually a marital one, complementary. At one extreme, as in "Going for Water," "A Prayer in Spring," and "Two Look at Two," the poet suggests that the man and woman are truly united. In some of these poems he refers to the couple simply as "we" or "they"–a unit, in other words–and although he makes their separateness evident in "Two

Look at Two" he nevertheless indicates that they form a pair. At the other extreme, men and women are represented as antagonistic. Frost seems to feel that cruelty forms part of love and that a lack of understanding and communication is not at all unusual. This is the case in "Home Burial" and "The Subverted Flower," and the intention of "giving and taking pain" can be part of a husband's thinking.[24]

The normal state of affairs or the most appropriate, considering the contrarieties inherent in existence, lies somewhere between those two extremes of unity and antagonism. This is the relationship between man and woman in "The Death of the Hired Man" and "The Master Speed." In these and other poems like them, the man and the woman are separate and retain their particular characteristics, but have a mutual understanding and respect, forming a truly complementary pair. "The Death of the Hired Man" and "West-Running Brook" indicate the potential disagreement between them. Warren at first does not want to take Silas in, and Mary does; Warren does not sympathize with Silas, while Mary pities him. In "West-Running Brook" Fred and his wife perceive the wave in the stream in different terms, realistically and philosophically on the one hand, and fancifully and personally on the other. The normal or most appropriate resolution of the differences between man and woman is represented by the final interchange in "West-Running Brook":

> "Today will be the day
> You said so."
>
> "No, today will be the day
> You said the brook was called West-Running Brook."
>
> "Today will be the day of what we both said."

What achieves this balance between the contrarieties of man and woman is mutual love,[25] and since their relationship is symbolic of all existential contrarieties love may be taken as the answer to the confusion of the world. Obviously love is not always attainable but it at least existed for Frost as an ideal.

Frost's principal means of confronting the contrarieties of existence nevertheless is poetry itself. As form, as a satisfying activity *per se*, it represents a passive stance, a "momentary stay against confusion." We can see him enjoying the creation of poetic form throughout his work in the active engagement in various prosodic forms, and the working out of the relationship between these and the ideas and images they embody as well as in the various poetic structures—the dramatic monologues and dialogues and the various lyric patterns—and in his development of a style appropriate to his role. This kind of activity is in a sense "play," and as Simon O. Lesser argues, the process of simply creating form no matter what it "contains" is a means of relieving anxiety.[26] Simply handling problematic material and sorting it into some kind of manageable form is satisfying and reassuring, irrespective of the particular solutions to the problems. However, this kind of play is secondary, a by-product of the attempts to solve the problems directly; it is valuable but it is not the thing to aim at immediately. The ideational struggle takes precedence and is real. No matter what Frost said, his poetry is not merely a momentary stay against confusion, an attempt to create form simply for that temporary pleasure. It is more because it embodies an active stance. The activity lies in the kind of definition and exploration of problems that we have been examining, particularly those of the contrarieties within Frost's world view. In his attempts to resolve the problems, his poetry represents a substantive coming to grips with the confusion. Lawrance Thompson suggested that this is what characterizes his best poetry,[27] and I think few would disagree.

Frost's consciousness of his art, both as an attempt to solve human problems and as satisfying form in itself, is evident in a great deal of his poetry. In fact, many of his poems are concerned immediately if not explicitly with the nature of poetry and the processes it involved, as Caspersson suggests. "After Apple-Picking," for example, is commonly and reasonably read as a symbolic exploration of the poet's feeling about his work, the apples sometimes being equated almost allegorically with poems. Another case in point, "The Mountain," has been analyzed by Laurence Perrine as a similar consideration of the nature of poetry, not only in the line "all the fun's in how you say a thing," but in the whole fabric of the poem.[28] It focuses particularly on "the contrast . . . between poetic and scientific truth, or imaginative insight and literal fact," by opposing the literal impossibility of the spring's location and temperature changes to their validity as imaginative ideals.

This kind of balancing is surely typical of Frost, especially in its opposition of a hardheaded rational and skeptical conception to an article of poetic faith, an "as if." We may note that the antithesis between reality and imagination in "The Mountain" is not resolved. The narrator and the farmer are both relatively sensible and practical men. Their lives are governed for the most part by reality; at the same time they are willing to enjoy the imagination embodied in the spring. Some readers take this kind of unresolved balance as a weakness, as an indication that the poet is unsure of himself, is diffident and therefore ambiguous. As we know, Frost has been called a "spiritual drifter" as well as one who lacks "a wholly coherent mes-

III

Frost's Literary Contexts
and Techniques

Frost's Literary Heritage

Robert Frost was influenced by a number of earlier writers and thinkers. Sometimes this influence was exerted in specific ways or is evident in particular passages or poems, but usually it was general, the connection between him and his forebears appearing as a matter of analogy or of similar traditions.[1] The main literary figures to affect him were Wordsworth, Emerson, and Thoreau. In addition, he was profoundly influenced by William James, as we have already seen. It is further evident that he was indebted to Emily Dickinson and to classical Greek and Latin literature as well.

Frost's literary forebears affected his ways of thinking, his general attitudes and perspectives, and this basic influence usually resulted in certain stylistic or technical similarities. Except in a relatively few cases, Frost did not directly imitate or emulate his predecessors. He read their work, found he sympathized with their views in various ways, and like them, shaped his work partly in accordance with those views thematically, in subject matter, or technically.

Frost never analyzed thoroughly or in detail his relationship to literary traditions or his poetic theory and practice. In the last decades, however, these have come to receive the attention they deserve and have begun to be explored and carefully analyzed. One can now see the main attitudes that derive from Frost's literary heritage, the conceptions he adapted to his own uses, and the literary theories and practice that made him "one of the most notable craftsmen" of his time.[2] It is appropriate here to deal with the three main literary figures to influence Frost—Wordsworth, Emerson, and Thoreau—and then the main technical features that characterized his work—form (including meter and rhyme), the "sound of sense," and metaphor.

William Wordsworth

Frost paid tribute to Wordsworth in a talk he gave at Cornell in 1950 which was transcribed and published later.[3] He expressed his admiration for the simplicity and clarity of Wordsworth's poetry, particularly his lyrics. He felt, moreover, that the "banality," as Frost called it, of the poetry enabled it to penetrate to the deepest levels of human consciousness. And he evidently felt there was an analogy between his own poetry and Wordsworth's; this is certainly evident in poems like the early "Gum-Gatherer" and "The Tuft of Flowers." He also said that he had been influenced by the "Ode to Duty," suggesting that it justified his change "from youthful rebel to adult conservative."[4] Clearly Frost's brief remarks only hint at his affinity with Wordsworth, not to mention the significant differences between them. The basic similarities lie in their attitudes toward nature, their use of common people, and their resultant styles.

Like Wordsworth, Frost writes often about external nature—the mountains, lakes, woods, and fields, and the animals found there. Obviously, both poets appreciated nature and felt it was important. Even more significant are the particular similarities and the differences between them, however. Frost had a much more varied and less optimistic view of nature[5]—he was not a "Wordsworthian" nature poet, describing pretty country scenes for their inspirational purport as Wordsworth did in "To the Cuckoo," for instance:

> While I am lying on the grass
> Thy twofold shout I hear;
> From hill to hill it seems to pass
> At once far off, and near . . .
>
> O blessed Bird! the earth we pace
> Again appears to be
> An unsubstantial, faery place /
> That is fit home for Thee!
> (11. 5–8, 29–32)

He was much more conscious of the violence and evil at least potential in nature; "Storm Fear" makes this clear, as does "Once by the Pacific":

> It looked as if a night of dark intent
> Was coming, and not only a night, an age.
> Someone had better be prepared for rage.
> There would be more than ocean-water broken
> Before God's last *Put out the Light* was spoken.
> (11. 10–14)

Yet at the same time he reacted in a number of different ways to all aspects of external nature as we have seen—he is uncertain or at least ambiguous in his perceptions of nature in all its variety, even to the point of celebrating that uncertainty in "A Boundless Moment."[6]

Wordsworth, because he believed as a pantheist that a benevolent divinity was embodied in all natural things, was more single-minded and optimistic in his attitude toward nature.

Also because of his pantheism, Wordsworth turned to nature for inspiration, for a vision of moral value that specific scenes such as Tintern Abbey could convey as symbols of spiritual values.[7] This is almost never the case with Frost. He insisted on the gulf, or some kind of barrier, between man and nature: Nature is "other" to man.[8] Even in "Two Look at Two" where the personae approach the deer and their realm closely, the humans are separated from nature by a wall, and it only *seems* "as if . . . the earth returned their love." In consequence, Frost focuses primarily on man in contrast to nature, even praising him for rising above his environment,[9] as in "The Wood-Pile" and "Sand Dunes":

> They are the sea made land
> To come at the fisher town
> And bury in solid sand
> The men she could not drown . . .
>
> Men left her a ship to sink:
> They can leave her a hut as well;
> And be but more free to think
> For the one more cast-off shell.
> ("Sand Dunes," 11. 5–8, 13–16)

Frost's typical locale may be rural, but his main concern is man's physical and psychological experience in his own terms, since there is little or no organic relationship between man and nature.

There is a real and important analogy between Wordsworth and Frost in their poetic use of nature, nevertheless. As Lynen points out, both poets employ local rural material for "pastoral" purposes —they use nature, and man in nature, to reveal human mores and experience by the contrast with sophisticated urban society.[10] And, most important, they take the rural point of view, the only effective means to this end. They make their rural subjects symbolically universal and thus avoid sentimental regionalism.

Like Wordsworth, Frost perceived a connection, as well as opposition, between natural surroundings and man's mind, as "Putting in the Seed" and "The Onset" will show. This is perhaps what makes Frost most nearly a Wordsworthian nature poet. But again there is a significant difference between the two writers. Whereas Wordsworth approaches nature as an introspective individual and reports meditatively on his own feelings and experiences in nature, most notably in

"The Prelude," Frost's persona speaks as a member of a community, despite his individualism. He is a New Englander, like most of the characters in his poetry; this is the particular value of Frost's public image of rural philosopher. This role further enables him to write both lyrics and dramatic poetry effectively. The speaker in Frost's poems is usually conversational at least, often speaking to another member of society, and it is a short step from that to a thoroughly dramatic interchange like "The Death of the Hired Man."

The focus in Frost's poetry is primarily on man, usually *in* nature, but not *of* it, in contrast to Wordsworth. Yet the poets share a basic concern with common people that differentiates them from other writers outside the pastoral tradition. Although Frost does not write as a farmer himself, he is a neighbor, and like Wordsworth, takes farmers and laborers seriously as types of basic humanity. It is worth noting, however, that Frost's people are quite different from the Romantics' humble and sometimes simple-minded rustics. Persons from north of Boston are typically hard-nosed, perceptive, even sophisticated; their characteristic understated language is intended to convey meanings beyond the obvious. "The Mountain" and "The Axe-Helve" reveal the typical qualities of Frost's rural people.

Some of the most important ways that Wordsworth's and Frost's shared views affected their poetic technique have already become evident. Most basic is their choice of simple diction and of common phrasing and sentence structures in contrast to the elaborate styles of the periods before them — neoclassical elegant poetic diction in Wordsworth's case, and the Victorians' fulsome sonority in Frost's. In both, the particular vehicle was the idiom of country speakers, free from the artificiality of sophisticated society, and possessing an expressive idiom and flavor of its own. This language is found both in the characters whose voices are presented dramatically and in the speech of the personae in the lyric poems, especially in Frost. There are significant differences in their languages due to differing perceptions of rural society and of nature, however. Wordsworth is more visionary, more expostulatory and vaguer, while Frost is typically more ironic, more restrained, and more precise. Frost would never have written,

> Wisdom and Spirit of the universe!
> Thou Soul that art the eternity of thought,
> That givest to forms and images a breath
> And everlasting motion, not in vain . . .
>   . . . didst thou intertwine for me
> The passions that build up our human soul . . .
>   (*The Prelude*, Book I, 11. 401–404, 406–407)

while Wordsworth would hardly have begun a poem, "Back out of all this now too much for us" ("Directive"). Wordsworth's voice and style reflect his belief that man and nature share organically in a beneficent deity; Frost's tone and phrasing are consistent with a bleaker conception of man and his surroundings.[11]

What is most important to an understanding of Frost is to see what he learned from Wordsworth and how he adapted it to his own circumstances and purposes. The rural locales and people, the connection between nature and man, the voice and language appropriate to both are what Frost adopted in principle from Wordsworth, while he modified the principles as he saw fit.

Ralph Waldo Emerson

Robert Frost expressed his opinion of Emerson in a speech in 1959 upon receiving the Emerson-Thoreau medal from the American Academy of Arts and Letters. There he gave credit to Emerson for helping to form his conception of poetic language—a declaration that is commonly taken to mean that Emerson helped him to see the importance of "the sound of sense," the principle that the rhythms and intonations of language by themselves suggest meanings. Emerson himself did not employ the principle in his verse, as Greiner points out,[12] but enunciated it in a passage in "Monadnoc" beginning:

> Yet, will you learn our ancient speech,
> These the masters who can teach,
> Fourscore or a hundred words
> All their vocal muse affords;
> But they can turn them in a fashion
> Past clerks' or statesmen's art or passion . . .

Later in his speech Frost stated that he owed a debt particularly to Emerson for his preoccupation with freedom, for teaching that one should have the "courage to be new," to embark on searches instead of remaining bound by conventionalities.[13] Thus Frost felt both linguistic and attitudinal influences. He differed basically from Emerson's philosophic views, however, as he did from Wordsworth's. Frost characterized the older poet as a "Monist" who believed in the organic unity of all things informed by an essentially beneficent divine spirit. But Frost was neither a Platonic idealist nor a Transcendentalist, and as he said, he conceived of the universe as a dichotomy between good and evil. Despite this basic difference, however, the attitudes and interests the poets shared led Frost to adopt stances and voices similar in several ways to Emerson's.

Like Wordsworth, Emerson held intense and positive religious convictions that gave direction to his work, especially since he developed and stated them explicitly, whereas Frost lacked this positive conviction.[14] Emerson, also like Wordsworth, believed that external nature was emblematic of spiritual and moral values inherent in the universe, whereas Frost, a realist in William Dean Howells's sense, believed that nature is "bound to no thesis . . . and it will not allow you to say precisely what its meaning or argument is."[15] Thus while Emerson's poetry manifested an interest in reality for the insights it could provide into the spiritual, and leapt quickly from experience to the meaning it embodied, Frost's skepticism led him to concentrate on experience in a more restricted perspective and in more concrete detail.[16]

Rather strangely, Emerson and Frost arrived at certain similar positions, though from different directions. They both believed in the privacy of the individual, maintaining in the first place that man can control nature to some extent, as we can see from "Riders" and "All Revelation," and that social progress comes from the thought and work of great individuals (as Frost's behavior in Washington late in his life, and especially in Russia with Khrushchev, indicates).[17] Men should therefore foster their particular natures before engaging in socially directed efforts. Emerson believed in more governmental control and social progress than Frost would subscribe to, but otherwise their positions were analogous. Especially, Frost adopted Emerson's (and William James's) belief in the necessity of self-reliance and the consequent distrust of bookish scholarship in favor of personal speculation and experience. And this led Frost to spurn scientism and intellectualism in general, preferring to write poetry based on observed reality. It may be partly because of this attitude that Frost left Harvard—and, possibly, Dartmouth, earlier—to write poetry in New Hampshire.[18]

It is Emerson's independence of mind, perhaps more than anything else, that Frost respected and clung to. This intellectual freedom was as boldly speculative as Emerson's and led him like Emerson to refuse to systematize or structure the pattern of his ideas and to use a "poetic" method of analyzing experience and phenomena.[19] Frost said in "The Door in the Dark," "I had my native simile jarred. / So people and things don't pair anymore / With what they used to pair with before"; he was indicating the process of seeing resemblances or "correspondences" as a natural imaginative means of correlating observations and experiences. Thus a woman may resemble a silken tent in important ways even though logically or "scientifically" the two do not belong in the same category.

There are considerable differences between Emerson's and Frost's poetic techniques attendant upon their philosophic differences, just as there were with Wordsworth and Frost. Emerson is more oracular and his tone more sermonlike, while Frost is more dramatic and immediate; Emerson is more suggestive and general, while Frost puts characters and personae into concrete literal action.[20] But the influence of Emerson can be seen in equally important similarities in their poetic theory and practice. They share a trust in metaphor, analogy, and symbolism as their basic means of analysis, as I have said. And Frost followed Emerson's advice about voice tones which led him toward the recognition and employment of the "sound of sense." Both of these are central to Frost's poetic technique.

Henry David Thoreau

Walden was one of Frost's favorite books—he had "a special shelf in [his] heart" for it, along with Defoe's *Robinson Crusoe* and Darwin's *Voyage of the Beagle*. He described it as "everything from a tale of adventure . . . to a declaration of independence and a gospel of wisdom," adding later in the same interview that in that declaration was where he found "most justification for [his] own propensities." Frost certainly knew more of Thoreau than *Walden*, but he maintained that "Thoreau's immortality may hang by a single book, but that book includes even his writing that is *not* in it."[21]

There were aspects of Thoreau, of course, that found no echo in Frost. Although they were both "parablists" in "their way of releasing an idea through an action from common experience,"[22] the same philosophic differences appear between them as in the cases of Emerson and Wordsworth: Frost was no Transcendentalist or pantheist. Where Thoreau found nature spiritually beneficent, Frost viewed it with more detachment, even suspicion at times.[23] To be sure, Frost sometimes finds a more than material satisfaction in nature, as in "Fragmentary Blue" and "Directive," where a hint of spiritual power is evident in nature. And in "The Axe-Helve," we seem to find an almost Romantic approbation of the "natural" man that corresponds to the description of the wood-chopper and the artist of Kouroo in *Walden*.[24]

Certainly the most important specific influence Frost felt came from Thoreau's independence, especially since he enacted it dramatically in his own behavior as well as expressing it in writing. What this independence meant to Frost was not "Liberty with a capital 'L' " so much as "the daily liberties he could take right under the noses of the high and mighty and the small and petty."[25] A desire for this kind of freedom appears throughout Frost's life—in his dislike of the restraints of undergraduate life at Dartmouth and Harvard, in the informality of his classes, in his reluctance to write poetry to order, and in his refusal to work for the Office of War Information in World War II. Nevertheless, Frost recognizes that *Walden* represented *"independence from society,"* whereas he himself wanted, and achieved, *"freedom in society."* He admired and emulated Thoreau's individuality and independence of mind, but believed that all men can and must reconcile their personal integrity with the needs of society. The development of one's own character was important not only for the individual's sake, but because society would thereby profit from his achievements.[26] It was Thoreau's originality and self-reliance that Frost approved as "independence" in *Walden*, as in Defoe's *Robinson Crusoe*.

Some of Frost's work shows the influence of Thoreau quite specifically and profoundly. "The Axe-Helve" is significant because its main theme echoes Thoreau's aversion to machinery (the machine-made helve is inadequate, and Baptiste's stove overheats) and to false education, artificially imposed from without.[27] The fine poem "Directive" is particularly notable both because of its preeminence in Frost's canon and because of the degree of influence that *Walden* exerted on it.[28] There are particular images and events that echo *Walden*, including walking back in time, getting lost, and reaching a spring at least in imagination. Most important, since it indicates Thoreau's influence on Frost's poetic endeavor, is the similarity to passages in *Walden* of Frost's insisting on metaphor as the key to the "momentary stay against confusion." The broken goblet (a borrowed image itself) comes to symbolize metaphor, language unattainable by "the wrong ones." Just as *Walden* for Frost was an adventure "always near the height of poetry,"[29] so Frost imaginatively attains the ultimate "height of the adventure" at the climax of "Directive." The kinship of Frost and Thoreau revealed in this poem should alert us to the influence to be found throughout Frost's work in less tangible forms.

It is clear that some Thoreauvian qualities in Frost's poetry are due to a general sympathy or analogy between the two writers' attitudes. They are both spokesmen for New England, they both prefer a rural environment to the city, and they are both conscious and appreciative of the wildness in nature, and of the wilderness that has become such a crucial symbol in American civilization. There are certain affinities between them, however, that draw them even closer, according to Lyle D. Domina. To begin with, they saw life as development, as a dynamic process in which a man takes an active part; and they also based their conceptions and behavior on their own observations and experiences. This self-reliance tended to keep them from extremism; they were more likely to gravitate to a mid-point between alternatives—spirituality and materialism, for example—and to try to maintain contact with both, one way or another. Though their methods were not always similar, they both pursued a "romantic" quest toward some kind of resolution of alternatives. This quest, argues Domina, takes the "reduced" form of a walk through the New England countryside. This walking becomes a trope for the process of life, offering new experiences, allowing time to observe the physical world and to speculate about a destination. Adopting such a myth enables them to maintain a "realistic," physical dimension in their work while investing it symbolically with significance beyond the obvious: The apples the speaker has picked in "After Apple-Picking" are real, but they also betoken an imaginative, intellectual and even spiritual endeavor that concerns the quest of the mythic hero (the speaker's alter ego) for wisdom.[30]

The mythic hero is usually far beneath the surface of Frost's and Thoreau's work. He emerges rather more clearly in "Directive," and, significantly, that poem reveals especially clearly the connection with Thoreau. In any case, it is becoming increasingly evident that Thoreau is just as important a literary forebear of Frost as Emerson and Wordsworth, if not more so.

The connections between Frost and these three writers, and especially the admiration he expressed for them, are ambiguous in a particular way. Certainly they exerted considerable influence on him, yet the difference between their Romantic faith in a beneficent spirit immanent in external nature and his more objective conception of nature seems fundamental. It looks as if Frost wished he could share their faith, and perhaps did so sometimes or in certain ways, as in "Directive" and "West-Running Brook." Whether he shared their particular metaphysical views or not, however, is less important to our understanding of Frost the poet than the fact that they helped shape his art—the tone, the attitudes, and even, in certain ways, his poetics.

Frost's Poetic Techniques

Robert Frost was a highly conscious artist and believed correctly that he had developed cogent and effective poetic theories. As early as 1913, he wrote to his friend John Bartlett, "I am one of the most notable craftsmen of my time ... I am possibly the only person going who works on any but a worn out theory (principle I had better say) of versification."[1] He went on to describe his principle of "the sound of sense" (see below); this was not original with him, but his emphasis on it was a significant contribution to modern poetic theory and practice. Frost's writings on his poetic theories and practice are occasional and scattered through letters, introductions to such volumes as Robinson's *King Jasper,* public speeches, and other prose works. He was always primarily a poet rather than a critic or any other kind of prose writer, and did not value his prose highly, never bothering to collect it. Now, however, it is being assembled and published, and the patterns of his critical thinking are beginning to reveal their significance to an increasing number of readers.

In contrast to Wordsworth, Emerson, and other Romantic writers, Frost tended to think of himself as a craftsman. He once said he considered the term "poet" a praise word, and was preoccupied with the technicalities of versification to a greater degree than they, at the same time considering his writings on the subject relatively unimportant.[2] He believed, moreover, that any critical writing a poet did was likely to distract him from his proper work. What was important to him were the principles and practices themselves, not his writing about them. Similarly, it is most important for us to understand the major features of his poetic theory and practice; these are his conceptions of form, particularly in terms of meter and rhyme, of the "sound of sense," and of metaphor.

Form

Frost's conception of form resulted from his general view of existence. To man, Frost believed, the universe seemed almost chaotic, a confusion in which he could find meaningful patterns of objects and ideas only with difficulty. Not that this "confusion" was inherently bad—it was simply raw material, the "crudity" for which Frost once expressed thanks,[3] partly because the poetic impulse itself, before it is shaped into a poem, is part of the confusion. Man's problem lies in achieving the right relationship with the confusion of his surroundings; in order to do this he must perceive himself and his situation clearly. For Frost, the achievement of some kind of form—an axe-helve or a poem—manifests a clarification of the confusion, and a "momentary stay" against it, as he put it in "The Figure a Poem Makes." Man must attain a middle ground between giving in to the confusion—going "with the drift of things" like Nitchie's passive "prudential man"—and resisting it too much by the artificial imposition of form as "anthropocentric" man does.[4] It is especially appropriate for the poet to attempt this achievement since his imagination affords him clearer perceptions and a better understanding of man's position than are generally available.[5]

To achieve form without imposing it artificially, the poet must generate it organically. Some sense of the form of a work should be part of the mood, the emotion from which a poem springs. The poet should not choose a verse form and try to fit the "content" into it, but should allow it to emerge "naturally" as the original emotion resolves itself progressively in his thoughts. This holds true for both meter and rhyme; neither should be forced. Just as the meter and rhythm should be part of the total experience of the poem, the rhymes should be unostentatious and appropriate; this is usually the case in Frost's own work. The form ultimately results from the conjunction of the poetic impulse and the exigencies of meter and rhyme to produce an organic whole.

Although Frost might seem, in his theory, to argue for vers-libre, this is not the case. For one thing, he believed that certain verse forms were natural to each culture or language; in English, the normal meters were "strict iambic and loose iambic," that is, iambic with one unstressed syllable or two (no more) before the stressed syllable.[6] It seemed to him inexcusably artificial to try, as in free verse, to avoid the forms natural to our culture. As he said, he would as soon play tennis without a net as write poetry without meter.

What gives Frost's poetic form its particular vitality in practice is a direct result of his theory. He maintained with Wordsworth and Emerson that certain general speech patterns were natural to a given language and culture and were to be found especially clearly in the talk of ordinary, common people, particularly in rural areas. The people "north of Boston," himself included in his role of rural thinker, have their way of talking, their natural speech rhythms. Frost worked largely with these rhythms and with formal meter simultaneously, and since they rarely matched perfectly or consistently, he achieved a "tune," as he called it, whose variety and tension make it constantly interesting. "The possibilities for tune from the dramatic tones of meaning struck across the rigidity of a limited meter are endless," Frost observed.[7]

This interplay between natural speech rhythms and formal meter can be seen both when a character is talking, and when the poem directly expresses the poet's—or his persona's—thoughts and feelings. In the following passage from "Home Burial," the meter is basically iambic, and almost perfectly regular in the first lines. We have the metrical rhythm in the backs of our minds by this point in the poem, and these lines from the husband's first longish speech are calm at first. As he pursues the subject, the tension rises partly because the speech rhythms override the formal meter to some degree. And when the wife speaks, the emotional tension reaches a peak:

> "The little graveyard where my people are!
> So small the window frames the whole of it.
> Not so much larger than a bedroom, is it?
> There are three stones of slate and one of marble,
> Broad-shouldered little slabs there in the sunlight
> On the sidehill. We haven't to mind *those*.
> But I understand: it is not the stones,
> But the child's mound—"
>
> "Don't, don't, don't, don't," she cried.
> (ll. 23–30)

A very different, later poem, "The Gift Outright" shows the same kind of variety in meter and rhythm though to a lesser degree. Most good poets modify the metrical rhythm by substituting exceptional feet, of course. What makes Frost relatively unusual is his deliberate dependence on conversational speech and the degree to which he insists on it. Even here, in a "public" and perhaps overly rhetorical poem, we can hear the accents of speech cutting across the iambic meter:

> Such as we were we gave ourselves outright
> (The deed of gift was many deeds of war)
> To the land vaguely realizing westward,
> But still unstoried, artless, unenhanced,
> Such as she was, such as she would become.
> (ll. 12–16)

The iambic—strict and loose—was clearly the most common meter for Frost; the exceptions are rare. One is "For Once, Then, Something," an experiment in hendecasyllabics, a classical meter often used by Catullus. The lines regularly have eleven syllables and are based on the trochaic foot:

> Others taunt me with having knelt at well-curbs
> Always wrong to the light, so never seeing
> Deeper down in the well . . .
>
> (ll. 1–3)

Other exceptions can be found in poems where certain variations of the iambic meter make it at least momentarily a recognizably different form. One such is "Blueberries," because it is so consistently of "loose" iambics that the meter should conventionally be called anapestic:

> "You ought to have seen what I saw on my way
> To the village, through Patterson's pasture today:
> Blueberries as big as the end of your thumb . . ."
>
> (ll. 1–3)

Another, perhaps, is the beginning of "Pan With Us," which begins in a glyconic, a verse form that Frost may well have found in Catullus or Horace:[8] "Pan came out of the woods one day."

Considering Frost's belief in the normality of iambics in English, however, it is hardly surprising that most of his poems are based on them. The number of feet varies considerably, nevertheless. Pentameter is easily most common, in blank verse, heroic couplets, sonnets, and stanzas of various kinds, as well as scattered through certain poems like "After Apple-Picking," whose line lengths are irregular. Almost equally common is tetrameter, mostly in couplets and various stanzas, especially quatrains. Then Frost uses the three-stress, and even an occasional single-stress line. Important poems can be cited as examples of most of these meters: "Directive" is in blank verse; "Once by the Pacific" is in heroic couplets; "Design" is a sonnet; "Stopping by Woods . . ." is in tetrameter stanzas; "Nothing Gold Can Stay" is in trimeter couplets; "Kitty Hawk" is in dimeter; "After Apple-Picking" is in a combination of meters, including pentameter, trimeter, dimeter, and even monometer.

Frost's rhyme schemes show the same kinds of variations as his meters. The most common are blank verse and quatrains of various sorts (abab, abba, aaba, and even aabb), but he also often employs couplets, with occasional tercets, and stanzas that have grown from the quatrain into five and six lines each. There are occasional experiments, like the *terza rima* of "Acquainted with the Night," and some ballad meter in "The Oft-Repeated Dream" from "The Hill Wife," for instance. There are poems like "Reluctance" in which Frost works with extrametrical syllables and feminine rhymes to produce an effect of lassitude. There is "Stopping by Woods," where the third line of each stanza indicates the beginning rhyme-sound for the following stanza, up to the last one: aaba, bbcb, ccdc, dddd. And there are a few poems like "After Apple-Picking," "The Grindstone," and "Storm-Fear" where the rhyme schemes are irregular in addition to the variation in line length. The effects of these variations always depend, in Frost's work, on the nature of the particular poem; the form is part of the meaning, even when we cannot easily describe the correlation.

One rhymed form, more or less predetermined, that Frost used often and well was the sonnet. Evidently he felt, as others have, that it was an inherently natural enough form for some poetic endeavors to be satisfying. At the same time he took considerable liberties with the form, demonstrating his desire to achieve organic unity in a poem almost despite the conventional structure. One can hardly specify a normal practice in Frost's sonnets. He used closed quatrains (abba, etc.) twice as often as alternately rhymed quatrains (abab, etc.), thus showing a preference for one feature of the rhyme scheme of the Italian sonnet form. Almost all of the twelve in the larger group, however, end in a rhymed couplet, as the English sonnet form does characteristically. In both groups—in fact, in almost all of Frost's sonnets—that couplet serves as a final comment set off to some degree from the body of the poem, again as in an English sonnet. But the general development of the meaning often breaks or changes quite commonly somewhere around lines seven to nine, as most Italianate, or at least Miltonic sonnets do. In other words, Frost's common forms embody features of the Italian sonnet form and the English form at the same time. What is more, Frost experimented further in several sonnets. Some are composed entirely of couplets, or couplets and triplets (e.g., "Into My Own," "Once by the Pacific"); a few have irregular rhyme schemes (e.g., "Mowing," "The Oven Bird"); and one ("Hyla Brook") has an extra line. It is worth noting, finally, that these twenty-five or so sonnets include some of his very best works. "Design," "The Oven Bird," and "The Silken Tent," for instance, rank among the best sonnets in English.

Frost is most often particularly praised for his handling of blank verse. He wrote over fifty pieces in this form, ranging in length from poems about the length of sonnets through the monologues and dialogues, to the long discourses like "Build Soil," and the *Masques*. More important, they range in genre and style from the briefly lyrical (e.g., "The Gift Outright") to the dramatic (e.g. "Home Burial," "A Servant to Servants," the *Masques*) to the discursive (e.g., "New

Hampshire"); Frost was very versatile and flexible in his handling of blank verse. In his hands it achieved a vitality for his poetry that few other poets have been capable of.

The Sound of Sense

A particular reason for this vitality was Frost's use of what he called "sentence sounds" or "the sound of sense." This is the meaning that resides in speech in everything except the denotations of the words themselves. It is the connotative meaning carried by the pitch, the stresses, the pauses of various kinds, and other less tangible tonal qualities. As Frost described it, the abstract sound of sense can best be heard "from voices behind a door that cuts off the words."[9] It may reside partly in the connotations of the words themselves, but mainly it appears in the speech patterns and their variations. The sound of sense can be illustrated in one way by a few lines of "nonsense" words arranged in normal syntactical patterns (though this does not do justice to the dramatic overtones found in Frost). Take the opening of Lewis Carroll's "Jabberwocky," from *Through the Looking Glass*; there is obviously meaning here, but it is "abstract," not precisely definable. It depends partly on the suggestions from the diction, but equally largely from the syntax, the phrasing and location of words, and the pauses.

> 'Twas brillig, and the slithy toves
> Did gyre and gimble in the wabe:
> All mimsy were the borogoves,
> And the mome raths outgrabe.
> (ll.1–4)

A better illustration is the sentence-sounds Frost once listed briefly:

My father used to say—

You're a liar!

Put it there, old man! (offering your hand)[10]

We can catch the tones of respect and assurance, of anger, and of gladness here; that is, given a normal context, we can imagine how these statements would sound, the feeling they would convey even if we could not distinguish the particular words. Similarly, the sentence-sounds of an argument between parents can be recognized by a child who overhears them even when a wall makes the words indistinct.[11]

What counted most in language for Frost was the feelings it embodied in the tones of voice which the words and phrases, and other indications of content, would signalize only with difficulty. A main problem is that many aspects of tones cannot be reproduced by written language. Some pauses can be represented by punctuation, and some stressing for emphasis can be indicated by word order and meter, but most tones of voice can only be suggested. This is what Frost meant when he gave the reader the responsibility of recognizing "sentence sounds" in his poetry. It was the poet's task to provide clues to those sounds as they were to be heard in speech.[12] Frost maintained that written language—especially in poetry—was at its best when it approached closely the nature of speech, and argued that a reader could recreate the sound of sense in a written sentence by drawing on his knowledge of the various speech patterns he had heard, partly because they are determined by the culture we live in—as Wordsworth and Emerson had indicated—and are therefore widely familiar.[13] These patterns also reflect individuals' ways of thinking, however, and the particular circumstances they find themselves in, concerns which make the rendering of sentence sounds difficult and their effect dramatically complex. Frost deserves special credit for the validity and precision readers have found in his handling of sentence sounds; he himself went so far as to declare that there was only one right—or possible—way to read one of his poems because of his management of the sound of sense, and while this seems to be wishful thinking, he obviously tried to provide clear clues to the voice tones.[14] Frost had little sympathy for the delight in pure sound exemplified by Swinburne and Poe. For him, the language of poetry should not be merely beautiful, but should have the significance and intensity he found in life itself; diction should be neither exotic nor peculiar to the individual poet but relatively simple, as the language of conversation is simple. Radically speaking, sentence sounds are meaning enacted, dramatized—"words that have become deeds," as Frost put it. They manifest the "fundamental emotional energy of human nature," as all human behavior should.[15] In order to avoid vitiating men's language further—it has already become so complex that abstraction from human vigor is a great danger—a poet must revert in a way to prelanguage communication, communicating vital meaning by acting it out through the voice tones.

The specific literary functions of the sounds of sense in Frost's poetry were several. First, they contributed to the vitality of the rhythm by their varying relationship with the regular meter, by "breaking ... with all their irregularity of accent across the regular beat of the metre."[16] This kind of vitality is evident in the dramatic lines from "Home Burial" quoted earlier. Such rhythmical variation hardly originated with Frost, but he deserves much credit for the way he was able to reproduce the flavor of speech so effectively (some people, in fact, complained that his poems were too conversational) while preserving the basic meter as a formal background. This tense compromise is a masterly handling of the relationship between confusion and form in poetic terms.

The sounds of sense also serve for characterization, since Frost succeeded in giving particular characters their own ways of speaking. The measured and restrained phrasing of the husband in "Home Burial" contrasts sharply with the rushed and incoherent speech of the wife:

> He said twice over before he knew himself:
> "Can't a man speak of his own child he's lost?"
>
> "Not you!—Oh, where's my hat? Oh, I don't need it!
> I must get out of here. I must get air.—
> I don't know rightly whether any man can."
>
> "Amy! Don't go to someone else this time.
> Listen to me. I won't come down the stairs."
> He sat and fixed his chin between his fists.
> (11.34–41)

It is clear from this passage, too, that the sound of sense creates emotion. The words themselves and the syntactical relationships can aim in that direction, but it is the tones and the connotations of the phrasing that achieve the most.

The overriding function of sentence sounds is dramatic—in this are involved the emotion, the characterization, and the rhythmic variety. "Everything written is as good as it is dramatic," Frost wrote, adding, "A dramatic necessity goes deep into the nature of the sentence. Sentences are not different enough to hold the attention unless they are dramatic ... All that can save them is the speaking tone of voice."[17] The drama in Frost's poetry, in other words, resides in more than the external form of the *Masques* and the dramatic poems, though these are certainly significant. Most essential, however, is the language itself. The drama in the language involves the emotional conflict between characters as embodied in the way they talk as well as in what they say. And similarly in Frost's lyrics and the discursive poems like "New Hampshire" there is a dramatic relationship between the sentences themselves, as Frost works out the poems "making the sentences talk to each other as two or more speakers do in drama."[18] The end of "New Hampshire" provides an amusing illustration:

> I choose to be a plain New Hampshire farmer
> With an income in cash of, say, a thousand
> (From, say, a publisher in New York City).
> It's restful to arrive at a decision,
> And restful just to think about New Hampshire.
> At present I am living in Vermont.
>
> (11. 408–13)

One comes to feel that almost all of Frost's poems except those in dramatic form represent his own voice—at least in one persona or another—performing dramatically for the reader's benefit. In "Directive" this takes the explicit form of addressing the reader:

> I have kept hidden in the instep arch
> Of an old cedar at the waterside
> A broken drinking goblet like the Grail
> Under a spell so the wrong ones can't find it,
> So can't get saved, as Saint Mark says they mustn't.
> (I stole the goblet from the children's playhouse.)
> Here are your waters and your watering place.
> Drink and be whole again beyond confusion.
>
> (11. 55–62)

Here, as elsewhere, such features as parenthetical remarks like asides in a play show that Frost is conscious of the sounds of sense that create drama in his poetic language.

Metaphor

The third and most basic feature of Frost's poetic technique is his dependence on metaphor (by "metaphor" he meant all kinds of figures of speech, including symbolism). Despite his insistence on the importance of diction, phrasing, and intonation, Frost believed that metaphor was the essence of poetry, first because poets naturally thought metaphorically, and second because they tended to convey their thoughts to others indirectly, by the suggestive power of metaphor.

"All thinking, except mathematical thinking, is metaphorical," wrote Frost in "Education by Poetry."[19] Men naturally think in terms

of resemblances, some trivial and some significant. The correspon-
dences between ideas and between objects, as Emerson had taught,
were what began the process of poetic creation for Frost. To "have a
think," as he put it, was to start toward a poem. All men perceive
their world, and some become enthusiastic about the beauty or the
strangeness of it. To "tame" this enthusiasm, the emotional response
to experience, by filtering it through the intellect into metaphor is to
subject it to artistic control. It is not enough for a poet simply to re-
spond to a sunset with "oh's" and "ah's"—he must exercise his crea-
tive imagination to perceive and reveal to others correspondences
with other phenomena which they may have noticed before but
never thought of expressing. "The subject [of poetry] should be
common in experience and uncommon in books. . . . It should hap-
pen to everyone but it should have occurred to no one before as ma-
terial."[20] He refused to accept the late Romantic notion that some
subjects were inherently more poetic than others. Like Wordsworth,
Frost believed that everyday subjects were the best, so that readers
could be surprised by new perceptions of familiar things and ideas.
Therein lies a main reason for his adopting the persona of a rural
thinker. Just as Wordsworth wrote about the English countryside
and its people, so Frost adopted rural New England as his pastoral
milieu—it was ordinary, and familiar in its basic experiences and
human types to a wide variety of readers, as the popularity of his
poetry shows.

Poets—even more than other men—not only find analogies, they
communicate them to readers by indirection:

> Poetry provides the one permissible way of saying one thing and meaning
> another. People say, "Why don't you say what you mean?" We never do
> that, do we, being all of us too much poets. We like to talk in parables and
> in hints and in indirections—whether from diffidence or some other in-
> stinct.[21]

A reliance on suggestion, on the power of metaphor and symbolism,
is natural to poets if not to all men as Frost saw it. It was certainly
very like him to wish to remain reticent, to hide, as it were, behind
his public image and his figurative language. He not only felt reluc-
tant to expose himself fully, but also believed on principle that a poet
should expect his best readers to be intelligent and perceptive. If the
poet has the creative imagination to perceive ideas and objects in
new relationships, his readers should be creative enough to ap-
preciate his perceptions when he hints at them. Like the drinking
goblet in "Directive," the real significance of good poetry should be
hidden "so the wrong ones can't find it."

Frost's beliefs about metaphor had further specific practical results. In addition to drawing on familiar subject matter as a means of affording him the kind of originality he sought, Frost placed great emphasis on his choice of simple image-making words and phrases for the same reason. He deliberately depended on simple diction in order to maintain an everyday, conversational sound of sense and to present immediately concrete images on which to build his metaphors, aiming as ever at providing a simple basis for original perceptions. We can all easily see the walls, the ponds, the trees, the snow, and other physical things that are the matter of so much of Frost's poetry.

The metaphors themselves are usually just as simple as the concrete diction. There is little in Frost that resembles Metaphysical figurative language. Rather, he sought the apt metaphor, one not too farfetched: a storm like a beast, a wood-pile wound round by clematis "like a bundle," a "snow-drop spider," "monolithic knees" of bedrock in an abandoned dirt road. Sometimes they are explicit like these, while often they are implicit, symbolistic, like the conception of man's nature implied in "A Cow in Apple Time," and the attitude toward death implied in "Stopping by Woods." Perhaps one reason for Frost's metaphoric restraint was that he was very conscious of the limitations of metaphor. No matter how apt a metaphor may seem, it will at some point reveal a defect in the analogy it is based on. "All metaphor breaks down somewhere. . . . It is touch and go with metaphor," wrote Frost, illustrating his point with a story of someone who compared the universe to a machine, admitting at the same time that in some ways they were different. Metaphor, in other words, like any other kind of form in Frost's broad sense was only a "momentary stay against confusion." One cannot reduce or simplify the richness and multiplicity of existence thoroughly or completely; man cannot "make sense" of everything.

Despite the simplicity of his typical metaphors, Frost sometimes used them as the structural foundation of whole poems. Rarely are any merely decorative; almost always they serve some purpose in the unity of the poem, as those mentioned above do. In "Stopping by Woods" and "A Cow in Apple Time," however, the symbolism provides one kind of form for the whole work. The same is true of the quest in "Directive," the life-voyage in "The Draft Horse," the turning of the world and experience in "The Grindstone," and other similar poems. In calling himself a synecdochist, Frost was not merely suggesting that he liked to use a part to represent the whole, as the classic description of the figure has it (though this occurs in such passages as "The heart is still aching to seek, / But the feet question 'whither?' " ["Reluctance," ll. 17–18]). Frost's main point was that he used small things and incidents, particular experiences like sharpening a scythe on a grindstone or looking into a geode to represent larger concerns symbolically. It is in this process of seeing resemblances between small phenomena and larger issues that we see most clearly how important metaphor was to Frost.

In the last analysis, Frost's metaphoric thinking was an attempt to "say matter in terms of spirit, or spirit in terms of matter, to make the final unity." According to Frost, this "is the height of poetry, the height of all thinking, the height of all poetic thinking."[22] The poet, even more than most men, has an almost Godlike role: It lies in "risking spirit / In substantiation."[23] All men are ultimately doomed to failure, but poetry is "the greatest attempt that ever failed," and the poet's task, like all men's, is to persist in the attempt.[24]

Notes*

Chapter 1

1. Information on Robert Frost's family and his life is from Thompson, *Robert Frost: The Early Years* (hereafter cited as *Early Years*); Thompson, *Robert Frost: The Years of Triumph, 1915–1938* (hereafter cited as *Years of Triumph*); Thompson and Winnick, *Robert Frost: The Later Years, 1938–1963* (hereafter cited as *Later Years*); and *Selected Letters of Robert Frost,* ed. Thompson (hereafter cited as *Letters*).

2. Film, *Robert Frost: A Lover's Quarrel with the World.*

3. As Thompson points out, Frost continued to think dualistically the rest of his life (*Early Years*, p.20).

4. *Early Years*, pp. 88–90; see also Evans, "A Literary Friendship: Robert Frost and Carl Burrell," in *Frost: Centennial Essays*, ed. Tharpe, pp. 504–517.

5. *Early Years*, p. 512.

6. Ibid., pp. 173–188. *Twilight* included "My Butterfly," "An Unhistoric Spot," "Summering," "The Falls," and "Twilight." It is important to note, however, that the evidence gathered by Robert S. Newdick for the biography of Frost that he was working on at the time of his death in 1939 suggests a somewhat different account of this episode. Sutton, ed., *Newdick's Season of Frost: An Interrupted Biography of Robert Frost.*

7. *Early Years*, pp. 231–232, 239–243, 294–295, 383–386. See also Thomas McClanahan, "Frost's Theodicy: 'Word I Had No One Left But God,'" in *Frost: Centennial Essays II*, ed. Tharpe, pp. 112–126.

8. *Early Years*, pp. 258–259, 546–547, 597–598.

9. Ibid., pp. 267–268. 550 n. 9.

10. For "Spoils of the Dead" and its significance, see *Early Years*, pp. 558–559, 308–310.

11. Ibid., pp. 375–376, 381–388, 581–582.

12. Ibid., pp. 389–390.

Chapter 2

1. *Letters*, p. 52.

2. *Early Years*, pp. 402–404.

3. Ibid., pp. 397 ff.

4. See Haynes, "The Narrative Unity of *A Boy's Will*," pp. 452–464; and Miller, "Design and Drama in *A Boy's Will*," *Frost: Centennial Essays,* ed. Tharpe, pp. 351–368.

---

*Complete publication information for works cited in the Notes can be found in the Bibliography.

5. *The Poetry of Robert Frost,* ed. Lathem, pp. 529-530 (hereafter cited as *Poetry*).

6. Greiner, *Robert Frost: The Poet and His Critics,* pp. 70–72.

7. O'Donnell, "Robert Frost and New England: A Revaluation," p.p. 704–705.

8. *Early Years,* pp. 166–167, 418–419, 434–436. Frost's principles and achievements in regard to the "sound of sense" are discussed in Part III below.

9. See Greiner, pp. 74–79, 207 ff.; Lynen, *The Pastoral Art of Robert Frost,* for evidence of some important ways symbolic breadth is achieved.

10. *Years of Triumph,* pp. 93–96.

11. Ibid., p.p. 12–20.

12. Ibid., pp. 61-62.

13. Ibid., p. 80.

14. Ibid., p. 539.

15. Sergeant, *Robert Frost: The Trial by Existence,* p. 188; *Years of Triumph,* pp. 540–542.

16. *Years of Triumph,* p. 108.

17. Ibid., pp. 139–140.

18. Ibid., pp. 151–152.

19. *Letters,* p. 272.

20. *Years of Triumph,* pp. 178–183.

21. Lynen, pp. 135–136; Shackford, "The Development of the Poetry of Robert Frost," pp. 30–35.

22. For a long time Frost mistakenly maintained that he had been born in 1875. In 1949, the correct date, 1874, was made clear. See *Letters,* pp. xlvii f.

23. *Years of Triumph,* pp. 272–279.

24. Lynen, p. 135; Shackford, pp. 45 ff.

25. *Years of Triumph,* p. 311.

Chapter 3

1. *Years of Triumph,* pp. 402–403; *The Later Years,* pp. 152–153.

2. *Ibid,* pp. 419–422.

3. Ibid., pp. 424, 429–430.

4. Ibid., pp. 432–433, 441–443, 448–464, 477–492.

5. *Poetry,* p. 557.

6. *Years of Triumph,* pp. 674–675.

7. *Later Years,* pp. 1–10, 23–24.

8. Ibid., pp. 92–93.

9. Sergeant, *Robert Frost: The Trial by Existence,* p. 385; *Later Years,* p. 93.

10. Van Egmond, *The Critical Reception of Robert Frost,* pp. 31–33; *Later Years,* pp. 157–160.

11. Pound had made broadcasts from Germany during World War II on behalf of the Nazi government. *Later Years,* pp. 174–176.

12. Ibid., pp. 266–270.

13. Ibid., p. 303; *Poetry,* p. 573.

14. *Years of Triumph*, p. 673; *Later Years*, p. 300.
15. *Later Years*, p. 306.
16. Ibid., pp. 306–326.

Chapter 4

1. See Dendinger, "Robert Frost, The Popular and the Central Poetic Images," pp. 792–804.
2. *Early Years* and *Years of Triumph*.
3. See articles on "Mending Wall" by John C. Broderick and Carson Gibbs in *The Explicator Cyclopedia* (Chicago, 1966), pp. 135–137; S. L. Dragland, "Frost's 'Mending Wall,' " *Explicator*, XXV (1967), item 39; Charles N. Watson, Jr. "Frost's Wall: The View from the Other Side."
4. Holland, "The 'Unconscious' of Literature: The Psychoanalytic Approach"; see also "Against the 'Mending Wall': The Psychoanalysis of a Poem by Frost," where Jayne argues that the men's cooperation in the poem, and the associated imagery such as that of stones as "loaves" or "balls" suggest latent homosexual impulses.
5. Trilling, "A Speech on Robert Frost: A Cultural Episode," p. 451.
6. *Years of Triumph*, pp. 304, 626, 725–726.
7. Ibid., p. 88.
8. Ibid., pp. 545–548.
9. *Early Years*, pp. 381–388, 582.
10. *Years of Triumph*, p. 388.
11. *Early Years*, pp. 396–397.
12. Ibid., p. 554.
13. See Judd, "Reserve in the Art of Robert Frost."
14. Letter of 10 March 1924, *The Letters of Robert Frost to Louis Untermeyer*, pp. 165–166.
15. See Perrine, "Frost's 'The Mountain': Concerning Poetry."
16. See also Chickering, "Robert Frost, Romantic Humorist," for a detailed discussion of the self-image that lies behind the distancing of Frost's poetry.
17. *Anatomy of Criticism*, p. 40.
18. See Greiner, "The Use of Irony in Robert Frost."
19. *Early Years*, p. 512.
20. See Lynen, *Pastoral Art*, pp. 21–24.

Chapter 5

1. *Years of Triumph*, pp. 560–561.
2. "Robert Frost: or the Spiritual Drifter as Poet."
3. *The Poetry of Robert Frost: Constellations of Intention*, pp. 23 ff.
4. Many studies of Robert Frost's theory and practice of "the sound of sense," among them Cook, *The Dimensions of Robert Frost*, pp. 61 ff.; Brower, *The Poetry of Robert Frost*, pp. 3 ff.; Lynen, *The Pastoral Art of Robert Frost*, pp.

80 ff.; Greiner, "Robert Frost's Theory and Practice of Poetry"; Vander Ven, "Robert Frost's Principle of 'Oversound.' "

5. *Years of Triumph,* p. 730.

6. Ibid., p. 485.

7. See Pritchard, "Diminished Nature," pp. 475–479.

8. See William R. Osborne, "Frost's 'The Oven Bird,' " *Explicator,* XXVI (1968), item 47; Jerry A. Herndon, "Frost's 'The Oven Bird,' " *Explicator,* XXVIII (1970), item 64.

9. Laurence Perrine, "Neither Out Far nor In Deep," *Explicator Cyclopedia* (Chicago, 1966), p. 138.

10. See Churchill, "Frost: The Sonnets."

11. Frye, *Anatomy of Criticism;* see Katz, "Irony in the Poetry of Robert Frost."

12. See Nitchie, *Human Values in the Poetry of Robert Frost,* pp. 68–109.

13. Ibid., p. 78.

14. Lynen, p. 19.

15. See Swennes, "Man and Wife: The Dialogue of Contraries in Robert Frost's Poetry."

16. Katz, p. 58.

17. See Frye, p. 60.

18. Preface to *A Way Out,* reprinted in *Selected Prose of Robert Frost,* Cox and Lathem, eds., p. 13.

19. "Birches," *Poetry,* p. 122; "Stopping by Woods on a Snowy Evening," *Poetry,* p. 225.

20. "It Bids Pretty Fair," *Poetry,* p. 392.

Chapter 6

1. "Conflict of Tradition," *Modern Drama,* X (1969), pp. 275–279.

2. Dendinger, "Robert Frost: The Popular and the Central Poetic Images," p. 804.

3. *Years of Triumph,* p. 485.

4. *Early Years,* p. 623.

5. Brown, "The Quest for 'all creatures great and small,' " *Frost: Centennial Essays,* ed. Tharpe, pp. 6–7.

6. *Years of Triumph,* pp. 722, 725, 728, 730.

7. Kyle, "Epistemological Dualism in the Poetry of Robert Frost."

8. E.g., Ryan, "Frost and Emerson: Voice and Vision," pp. 5–23; Duvall, "Robert Frost's 'Directive' out of *Walden*"; McClanahan, "Frost's Theodicy: 'Word I Had No One Left But God,' " *Frost: Centennial Essays II,* ed. Tharpe, pp. 112–126.

9. See Childs, "Reality in Some of the Writings of Robert Frost and William James"; Lornell, "Robert Frost: Reality and Form"; Kyle.

10. "Painterly Qualities in Frost's Lyric Poetry," p. 10.

11. Montgomery, "Robert Frost and His Use of Barriers: Man *vs.* Nature Toward God," p. 339.

12. Perrine, "Frost's 'The Mountain': Concerning Poetry."

13. *Years of Triumph,* pp. 324 ff.

14. Greiner, "Confusion and Form: Robert Frost as Nature Poet"; Childs; Heibel, "The Skepticism of Robert Frost."

15. *Years of Triumph,* p. 601, n. 30; Lynen, *The Pastoral Art of Robert Frost, passim,* esp. pp. 9–11.

Chapter 7

1. See Nitchie, *Human Values in the Poetry of Robert Frost,* p. 43; Brower, *The Poetry of Robert Frost,* p. 125; Sampley, "The Myth and the Quest: The Stature of Robert Frost."

2. "A Passing Glimpse," p. 248.

3. *The Pastoral Art of Robert Frost,* p. 149.

4. Gwynn, "Analysis and Synthesis of Frost's 'The Draft Horse.' "

5. Lane, "Agnosticism as Technique: Robert Frost's Poetic Style"; see also Nilakantan, " 'Something Beyond Conflict': A Study of the Dual Vision of Robert Frost."

6. For example, Nitchie, pp. 68–109; Lynen, pp. 42, 153–154, 158; Pritchard, "Diminished Nature."

7. *Early Years,* pp. 291–292.

8. "Happiness Makes Up in Height for What It Lacks in Length," *Poetry,* p. 333.

9. See Hartsock, "Robert Frost: Poet of Risk"; also Sampley.

10. "Neither Out Far nor In Deep," and "The Star-Splitter," *Poetry,* pp. 301, 179.

11. See Childs, "Reality in Some of the Writings of Robert Frost and William James"; and Greiner, "Confusion and Form: Robert Frost as Nature Poet."

12. Heibel, "The Skepticism of Robert Frost."

13. "Man and Wife: The Dialogue of Contraries in Robert Frost's Poetry."

14. Sasso, "Robert Frost: Love's Question."

15. *Years of Triumph,* pp. 64, 108.

16. Nitchie, pp. 49 ff.

17. Juhnke, "Religion in Robert Frost's Poetry: The Play for Self-Possession."

18. *Years of Triumph,* pp. 728, 729–730: "Religious Belief" and "Skeptic."

19. Nitchie, pp. 49 ff.

20. Irwin, "The Unity of Frost's Masques," pp. 308-309.

21. "Permutations of American Romanticism," pp. 260–261.

Chapter 8

1. Childs, "Reality in Some of the Writings of Robert Frost and William James," p. 153.

2. Kyle, "Epistemological Dualism in the Poetry of Robert Frost," pp. xiii-xiv.

3. Mastendino, "Dualism in the Poetry of Robert Frost."

4. "Diminished Nature," p. 481.

5. Dowell, "Counter-Images and Their Function in the Poetry of Robert Frost," p. 16.

6. "Robert Frost's Ideas of Order."

7. "Confusion and Form: Robert Frost as Nature Poet," p. 396.

8. Ibid., p. 397.

9. *Years of Triumph,* pp. 413, 664, 290.

10. Lynen, *The Pastoral Art of Robert Frost,* pp. 90–98.

11. See Caspersson, "Robert Frost: Parables of Poetic Experience."

12. Nitchie, *Human Values in the Poetry of Robert Frost,* pp. 160, 169–170, 184.

13. Domina, "The Experiential Mode in Robert Frost."

14. Sampley, "The Tensions of Robert Frost," p. 434.

15. "Parnassus Divided," p. 68.

16. Childs, p. 157.

17. "The Myth and the Quest: The Stature of Robert Frost."

18. Morrow, "The Greek Nexus in Robert Frost's 'West-Running Brook,'" pp. 25, 27–28.

19. See Weinstein, *passim.*

20. Domina, esp. pp. 53–54.

21. Nitchie, pp. 19–20; see also Duvall, "Robert Frost's 'Directive' Out of Walden."

22. See also Peters, "The Truth of Frost's 'Directive,'" and Blum, "Robert Frost's 'Directive': A Theological Reading."

23. Knox, "A Backward Motion Toward the Source."

24. Sasso, "Robert Frost: Love's Question."

25. Swennes, "Man and Wife: The Dialogue of Contraries in Robert Frost's Poetry," pp. 371–372.

26. *Fiction and the Unconscious,* p. 126.

27. *Early Years,* pp. xix-xx.

28. "Frost's 'The Mountain': Concerning Poetry," pp. 5–11.

29. Winters, "Robert Frost: or, The Spiritual Drifter as Poet"; Nitchie, p. 218.

Chapter 9

1. Greiner, *Robert Frost: The Poet and His Critics,* pp. 141–142.

2. *Letters,* p. 79.

3. "A Tribute to Wordsworth," cited in Greiner, p. 142.

4. Greiner, p. 143.

5. Lynen, *The Pastoral Art of Robert Frost,* pp. 141 ff.

6. Brower, *The Poetry of Robert Frost: Constellations of Intention,* pp. 92–95.

7. Baker, "Frost on the Pumpkin," cited in Greiner, p. 216.

8. Nitchie, *Human Values in the Poetry of Robert Frost,* pp. 28 ff., cited in Greiner, p. 223; Montgomery, "Robert Frost and His Use of Barriers: Man vs. Nature Toward God."

9. Lynen, pp. 143 ff.

10. Ibid., pp. 58–59.

11. Brower, pp. 76–77, cited in Greiner, p. 149.

12. Greiner, p. 156.

13. Frost, "On Emerson," p. 715; cited in Greiner, p. 156.

14. See Winters, "Robert Frost: or, The Spiritual Drifter as Poet," cited in Greiner, p. 160.

15. Baker, p. 125; William Dean Howells, cited in Dendinger, "Emerson's Influence on Frost through Howells," in *Frost: Centennial Essays,* ed. Tharpe, p. 269.

16. Brower, pp. 83–87.

17. Thompson, *Emerson and Frost: Critics of Their Times,* cited in Greiner, p. 154.

18. Waggoner, "The Humanistic Idealism of Robert Frost," pp. 209–211.

19. Cook, "Emerson and Frost: A Parallel of Seers," p. 216; cited in Greiner, p. 162.

20. Ryan, "Frost and Emerson: Voice and Vision," pp. 20–21; cited in Greiner, p. 165.

21. *Interviews with Robert Frost,* ed. Lathem, pp. 142, 146, 143.

22. Cook, "A Parallel of Parablists: Thoreau and Frost," in *The Thoreau Centennial,* ed. Harding; Greiner, p. 171, referring to Cook, p. 72.

23. Cook, pp. 74, 77.

24. Monteiro, "Redemption Through Nature: A Recurring Theme in Thoreau, Frost and Richard Wilbur," pp. 799–800.

25. *Interviews,* p. 145.

26. Stanlis, "Robert Frost: The Individual and Society," pp. 218 (italics in the original); 213, 215.

27. Monteiro, p. 801.

28. See Duvall, "Robert Frost's 'Directive' out of *Walden*"; also worth consulting is Dougherty, "Robert Frost's 'Directive' to the Wilderness."

29. *Books We Like,* pp. 141–142; cited in Duvall, p. 483.

30. "Frost and Thoreau: A Study in Affinities," pp. 223, 225.

Chapter 10

1. *Letters,* p. 79.

2. Film, *A Lover's Quarrel with the World.*

3. *Letters,* p. 465.

4. Frost, "Reluctance," *Poetry,* p. 30; Nitchie, *Human Values in the Poetry of Robert Frost,* pp. 169-170.

5. Greiner, "Robert Frost's Theory and Practice of Poetry," p. 145.

6. Frost, "The Figure a Poem Makes," *Selected Prose,* ed. Cox and Lathem, pp. 17–18.

7. Ibid., p. 18.

8. Bacon, "In- and Outdoor Schooling," *Robert Frost: Lectures on the Centennial of His Birth,* p. 6.

9. *Letters,* p. 80.

10. Anderson, *Robert Frost and John Bartlett: The Record of a Friendship*, p. 84.

11. Vander Ven, "Robert Frost's Dramatic Principle of 'Oversound,' " p. 244.

12. Ibid., pp. 249–250.

13. *Letters*, pp. 159, 109.

14. *Years of Triumph*, p. 427.

15. Vander Ven, p. 244.

16. *Letters*, p. 80.

17. Preface to "A Way Out," *Selected Prose*, p. 13.

18. *Letters*, p. 427.

19. *Selected Prose*, pp. 36–37.

20. *Letters*, p. 426.

21. From "Education by Poetry," *Selected Prose*, pp. 36–37.

22. Ibid., p. 41.

23. From "Kitty Hawk," *Poetry*, p. 435.

24. "Education by Poetry," *Selected Prose*, p. 41.

Bibliography

The following list includes works referred to in the text and additional works that should be interesting to readers of Frost's poetry. It is selective—and must inevitably lack some worthwhile material—but it should constitute a useful working bibliography. The annotations are intended to indicate the central thesis or subject of each work; some entries (particularly the works cited in the text) are not annotated when they are not widely available. In Section F, Analyses of Particular Poems, reference is made to *Explicator* magazine by volume, date, and item number or the issue and page numbers; and to *The Explicator Cyclopedia,* I (Chicago, 1966) (cited as Explicator Cyclopedia, I) by the page numbers of entries therein; some of these articles are very brief, though all are worth noting. I have also tried to indicate in Section F when a poem has been significantly analyzed in an article in E, General Articles and Reviews. It should be noted too that most of the books in the first section contain discussions of many of Frost's poems.

A. *Works by Frost: Poetry, Letters, Talks, Recordings*

1. Barry, Elaine, ed., *Robert Frost on Writing* (New Brunswick, N.J., 1973). An analysis of Frost's critical theory and practice, and an anthology of his letters, essays, and talks that contain many of his most important comments on writing and criticism.
2. Cook, Reginald L., *Robert Frost: A Living Voice* (Amherst, Mass., 1974). A combination of twelve transcribed talks by Frost at the Bread Loaf School of English (and reports on other talks) with biographical and (mainly) critical analyses of Frost as man and poet, based on Cook's personal experiences and on the talks.
3. Frost, Robert, *The Letters of Robert Frost to Louis Untermeyer,* ed. Louis Untermeyer (New York, 1963). About 270 letters covering nearly fifty years of Frost's relationship with one of his best friends. Reveals Frost's personality and especially his views on literature.
4. _____, "On Emerson," *Daedalus* (Cambridge, Mass.), LXXXVIII (1959), 712–718. See above, Chapter 9.
5. _____, *The Poetry of Robert Frost,* ed. Edward C. Lathem (New York, 1969). The best and most complete collection of Frost's poetry to date.
6. _____, *Selected Letters,* ed. Lawrance Thompson (New York, 1964). The most authoritative and scholarly collection (over 560 letters to over 120 persons) to date, covering most of Frost's life. Excellent index, and detailed chronology of Frost's life.

7. _____, *Selected Prose,* eds. Hyde Cox and E. C. Lathem (New York, 1966). Fifteen of Frost's most important essays, mainly on literature, from 1929 to 1966.

8. _____, "A Tribute to Wordsworth," *Cornell Library Journal,* No. 11 (1970), 78–99. See above, Chapter 9.

9. Grade, Arnold, ed., *Family Letters of Robert and Elinor Frost* (Albany, 1972). Over 180 letters from 1914 on, fifty by Elinor, mainly to the children. Reveal Frost particularly as loving and concerned father, and Elinor as the mainstay of the family.

10. Lathem, Edward C., ed., *Interviews with Robert Frost* (New York, 1966). The most important interviews from 1915 to 1963.

11. *Robert Frost Reading His Own Poems* (record). Library of Congress, Recording Laboratory PL6 [1953] (33⅓ rpm).

12. *Robert Frost Reads From His Own Works* (record). Carillon Records YP320 [1961] (33⅓ rpm).

13. *Robert Frost Reads His Poetry* (record). Caedmon 1060 [1957] (33⅓ rpm).

14. "Thoreau's *Walden*: A Discussion between Robert Frost and Reginald Cook." *Listener* (1954), pp. 319-320. See above, Chapter 9.

B. *Biographies, Memoirs, Film*

1. Anderson, Margaret Bartlett, *Robert Frost and John Bartlett: The Record of a Friendship* (New York, 1964). By the daughter of two students at Pinkerton Academy who remained Frost's friends. Reprints many letters from Frost; provides personal insight into Frost and some literary discussion and gossip.

2. Beach, Joseph Warren, "Robert Frost," *Yale Review,* XLIII (1954), 204–217. Memoir and personal/poetic analysis stressing Frost's insistence on individualism and the dialectic tensions in his temperament.

3. Cox, Sidney, *A Swinger of Birches: A Portrait of Robert Frost* (New York, 1957). An account of Frost's ideas and behavior based on letters, observations, and conversations from a forty-year friendship. Cox idealized Frost, seeing mainly the mythic figure of the rural thinker, but provides valuable insights into Frost's sense of realism, his teaching, and his humor.

4. Frost, Lesley, *New Hampshire's Child: The Derry Journals of Lesley Frost* (Albany, 1969). Facsimile reproduction of journals kept by Frost's eldest daughter between 1905 and 1909.

5. *A Lover's Quarrel with the World* (film), WGBH-TV (Holt, Rinehart and Winston, 1967). A fairly realistic presentation of Frost speaking and reading in public, visiting classes, at Ripton, and reminiscing about his life and his way of life.

6. Mertins, Louis, *Robert Frost: Life and Talks-Walking* (Norman, Okla., 1965). An account of the book collector's long friendship, containing many interesting anecdotes, conversations, and letters not available elsewhere; some general biographical information. Generally admiring,

even when Frost's bad side is reported. Some errors in fact, and considerable unreliability in quoting Frost.

7. Morrison, Kathleen, *Robert Frost: A Pictorial Chronicle* (New York, 1974). A personal and warm biographical memoir particularly of the twenty-five years Mrs. Morrison was closely associated with Frost; notable for the many photographs of the poet in various circumstances.

8. Morse, Stearns, "Lament For a Maker: Reminiscences of Robert Frost," *The Southern Review*, n. s., IX (1973), 53–68. A memoir spanning forty years, providing sharp and unusual insight into Frost's personality, such as the perception of his "bisexualism."

9. Reeve, F. D., *Robert Frost in Russia* (Boston, 1964). A detailed, reliable report of Frost's trip of 1962 by a Russian-speaking escort who describes and explains events and situations not adequately understood or reported by news media.

10. Sergeant, Elizabeth S., *Robert Frost: The Trial by Existence* (New York, 1960). Knowledgeable and affectionate biography marred by sentimental rhetoric, unreliability in details and dates, and questionable documentation.

11. Smythe, Daniel, *Robert Frost Speaks* (New York, 1964). A record of Frost's conversations with Smythe from 1939 to 1962. Interesting variant accounts of episodes in Frost's life and opinions of other poets and of his own poems.

12. Sokol, B. J., "What Went Wrong Between Robert Frost and Ezra Pound," *New England Quarterly*, XLIX (1976), 521–541. A satisfying attempt to reconstruct the actual events of Frost's first acquaintance with Pound, and to analyze their relationship.

13. Sutton, William A., ed., *Newdick's Season of Frost: An Interrupted Biography of Robert Frost* (Albany, 1976). An account of the work done on a biography of Frost by Professor Newdick before his sudden death at the age of forty. Includes a narrative of the five-year relationship between Frost and the Newdicks and an abbreviated selection of the notes and material Newdick had gathered on Frost.

14. Thompson, Lawrance, *Robert Frost: The Early Years, 1874–1915* (New York, 1966); ———, *Robert Frost: The Years of Triumph, 1915–1938* (New York, 1970); ———, and R. H. Winnick, *The Later Years, 1938–1963* (New York, 1976). The authorized biography. Detailed, accurate, impressive, fascinating, evidently slanted against Frost.

15. Udall, Stewart L., "Robert Frost, Kennedy, and Khrushchev: A Memoir of Poetry and Power," *Shenandoah*, XXVI (1975), 52–68. An account by the former Secretary of the Interior of Frost's friendship with him, Frost's problematic relationship with President Kennedy, and Frost's meeting with Khrushchev.

16. Untermeyer, Louis, "The Northeast Corner," in *From Another World* (New York, 1939). A chapter in the autobiography of one of Frost's closest friends, admiring and tolerant of the poet's faults, but recognizing his complexity.

17. See also D.26, D.9, A.2.

C. General and Reference Works

1. Greiner, Donald J., *Robert Frost: The Poet and His Critics* (Chicago, 1974). A "selective and evaluative study" of much important critical and scholarly work on Frost, grouped according to particular concerns, such as biography, "Negative Criticism," and "Nature Poet." Includes bibliographies and study guides.
2. Lathem, Edward C., *A Concordance to the Poetry of Robert Frost* (New York, 1971). Concordance; omits nonsignificant works.
3. Lentricchia, Frank, and M. L. Lentricchia, *Robert Frost: A Bibliography, 1913–1974* (Metuchen, N.J., 1976). The most complete and accurate bibliography to date of works by and about Frost. Not annotated.
4. Van Egmond, Peter, *The Critical Reception of Robert Frost* (Boston, 1974). Annotated bibliography of works related to Frost (though not his own, except for talks and interviews). Notes usually helpful, though vague and sometimes inaccurate.

D. Books of Criticism and Analysis

1. Barry, Elaine, *Robert Frost* (New York, 1973). A critical study of Frost's poetry explicitly assuming that most of it should be approached in terms of the various speaking voices and personae through which the poet filtered his beliefs. Chapters on "The Lyric Voice," "The Dramatic Narrative," "Frost and the Sonnet Form," and "The Meditative Voice."
2. Brower, Reuben A., *The Poetry of Robert Frost: Constellations of Intention* (New York, 1963). An analysis of Frost's poems, in relation to various patterns of "intentions" of "form and meaning" in his work, and in relation to writers such as Wordsworth, Emerson, and William James. Chapters on voice and prosody, metaphor, Frost's relation to nature and to other nature poetry, on his "dramatic eclogues," etc.
3. Caspersson, Joanne, "Robert Frost: Parables of Poetic Experience," M.A. thesis, Trinity College (Hartford, Conn.), 1974. Not widely available.
4. Churchill, Faith S., "Frost: The Sonnets," M.A. thesis, Trinity College (Hartford, Conn.), 1971. Not widely available.
5. Cook, Reginald L., *The Dimensions of Robert Frost* (New York, 1958). An analysis of Frost's poetry and of Frost as man and poet, based partly on conversations with the poet over thirty years. Rather sentimental and too close to the Frost "myth" of benevolent rural thinker, but informative and sensitive.
6. Cox, James M., ed., *Robert Frost: A Collection of Critical Essays* (Englewood Cliffs, N.J., 1962). Reprinted critical articles and essays, all significant.
7. Domina, Lyle D., "Frost and Thoreau: A Study in Affinities," Ph.D. dissertation, University of Missouri, 1969. Not widely available.
8. Doyle, John R., Jr., *The Poetry of Robert Frost* (New York, 1962). Mostly close analyses of particular poems, whole or in part, to reveal aspects of Frost's work and thought; brief chapters on Frost's life and his relation to major modern poets.

9. *Frost: Centennial Essays,* ed. Jac L. Tharpe (Jackson, Miss., 1974); *Frost: Centennial Essays II,* ed. Jac L. Tharpe (Jackson, Miss., 1976); *Frost: Centennial Essays III,* ed. Jac L. Tharpe (Jackson, Miss., 1978). Collections of articles and essays, many important and some not so significant, by well-known and less known critics, on various aspects of Frost and his work.
10. Frye, Northrop, *Anatomy of Criticism* (Princeton, 1957). General theoretical approach to criticism, largely archetypal.
11. Gerber, Philip C., *Robert Frost* (New York, 1966). A general introduction to the poet and his work. Fairly useful, but dated (before Thompson's biography, for example) and rather superficial.
12. Greiner, Donald J., "Robert Frost's Theory and Practice of Poetry," Ph.D. dissertation, University of Virginia, 1968. Not widely available.
13. Heibel, William R., "The Skepticism of Robert Frost," Ph.D. dissertation,.Northwestern University, 1966. Not widely available.
14. Isaacs, Elizabeth, *An Introduction to Robert Frost* (Denver, 1962). A brief analysis of Frost's life and general reputation, a more extended "synthesis" of his poetic theory and practice, and close analyses of twelve poems representing Frost's "lyrics," "dramatic narratives," and "satires."
15. Katz, Sandra L., "Irony in the Poetry of Robert Frost," M.A. thesis, Trinity College (Hartford, Conn.), 1971. Not widely available.
16. Kemp, John C., *Robert Frost and New England: The Poet as a Regionalist* (Princeton, 1979). Important study of the development of Frost's regional personae, with special emphasis on the tension between Frost's regionalism and his wider imaginative vision.
17. Kyle, Carol A., "Epistemological Dualism in the Poetry of Robert Frost," Ph.D. dissertation, University of Pennsylvania, 1968. Not widely available.
18. Lane, Millicent T., "Agnosticism as Technique: Robert Frost's Poetic Style," Ph.D. dissertation, Cornell, 1967. Not widely available.
19. Lentricchia, Frank, *Robert Frost: Modern Poetics and the Landscapes of Self* (Durham, N.C., 1975). A phenomenological and structural analysis of Frost, recognizing that he believed in an interaction between objective reality and the perceiving mind. The book describes how the "landscapes" of Frost's mind are manifested in basic images in his work (especially brook, house, and woods), and in his handling of language.
20. Lesser, Simon O., *Fiction and the Unconscious* (Boston, 1957). General psychoanalytic approach to literary criticism.
21. Lornell, Ruby, "Robert Frost: Reality and Form," M.A. thesis, Trinity College (Hartford, Conn.), 1972. Not widely available.
22. Lynen, John F., *The Pastoral Art of Robert Frost* (New Haven, 1960). A thorough and thoughtful analysis of Frost as a nature poet, based on the observation that the rural world provides Frost not merely with material but with a symbolic mode or perspective as a means of commenting on sophisticated, urban problems as well as simple or fundamental ones.
23. Mastendino, Alfred C., "Dualism in the Poetry of Robert Frost," Ph.D. dissertation, University of Massachusetts, 1971. Not widely available.
24. Nitchie, George W., *Human Values in the Poetry of Robert Frost* (Durham,

N.C., 1960). A well argued and careful study of Frost's poetry to show that although it is significant, it oversimplifies human problems and lacks a coherent world view. Because Frost has no governing "myth" like Yeats's or Eliot's, his stature is less, despite the greatness of his poems.

25. Poirier, Richard, *Robert Frost: The Work of Knowing* (New York, 1977). Careful, detailed study of Frost's poetry demonstrating his "complexity of mind and technique," indicating his fundamental skepticism, and identifying the relationship in his poetry of the need for "home" (physical center, form) and for "excursion beyond . . . home."

26. *Recognition of Robert Frost*, ed. Richard Thornton (New York, 1937). Reprinted reviews and criticism from 1913 to 1937.

27. Shackford, John S., "The Development of the Poetry of Robert Frost," Ph.D. dissertation, Indiana University, 1971. Not widely available.

28. Squires, Radcliffe, *The Major Themes of Robert Frost* (Ann Arbor, Mich., 1963). Concerned with certain aspects of Frost's work: "Its legality of language, its relevance to life, . . . its truth and honor of concept—the philosophic muse that speaks in the center of his poetry." Thoughtful and sensitive, though rather sentimental and somewhat dated.

29. Thompson, Lawrance, *Emerson and Frost: Critics of Their Times* (Philadelphia, 1940; reprinted 1969). A valuable but not widely available brief study of the analogies and differences between the two writers as thoughtful and "plain-spoken" critics of contemporary America.

30. _____, *Fire and Ice* (New York, 1942). An excellent basic analysis of the main facets of Frost's work, including his poetics, in theory and practice, and his "attitude toward life."

E. General Critical Articles and Reviews

1. Adams, Richard P., "Permutations of American Romanticism," *Studies in Romanticism*, IX (1970), 249–268. The basic impulse of American romanticism is the shift from conceiving of the universe as static to conceiving of it as dynamic, with means sought to control it. Emerson, Frost, and Stevens are discussed as "romantic" poets, and Eliot as a "classical" one.

2. Auden, W. H., "Robert Frost," in *A Dyer's Hand and Other Essays* (New York, 1962). General definition of Frost's poetry as concerned with truth rather than beauty ("Prospero-" rather than "Ariel-dominated"), and analysis of its functional style and imagery.

3. Bacon, Helen, "In- and Outdoor Schooling," *Robert Frost: Lectures on the Centennial of His Birth* (Washington, D.C., 1975), pp. 3–25. An analysis of Frost's use, explicit and implicit, of Greek and Latin classical literature and myth.

4. Baker, Carlos, "Frost on the Pumpkin," *Georgia Review*, XI (1957), 117–131. A general appreciation of Frost; significant discussion of his nature poetry.

5. Bartini, Arnold G., "Robert Frost and Moral Neutrality," *CEA Critic*, XXXVIII (1976), 22–24. Argues that "Frost's work reveals . . . an essen-

tial indifference to moral perspective": neither nature, man, nor God is a moral arbiter.

6. Baym, Nina, "An Approach to Robert Frost's Nature Poetry," *American Quarterly,* XVII (1965), 713–723. Discussion of Frost's concern with "mutability"–"flux" or "alternation," as Frost calls it–and especially with decay or entropy in nature, and man's momentary resistances to it.

7. Berger, Harry, Jr., "Poetry as Revision: Interpreting Robert Frost," *Criticism,* X (1968), 1–22. Demonstrates how Frost reenacts, reperceives, revises raw experiences in the present time of the poem, producing a complex momentary resolution of such problems as human conceptions of, attitudes toward, and behavior in life.

8. Borkat, Roberta F. S., "The Bleak Landscape of Robert Frost," *Midwest Quarterly,* XVI (1975), 453–467. The bleakness of Frost's conception of the universe and man's relations with God as seen particularly in the *Masques.*

9. Borroff, Marie, "Robert Frost's New Testament: Language and the Poem," *Modern Philology,* LXIX (1971), 36–56. The "simplicity" of Frost's diction and its implications in terms of "dramatic strategy and structure."

10. Bort, B. D., "Frost and the Deeper Vision," *Midwest Quarterly,* V (1963), 59–67. In contrast to Wordsworth, Frost is "wary" of claiming "a reciprocity that nature may be unwilling or unable to give."

11. Brown, Marice C., "The Quest for 'all creatures great and small,' " in D.9, (Vol. I).

12. Carruth, Hayden, "The New England Tradition," *American Libraries,* 1971, pp. 690–700, 938–940; reprinted in *Regional Perspectives: An Examination of America's Literary Heritage,* ed. John G. Burke (Chicago, 1973), pp. 1–48. Describes the New England tradition as a spiritual heritage beginning with the Puritans and having its vitality in the rural milieu; relates Frost to this tradition, especially in a penchant for understatement even in the face of horror, as in "The Vanishing Red."

13. Chabot, C. Barry, "The 'Melancholy Dualism' of Robert Frost," *Review of Existential Psychology & Psychiatry,* XIII (1974), 42–56. Finds that in the course of his life Frost came to accept the conflict between himself and the world, but still continued to need "protective solitude" at times.

14. Chickering, Howell D., Jr., "Robert Frost, Romantic Humorist," *Literature and Psychology,* XVI (1966), 136–150. The self-image behind the distancing in Frost's poetry: through his poetry, he forms his "ego ideal," which is served particularly by his humor.

15. Childs, Kenneth W., "Reality in Some of the Writings of Robert Frost and William James," *Proceedings of the Utah Academy of Sciences, Arts and Letters,* XLIV, No. 1 (1967), 150–158. Discussions of the reflections in Frost's poetry of his interest in his mind's "attempt to cooperate with nature in a mutual effort to impose a meaningful pattern on existence"; he and James share a "duality in empiricism."

16. Cook, Reginald L., "Emerson and Frost: A Parallel of Seers," *New England Quarterly,* XXXI (1958), 200–217. Analysis of the similarities and differences between the two writers' basic beliefs and attitudes.

17. _____, "A Parallel of Parablists: Thoreau and Frost," in *The Thoreau Centennial*, ed. Walter Harding (Albany, 1964), pp. 65–79. Though both writers are parablists, Thoreau's parables are "aspiratory," idealistic, because of his Transcendentalism, while Frost's are more realistic projections of "felt experience" which points toward an idea.

18. _____, "Robert Frost: An Equilibrist's Field of Vision," *Massachusetts Review*, XV (1974), 385–401. Frost's poetry reflects a dynamic, sensitive continuing adjustment to opposed forces and tendencies in a pluralistic universe.

19. Coursen, Herbert R., Jr., "A Dramatic Necessity: The Poetry of Robert Frost," *Bucknell Review*, X (1961), 138–147. The movement from voice to voice in Frost's poems dramatizes his basic attempt to balance alternatives, especially retreat and confrontation.

20. Cowley, Malcolm, "Frost: A Dissenting Opinion," and "The Case Against Mr. Frost: II," *New Republic*, CXI (1944), 312–313, 345–347. Reprinted in part, D.6. Criticizes Frost's social and political conservatism, and his failure to "strike . . . inward into . . . human nature."

21. Cox, James M., "Robert Frost and The Edge of the Clearing," *Virginia Quarterly Review*, XXXV (1959), 73–88. Argues that Frost as public performer is the persona in many of his poems: the "mythic" New England farmer as poet.

22. Dendinger, Lloyd N., "Emerson's Influence on Frost through Howells," in D.9, (Vol. I).

23. _____, "The Ghost-Haunted Woodland of Robert Frost," *South Atlantic Bulletin*, XXXVIII (1973), 87–94. Affinities between Poe and Frost: Poe's "Philosophy of Composition" is applicable to several of Frost's poems, and the two poets make similar "allegorical use . . . of the natural world."

24. _____, "The Irrational Appeal of Frost's Dark Deep Woods," *Southern Review*, n.s., II (1966), 822–829. Frost's fascination with the woods is in the American tradition of the appeal of the wilderness, which mature judgment nevertheless rejects.

25. _____, "Robert Frost: The Popular and the Central Poetic Images," *American Quarterly*, XXI (1969), 792–804. Provides insights into American culture by analyzing the bases of Frost's popularity in terms of his images—as New England sage, as grim regional realist, as "traveler through the natural world" (the "central image," connected with the recurrent image in American literature of the solitary man confronting the wilderness).

26. Domina, Lyle, "The Experiential Mode in Robert Frost," *Re: Arts and Letters*, IV, No. 1 (1970), 53–63. Because Frost feels strongly "the conflicting claims of the universe," especially those of the physical and the spiritual, he adopts a mediating position between them, embracing neither completely but participating in both.

27. Dowell, Peter W., "Counter-Images and Their Function in the Poetry of Robert Frost," *Tennessee Studies in Literature*, XIV (1969), 15–30. A number of images in Frost poems convey dual, antithetical ideas, pro-

viding "a compact means of seeing more than one dimension of the poem."

28. Greiner, Donald J., "Confusion and Form: Robert Frost as Nature Poet," *Discourse,* XI (1968), 390–402. The "confusion" of man's natural milieu must be accepted as source and stimulus for creativity through the clarifying power of form; man should not expect nature to respond to him nor correspond to his human attitudes.

29. _____, "The Use of Irony in Robert Frost," *South Atlantic Bulletin,* XXXVIII (1973), 52–60. Frost's persona rejects the "traditional defenses against the unknown: God, nature communion, and . . . human companionship"; his main defense is an ironic stance—usually affirmative, even humorous.

30. Griffith, Clark, "Frost and the American View of Nature," *American Quarterly,* XX (1968), 21–37. Like the later Romantics, Frost would like to learn from Nature, but as a modernist, he realizes nature is opaque, "other" than man. Important analysis of Frost's relation to a peculiarly American tradition.

31. Hall, Dorothy Judd, "The Height of Feeling Free: Frost and Bergson." *Texas Quarterly,* XIX (1976), 128–143. Demonstrates that Frost's adaptations from Bergson invalidate the accusation that the poetry suffers from a lack of philosophical commitment. Emphasizes the effect on Frost's work of his belief in a freely creative process implementing the *élan vital.*

32. _____, "Painterly Qualities in Frost's Lyric Poetry," *Ball State University Forum,* II (1970), 9–13. Demonstrates that through his "competence in visual design" Frost "achieves some of his subtlest shadings of meaning."

33. Hart, Jeffrey, "Frost and Eliot," *Sewanee Review,* LXXXIV (1976), 425–447. Comparative analyses of Frost's and Eliot's beliefs and work. In both, the central theme is "metaphysical desolation"; Frost "finds ways to live with" it, while Eliot "lives through and finally beyond it." In Frost "the voice of reason and skepticism is paramount," . . . while Eliot "mesmeriz[es] us with mysteries and incantations."

34. Hartsock, Mildred E., "Robert Frost: Poet of Risk," *Personalist,* XLV (1964), 157–175. Frost "confronts the intellectual and emotional dilemmas of our age" and maintains that man must "trust his values and venture action in a context of limited knowledge."

35. Haynes, Donald T., "The Narrative Unity of *A Boy's Will*," *PMLA,* LXXXVII (1972), 452-464. Demonstrates just how Frost's first volume traces "the development of a poet from initial withdrawal to final return to society, and from initial interest in, to final, mature acceptance of his poetic vocation."

36. Hearn, Thomas K., Jr., "Making Sweetbreads Do: Robert Frost and Moral Empiricism," *New England Quarterly,* XLIX (1976), 65–81. Indicates similarities between Frost and the eighteenth-century philosopher David Hume. Frost believed that morality is grounded in human experience, particularly in the individual's "desires, feelings, and affec-

tions," and that poetry can help make those reliable bases by heightening our awareness of our total environment.

37. Howarth, Herbert, "Frost in a Period Setting," *Southern Review*, n.s., II (1966), 789-799. Argues that Frost's technical innovations between 1905 and 1925 were just as great as those of Eliot and Pound: Frost's brevity in diction, his prosody, his "well-restrained rhetoric" mark his importance and modernity.

38. Jarrell, Randall, "To the Laodiceans," *Kenyon Review*, XIV (1952), 535-561. Reprinted in his *Poetry and the Age* (New York, 1953), and in D.6. An important appreciation of Frost in his own terms rather than in comparison with other contemporary poets.

39. Judd, Dorothy, "Reserve in the Art of Robert Frost," *Texas Quarterly*, VI (1963), 60-67. The poet's reserve has "triple motivation: emotional, intellectual, and moral." Even more fundamentally "it manifests itself in his refusal finally to commit himself to any philosophical system, poetic myth, or religious belief."

40. Juhnke, Anna K., "Religion in Robert Frost's Poetry: The Play for Self-Possession," *American Literature*, XXXVI (1964-65), 153-164. Frost "plays" in poetic forms with religious doubts, hopes, and fears to control and distance them, thereby mastering the impulse "either to reject religion absolutely or to commit oneself to it," and "finally making his own kind of salvation."

41. Knox, George, "A Backward Motion Toward the Source," *Personalist*, XLVII (1966), 365-381. The theme of the "return . . . to a source in self" as it runs through Frost's poetry, with accompanying imagery of the quest, the mountain and its stream, and others, culminating in "Directive." Relates the theme also to Eliot's version of it, especially in *Four Quartets*.

42. Langbaum, Robert, "The New Nature Poetry," *American Scholar*, XXVIII (1959), 323-340. Argues that Frost is closer to the nineteenth-century conception of nature than most modern poets, who insist on its "mindlessness, [and] . . . its non-human otherness."

43. Lentricchia, Frank, "Robert Frost: The Aesthetics of Voice and the Theory of Poetry," *Criticism*, XV (1973), 28-42. Frost's theory of voice held that the phonetic structure of a poem is a kind of symbolic form manifesting the persona's and the poet's self.

44. Leiber, Todd, M., "Robert Frost and Wallace Stevens: 'What to make of a Diminished Thing,' " *American Literature*, XLVII (1975), 64-83. Compares the two poets on the basis of their metaphysical concern with the modern "wasteland" and their solutions to it, particularly through poetic activity.

45. Miller, Lewis H., Jr., "Design and Drama in *A Boy's Will*," in D.9.

46. ———, "The Poet as Swinger: Fact and Fancy in Robert Frost," *Criticism*, XVI (1974), 58-72. Defines "a central poetic strategy" in Frost by which he comes to terms with "alien" nature: a sustained alternation between a factual or realistic approach to nature and a fanciful one.

47. Monteiro, George, "Redemption Through Nature: A Recurring Theme

in Thoreau, Frost and Richard Wilbur," *American Quarterly*, XX (1968), 795–809. Some profound affinities between Thoreau and Frost (and Wilbur) in their conception of nature as exemplar to man; particular focus on "The Axe-Helve" and "For Once, Then, Something."

48. Montgomery, Marion, "Robert Frost and His Use of Barriers: Man *vs.* Nature Toward God," *South Atlantic Quarterly*, LVII (1958), 339–353; reprinted in D.6. Because Frost's attitude toward nature is one of "armed and amicable truce and . . . respect," walls, fences, and windows are important in separating man from nature's—and God's—otherness; man can then accept the confusion of experience and impose momentary order on it.

49. Morris, John, "The Poet as Philosopher: Robert Frost," *Michigan Quarterly Review*, XI (1973), 127–134. Analyses some ways in which Frost developed philosophical problems in his poetry.

50. Morrison, Theodore, "Frost: Country Poet and Cosmopolitan Poet," *Yale Review*, LIX (1970), 179–196. Frost is a "country," rather than simply a nature poet, for a penchant for and practical experience with country life is essential to much of his poetry. Yet Frost reveals his cosmopolitanism in many poems where localization, especially in the country, is less important.

51. Munson, Gorham, "The Classicism of Robert Frost," *Modern Age*, VIII (1964), 291–305. A reassertion of the view represented in Munson's biography of 1927 *(Robert Frost: A Study in Sensibility and Good Sense)* that Frost is basically a classical poet, though not a Humanist in Irving Babbitt's sense as maintained earlier.

52. Nilakantan, Mangalam, "Something Beyond Conflict: A Study of the Dual Vision of Robert Frost," *Indian Journal of American Studies*, I (1969), 25–34. Not widely available.

53. O'Donnell, W. G., "Robert Frost and New England: A Revaluation," *Yale Review*, XXXVII (1948), 698–712. Reprinted in D.6. Traces Frost's development as a New England voice, acquiring an ability to "make local truth" serve the general purpose of a poem, and at his best, achieving a significant universality through local experience.

54. Ogilvie, John, "From Woods to Stars: A Pattern of Imagery in Robert Frost's Poetry," *South Atlantic Quarterly*, LVII (1959), 64–76. Traces the uses of woods and star imagery in Frost as general symbols of "the introspective life" and of "more impersonal, intellectual considerations," and particularly the general shift from the one to the other in his career.

55. Pritchard, William H., "Diminished Nature," *Massachusetts Review*, I (1960), 475–492. Defines Frost's poetic "stay against confusion" in terms of the calm and informed acceptance of "diminished nature."

56. _____, "The Grip of Frost," *Hudson Review*, XXIX (1976), 185–204. An appreciation of Frost and his work with particular emphasis on the voice in the poems bringing them to life while allowing them to remain essentially ambiguous and complex.

57. Ryan, Alvan S., "Frost and Emerson: Voice and Vision," *Massachusetts Review*, I (1959), 5–23. Significant similarities and differences between

the two poets' theory and practice of poetry and their "vision or interpretation of experience."

58. Sampley, Arthur M., "The Myth and The Quest: The Stature of Robert Frost," *South Atlantic Quarterly*, LXX (1971), 287–298. Argues that Frost, like Yeats and Eliot, has created a sustaining myth, that of enduring man in an uncertain universe, and a related quest back to nineteenth-century New England village life in order to reassert values inherent in our national origins.

59. _____, "The Tensions of Robert Frost," *South Atlantic Quarterly*, LXV (1966), 431–437. Basic in Frost's poetry is the tension between opposites, "quandary" in the relation between self and God, and between the self and the world. Frost's convictions result from or "are held in suspense between opposing tensions."

60. Sasso, Laurence J., "Robert Frost: Love's Question," *New England Quarterly*, XLII (1969), 95–107. Argues that Frost conceived of lovers as "wary, skeptical competitors" involved with the question of masculine dominance and feminine resistance.

61. Sears, John F., "William James, Henri Bergson, and the Poetics of Robert Frost," *New England Quarterly*, XLVIII (1975), 341–361. An analysis of the ideas Frost drew on in James and Bergson which influenced his poetics.

62. Stanlis, Peter J., "Robert Frost: The Individual and Society," *Intercollegiate Review* (Bryn Mawr), VIII, No. 5 (1973), 211–234. Frost believed that "there was a natural identity of self-interest and social benevolence in both individuals and society which kept men together or in society," though the relationship between self-interest and benevolence, the individual and society, freedom and authority, was "subject to perpetual adjustments."

63. Swennes, Robert H., "Man and Wife: The Dialogue of Contraries in Robert Frost's Poetry," *American Literature*, XLII (1971), 363–372. The monologues and dialogues representing relations between man and woman represent Frost's theory of reality in the acceptance of the difference between the sexes, and the evident desirability of communication, sometimes achieved but often not.

64. Traschen, Isadore, "Robert Frost: Some Divisions in a Whole Man," *Yale Review* (1965), 57–70. Argues that Frost "never risked his life," by "keeping himself from the deepest experiences"; this is reflected in various divisions in his poetry, as between "image and idea, matter and rhythm, the naturalist and the rationalist."

65. Trilling, Lionel, "A Speech on Robert Frost: A Cultural Episode," *Partisan Review*, XXVI (1959), 445–452; reprinted in D.6. Reproduces with preliminary comments the remarks on Frost's eighty-fifth birthday contrasting the Frost myth with Trilling's sense of Frost as a "terrifying poet" because of the universe he portrays.

66. Twombley, Robert F., "The Poetics of Demur: Lowell and Frost," *College English*, XXXVIII (1976), 373–392. Argues that the poetics of Robert

Lowell and of Frost is one "of affect rather than of form, in which closure is achieved . . . by a tacit agreement between poet and audience that their social interaction cannot . . . proceed any further."

67. Vander Ven, Tom, "Robert Frost's Dramatic Principle of 'Oversound,' " *American Literature*, XLV (1973), 238–251. Reviews Frost's pronouncements on "sentence-sounds"; defines them negatively, then as "tones of . . . voice, the vibrations of feeling" in poetry, recognizable to the reader from his own experience.

68. Viereck, Peter, "Parnassus Divided," *Atlantic Monthly*, LXV (1966), 434. Brief assessment of the current state of poetry in America.

69. Vitelli, James R., "Robert Frost: The Contrarieties of Talent and Tradition," *New England Quarterly*, XLVII (1974), 351–367. The tension between Frost's poetic talent and his chosen mythic role as popular poet is manifested in his work, especially in the "voice," and affects the reader's understanding and appreciation of it.

70. Waggoner, Hyatt H., "The Humanistic Idealism of Robert Frost," *American Literature*, XII (1941), 207-223. Analyses Frost's philosophy in terms of his affinity with Emerson's and James's "tradition of pragmatic idealism" and his opposition to contemporary determinism and scientism.

71. Warren, Robert P., "The Themes of Robert Frost," in *The Writer and His Craft: The Hopwood Lectures, 1932–1952* (Ann Arbor, Mich., 1954), pp. 218–233. Identifies the poet's principal overriding theme as man's concern with "the dream" and "the fact," reality and the ideal, and indicates some important verifying manifestations of it.

72. Weinstein, Norman, "Robert Frost's Ideas of Order," *Language and Literature*, I (1972), 5–21. Interesting, though often wrongheaded attempt to describe Frost's "world" and the structure of his poems in mathematical terms.

73. Winters, Ivor, "Robert Frost: or, The Spiritual Drifter as Poet," *Sewanee Review*, LVI (1948), 564–596. Reprinted in D.6. Attacks Frost for his "skepticism and uncertainty," for lacking social and philosophical commitment and direction.

F. *Analyses of Particular Poems*

"Acceptance"
1. See E.29.

"Accidentally on Purpose"
2. *Explicator*, XXXVI (1978), ii, 17.

"Acquainted with the Night"
3. *Explicator*, XXV (1967), 50; XXVI (1968), 64; XXXVII (1978), i, 13; XXXV, iii (1977), 28.
4. See E.29.

"After Apple-Picking"

5. Brooks, Cleanth and R. P. Warren, *Understanding Poetry*, 3d ed. (New York, 1960), pp. 363–369. The poem is fundamentally about the relationship between the ideal and reality, the former a "projection, a development of the literal experience."
6. Stein, William B., " 'After Apple-Picking': Echoic Parody," *University Review*, XXXV (1969), 301–305. The poem is "an insidious burlesque of the traditional religious vision," "negating the Christian arguments for belief in immortality."
7. *Explicator*, XXII (1964), 53; XXX (1972), 62.
8. See E.27, E.42, E.71.

"All Revelation"

9. See E.15, E.50, E.72.

"The Axe-Helve"

10. See E.47, E.69.

"The Bear"

11. See E.51.

"Bereft"

12. McClanahan, Thomas, "Frost's Theodicy: 'Word I Had No One Left But God,' " D.9, Vol. II, pp. 112–126.
13. See E.28, E.30.

"Birches"

14. Boyd, John D., "Frost's Grafting in His 'Birches,' " *Descant*, XVI (1972), 56-60. Studies the fusion of the two fragments composing the poem and the light it throws on the meaning, and on "Frost's characteristic manner of expression."
15. See E.7, E.33, E.46, F.142.

"Brown's Descent"

16. *Explicator Cyclopedia*, I, 128–129.

"Build Soil"

17. See E.42, E.62, E.73.

"Come In"

18. *Explicator Cyclopedia*, I, 129.
19. See E.14, E.54, E.71.

"A Concept Self-Conceived"

20. *Explicator*, XXV, iii (1967) 19.

"The Death of the Hired Man"

21. Marcus, Mordecai, "Motivation of Frost's Hired Man," *College Literature*, III (1976), 63–68. Emphasizes Silas's implied sense of "guilt and insecurity," especially in relation to the mother and father figures of Mary and Warren.

22. *Explicator Cyclopedia,* I, 129–130.
23. See E.23.

"The Demiurge's Laugh"
24. See E.17, E.54.

"Desert Places"
25. Brooks, Cleanth and R. P. Warren, *Understanding Poetry,* 3d ed. (New York, 1960), pp. 105–106. The speaker in the poem "is so truly mature" that he "cannot be frightened . . . by mere desolation in nature."
26. See E.7, E.29, E.42.

"Design"
27. *Explicator,* XXVIII (1970), 41.
28. See E.38.

"Devotion"
29. *Explicator Cyclopedia,* I, 130.

"Directive"
30. Blum, Margaret M., "Robert Frost's 'Directive': A Theological Reading," *Modern Language Notes,* LXXVI (1961), 524–525.
31. Dougherty, James P., "Robert Frost's 'Directive' to the Wilderness," *American Quarterly,* XVIII (1966), 208–219. The poem's theme is the retreat out of complexity into the simplicity of the wilderness, though it here lacks the Edenic quality common in American literature.
32. Doyle, John R., Jr., "A Reading of Frost's 'Directive,' " *Georgia Review,* XXII (1968), 501–508. The "controlling purpose . . . is to hint that there is something outside of man, beyond man, to which he must finally turn"; his theme "is the personal salvation of the individual."
33. Duvall, S. P. C., "Robert Frost's 'Directive' out of Walden," *American Literature,* XXXI (1960), 482–488. The poem as a direct descendent of Walden; the similarities in Frost's and Thoreau's art and ideas as represented in the poem.
34. Peters, Robert, "The Truth of Frost's 'Directive,' " *Modern Language Notes,* LXXV (1960), 29–32. The religious nature of the poem.
35. Water, Gregory, " 'Directive': Frost's Magical Mystery Tour," *Concerning Poetry,* IX (1976), No. 1, pp. 33–38. Describes the poem as a "terrifying" one which lures the reader into accepting a desolating and "shallow" experience as a metaphor for salvation.
36. *Explicator,* XXI (1963), 71; *Explicator Cyclopedia,* I, 130–131.
37. See E.3, E.9, E.21, E.26, E.33, E.38, E.44, E.53, E.58.

"The Draft Horse"
38. Gwynn, Frederick L., "Analysis and Synthesis of Frost's 'The Draft Horse,' " *College English,* XXVI (1964), 223–225. A careful attempt to indicate all the main formal structures of the poem, especially the archetypal, as they contribute to the theme.
39. *Explicator,* XXIV (1966), 79: XXV (1967), 60.

"A Dream Pang"
40. See E.35.

"A Dust of Snow"
41. *Explicator,* XXVIII (1969), 9; XXIX (1971), 61.
42. See E.7.

"The Egg and The Machine"
43. See E.27.

"An Empty Threat"
44. *Explicator,* XXX (1972), 63.

"The Figure in the Doorway"
45. See E.27.

"For Once, Then, Something"
46. *Explicator Cyclopedia,* I, 131–132.
47. See E.10, E.33, E.47.

"Ghost House"
48. *Explicator,* XXX (1971), 11.

"The Gift Outright"
49. Bosmajian, Hamida, "Robert Frost's 'The Gift Outright': Wish and Reality in History and Poetry," *American Quarterly,* XXII (1970), 95–105. The poem is more of an expression of a wish than a prediction, a less optimistic and more qualified resolution than it appears.
50. See E.62.

"Home Burial"
51. See E.60, E.72.

"How Hard It Is To Keep From Being King"
52. See E.31.

"Hyla Brook"
53. See E.3, E.55.

"I Could Give All to Time"
54. See E.50.

"I Will Sing You One-O"
55. *Explicator,* XXXIV (1976), 48.

"In White"
56. *Explicator,* XXVIII (1970), 41.

"In Winter in the Woods"
57. See E.32.

"Into My Own"
58. See E.14, E.35.

"Iris by Night"
59. See E.7.

"The Last Mowing"
60. *Explicator Cyclopedia,* I, 132–133.

"The Lesson for Today"
61. See E.44.

"Looking for a Sunset Bird in Winter"
62. See E.32.

"The Lovely Shall Be Choosers"
63. *Explicator Cyclopeda,* I, 133–134.

"Maple"
64. See E.49.

A Masque of Mercy
65. Irwin, W. R.,"The Unity of Frost's Masques," *American Literature,* XXXII (1960), 302–312. Demonstrates that the rationalistic paradoxes left unresolved in *A Masque of Reason* are "brought to a solution in an . . . unsentimental faith" in *A Masque of Mercy*; the pieces are complementary.
66. O'Donnell, William B., "Parable in Poetry," *Virginia Quarterly Review,* XXV (1949), 269–282. The *Masque of Mercy,* very different from and superior to the *Masque of Reason,* contains "standard Thomistic doctrine, counterbalanced by an underlying skepticism," but "Frost's . . . transforming wit" makes the material "suitable to the whimsicality of the plot."

A Masque of Reason
67. Stock, Ely, "*A Masque of Reason* and *JB*: Two Treatments of the Book of Job," *Modern Drama,* III (1961), 378–386. Indicates how each poet—Frost and MacLeish—answers the questions in the Book of Job, each modifying it according to "his own poetic vision," and with appropriately different techniques.
68. *Explicator Cyclopedia,* I, 134–135.
69. See E.5, E.8, E.40, E.48, E.53, E.73, F.65.

"Mending Wall"
70. Holland, Norman, "The 'Unconscious' of Literature: The Psychoanalytic Approach," in *Contemporary Criticism,* Stratford-Upon Avon Studies 12 (London, 1970), pp. 130–153. Demonstrates psychoanalytic literary analysis, finding in the poem an oral "nucleus of fantasy," that of symbolically breaking down the "individuated self."
71. Hunting, Robert, "Who Needs Mending," *Western Humanities Review,* XVII (1963), 88–89. The poem suggests that the mending of the wall is valuable because it brings the two men together, and the neighbor ironically is rebuking the narrator for the wall of arrogance in himself.
72. Jayne, Edward, "Against the Mending Wall: The Psychoanalysis of a Poem by Frost," *College English,* XXXIV (1973), 934–951. Argues that

the poem centers psychologically on an implicitly revealed latent homo-
sexuality which is repressed and denied.

73. Lentricchia, Frank, "Experience as Meaning: Robert Frost's 'Mending Wall,' " *CEA Critic*, XXXIV (1972), 8–12. Analysis particularly in terms of the "governing presence of the persona" especially in the tones of voice reflecting the imaginative play of his mind.

74. Watson, Charles N., "Frost's Wall: The View from the Other Side," *New England Quarterly*, XLIV (1971), 653–656. The "mode of the poem is . . . dramatic irony"; the "dramatized failure of perception is not the neighbor's but the speaker's."

75. *Explicator*, XXV (1967), 39; *Explicator Cyclopedia*, I, 135–137.

76. See E.9, E.48.

"Moon Compasses"
77. *Explicator*, XXXII (1974), 66.

"The Most of It"
78. Borroff, Marie, "Robert Frost's 'The Most of It,' " *Ventures: Magazine of the Yale Graduate School*, IX (1969), 76–82. Brilliant analysis of the poem as "thematic drama" of the relationship between subjective perception and demand on the one hand and objective reality on the other.

79. See E.10, E.15, E.28, E.56.

"The Mountain"
80. Perrine, Laurence, "Frost's 'The Mountain': Concerning Poetry," *Concerning Poetry*, XLI (1971), 5–11. The poem concerns poetry; it contrasts "poetic and scientific truth," "imaginative insight and literal fact."

81. See E.3.

"Mowing"
82. Chatman, Seymour, "Robert Frost's 'Mowing': An Inquiry Into Prosodic Structure," *Kenyon Review*, XVIII (1956), 421–438. Analysis of the poem in terms of Trager-Smith notation to study the relationship between meter and linguistic structure.

83. See E.9, E.35, E.46, E.56, E.69.

"The Need of Being Versed in Country Things"
84. See E.42, E.55.

"Neither Out Far nor In Deep"
85. *Explicator Cyclopedia*, I, 137–138.
86. See E.15, E.30, E.38, E.56, E.72.

"New Hampshire"
87. See E.33, E.69.

"Not All There"
88. *Explicator*, XXXI (1973), 33.

"Nothing Gold Can Stay"
89. *Explicator*, XXII (1964), 63.

"An Old Man's Winter Night"
90. *Explicator*, XXVII (1968), 19.
91. See E.42.

"On a Tree Fallen Across the Road"
92. See E.27.

"Once by the Pacific"
93. See E.30.

"One More Brevity"
94. See E.39.

"The Onset"
95. See E.64.

" 'Out, Out–' "
96. Henderson, Archibald, "Robert Frost's 'Out, Out,' " *American Imago*, XXXIV (1977), 12–27. A psychoanalytic critical analysis of the poem indicating why the boy's death was a kind of suicide.
97. *Explicator*, XXV (1967), 71; XXIX (1971), 70.
98. See E.23, E.56.

"The Oven Bird"
99. Monteiro, George, "Robert Frost's Solitary Singer," *New England Quarterly*, XLIV (1971), 134–140. Illuminates "The Oven Bird" by relating it to earlier New England writers, especially Thoreau and his editor, Torrey, and Mildred Howells.
100. *Explicator*, XXII (1963), 17; XXVI (1968), 47; XXVIII (1970), 64; XXXI (1972), 3; *Explicator Cyclopedia*, I, 138–139.
101. See E.55.

"The Pasture"
102. Horton, Rod W. and Lawrance Thompson, "The Pasture," *CEA Critic*, XI (1949), 4-5. The poem is a love poem, a metaphoric invitation to readers of Frost's poetry, and a representation of his search for truth.
103. *Explicator*, XXIX (1971), 80.
104. See E.36.

"Provide, Provide"
105. See E.38.

"Putting in the Seed"
106. *Explicator*, XXXI (1973), 59.
107. See E.61.

"Quandary"
108. See E.36.

"Questioning Faces"
109. See E.32.

"Range-Finding"

110. *Explicator*, XXIV (1966), 63.
111. See E.27.

"The Road Not Taken"

112. Mood, John J. L., "Frost's Dark Road—A Pedagogical Inquiry," *Rendezvous*, X (1975), 11–14. Attacks the common "moral cotton candy" interpretation, finding the poem "honest" and iconoclastic.
113. *Explicator*, XXIV (1965), 27; *Explicator Cyclopedia*, I, 139–141.
114. See E.49.

"The Rose Family"

115. *Explicator*, XXVI (1968), 43.

"Rose Pogonias"

116. See E.32.

"Sand Dunes"

117. Rooke, Constance, "The Elusive/Allusive Voice: An Interpretation of Frost's 'A Servant to Servants.' " *Cimarron Review*, XXXVIII (1976), 13–23. Demonstrates the "sexual and imaginative" imprisonment of the speaker, and the "elusive" role of Frost as the "implied ideal companion."
118. *Explicator Cyclopedia*, I, 141.

"The Silken Tent"

119. *Explicator*, XXX (1971), 10.

"Sitting By a Bush in Broad Sunlight"

120. *Explicator Cyclopedia*, I, 142.

"Spring Pools"

121. *Explicator*, XXVIII (1969), 28; XXX (1971), 27.
122. See E.32.

"Stopping by Woods on a Snowy Evening"

123. Armstrong, James, "The 'Death Wish' in 'Stopping by Woods,' " *College English*, XXV (1964), 440, 445. Indicates other implicit "death-wishes" in Frost's poetry and suggests the influence of T. L. Beddoes on "Stopping by Woods."
124. Ciardi, John, "Robert Frost: The Way to the Poem," *Saturday Review of Literature*, XLI (1958), 13–15, 65. Exemplifies reading poetry "in depth" by analyzing "Stopping by Woods"; provides the earliest widely known identification of the momentary "death-wish" in the poem.
125. Coursen, Herbert R., Jr., "The Ghost of Christmas Past: 'Stopping by Woods on a Snowy Evening,' " *College English*, XXIV (1962), 236–238. Parody of too-speculative interpretation: The speaker in the poem is Santa Claus.
126. Poss, Stanley, "Frost, Freud, and Delmore Schwartz," *CEA Critic*, XXX (1968), 6–7. The similarity in Freudian terms of "Stopping by Woods" and Schwartz's "A Dog Named Ego."

127. Shurr, William H., "Once More to the Woods: A New Point of Entry into Frost's Most Famous Poem," *New England Quarterly,* XLVII (1974), 584–594. Summary of the main traditions of interpretations of "Stopping . . ." and proposing a religious interpretation: the speaker refuses to be absorbed by the "divine darkness."
128. *Explicator,* XXVII (1968), 7; XXXII (1974), 33.
129. See E.14, E.21, E.24, E.42, E.50, E.54, E.71.

"The Subverted Flower"
130. *Explicator Cyclopedia,* I, 142–145.

"To Earthward"
131. *Explicator Cyclopedia,* I, 145.

"To the Thawing Wind"
132. *Explicator,* XXXI (1972), 31.

"The Tuft of Flowers"
133. See E.18, E.35.

"Two Look at Two"
134. See E.10, E.23, E.28.

"Two Tramps in Mud Time"
135. *Explicator,* XXIX (1970), 25; *Explicator Cyclopedia,* I, 145–146.

"Two Witches"
136. Marcus, Mordecai, "The Whole Pattern of Robert Frost's 'Two Witches': Contrasting Psycho-Sexual Modes," *Literature and Psychology,* XXVI (1976), 69–78. Demonstrates that the two poems are "mutually illuminating . . . companion pieces": " 'Coös' is a study of sexual failure . . . and 'Grafton' is a study of sexual triumph."

"The Vanishing Red"
137. See E.12.

"West-Running Brook"
138. Morrow, Patrick, "The Greek Nexus in Robert Frost's 'West-Running Brook,' " *Personalist,* XLIV (1968), 24–33.
139. *Explicator,* XXXV, iv (1977), 26.
140. *Explicator Cyclopedia,* I, 146–148.
141. See E.44, E.60, E.63, E.72.

"Wild Grapes"
142. Bacon, Helen, "For Girls: From 'Birches' to 'Wild Grapes,' " *Yale Review,* LXVII (1977), 13–29. Varied unifying themes and motifs (particularly the Dionysiac) are analyzed in "a poem whose richness and complexity have . . . gone unnoticed."

"The Witch of Coös"
143. *Explicator,* XXVII (1969), 40; XXXIII (1974), 19.
144. See F.136.

"The Witch of Grafton"
145. See F.136.

"A Witness Tree'
146. *Explicator Cyclopedia,* I, 148.

"The Wood Pile"
147. Narveson, Robert, "On Frost's 'The Wood Pile,' " *English Journal,* LVII (1968), 39–40. The point of the poem lies in the superiority of the woodcutter's motives for action over the narrator's and the bird's.
148. *Explicator,* XXXVIII (1970), 49: *Explicator Cyclopedia,* I, 148–149.
149. See E.46.

Index

Dartmouth College, xiii, xv, xvi, 7, 9, 21, 22, 37, 39, 152, 154

Darwin, Charles; *The Voyage of the Beagle,* 153

Davies, W. H., 18

Davison, Edward, 27

Davison, Wilfred, 27

Defoe, Daniel; *Robinson Crusoe,* 153, 154

Dendinger, Lloyd N., 47, 85, 171, 172, 175

Derry (New Hampshire), xiii, xiv, 7, 10, 11, 12, 13, 17, 19, 20, 21

Detroit, University of, xvi

deValera, Eamon, 40

DeVoto, Bernard, 33, 34, 37, 44

Dickinson, Emily, 7, 147

Dismal Swamp (Virginia), xiii, 8, 17, 35

Domina, Lyle P., 136, 139, 154, 155, 174, 175

Dowell, Peter W., 128, 174

Dragland, S. L., 49, 171

Duke University, xv

Durham (England), University of, xvi

Duvall, S. P. C., 139, 154, 174, 175

Dymock, Gloucestershire (England), xiv, 18, 40

Eisenhower, Dwight D., xvi, 39, 41, 42, 43

Eliot, Thomas Stearns, 25, 28, 32, 40, 41, 48, 71, 79, 138; *The Waste Land,* 25, 79

Elliott, George R., 24

Emerson, Ralph Waldo, x, 11, 35, 36, 37, 87, 90, 147, 151-153, 155, 156, 157, 162, 165, 172, 175; "Monadnoc," 151

England, xiv, xvi, 14, 15, 16, 21, 28, 42, 165

Europe, 28, 29

Evening Transcript, The, 19, 20

Faulkner, Williams, 40

Fisher, Dorothy Canfield, 23

Flint, F. S., 16, 17, 40; *Poetry and Drama,* 17

Florida (State), xv, 32, 34, 35, 42

Florida, University of, xvi

Forster, E. M., 40

Francis, James D., xiv

Francis, Lesley Frost; see Frost, Lesley

Franconia (New Hampshire), xiv, 12, 20, 21, 23

Fraser, Marjorie Frost, xiii, xiv, xv, 12, 24, 27, 28, 31, 32, 36

Fraser, Willard E., xv, 36

Frost, Carol, xiii, xiv, xv, 12, 23, 24, 25, 26, 27, 30, 31, 34, 35, 36

Frost, Elinor Bettina, xiv, 13

Frost, Elinor White, xiii, xiv, xv, 4, 6-10, 12-14, 19, 21, 22, 23, 27, 29, 31, 32, 33, 34, 35, 63

Frost, Elliot, xiii, 9, 10

Frost, Irma; see Cone, Irma Frost

Frost, Isabelle Moodie, xiii, 4, 5, 8, 10, 54, 55

Frost, Jeanie, xiii, xiv, 4, 5, 19, 23, 29

Frost, Lesley, xiii, xiv, 10, 23, 24, 25, 29, 34

Frost, Lillian LaBatt, xiv, xv, 26, 30, 31, 32, 35, 36

Frost, Marjorie; see Fraser, Marjorie Frost

Frost, Prescott, 31, 35

Frost, Robert Lee

  Books of Poetry:

    A Boy's Will, xiv, 16, 17, 18, 29, 54, 169; *Collected Poems* (1930), xv, 15, 30; *Collected Poems* (1939), xv, 35, 93; *Complete Poems* (1949), xv, 39; *A Further Range,* xv, 33, 34, 36; *In the Clearing,* xvi, 42, 43, 44; *A Masque of Mercy,* see Poems and Plays: *A Masque of Mercy; A Masque of Reason,* see Poems and Plays: *A Masque of Reason; Mountain Interval,* xiv, 21, 24, 26; *New Hampshire,* xiv, 25, 26, 28, 29; *North of Boston,* xiv, 11, 17, 18, 19, 22, 39, 56, 57, 125; *Selected Poems,* xiv; *Steeple Bush,* xv, 38, 42; *Twilight,* xiii, xv, 8, 35, 37, 169; *West-Running Brook,* xiv, 28; *A Witness Tree,* xv, 36, 88

  Honors and Prizes:

    see American Academy of Arts and Letters, American Philosophical Society, Bollingen Prize, Congressional Medal, Huntington Hartford Foundation Award, Limited Editions Club, National Institute of Arts and Letters, Nobel Prize nomination, Poetry Society of America medals, Pulitzer Prizes; see honorary degrees cited in Chronology, xiii-xvi

  Poems and Plays:

    "Acceptance," 29, 78, 136; "Accidentally on Purpose," 42; "Acquainted With the Night," 28, 29, 60, 101, 106, 115, 131, 159; "After Apple-Picking," 64, 65, 70, 86, 87, 88, 137, 143, 155, 159, 160; "The Aim Was Song," 94, 103; "All Revelation," 37, 64, 91, 138, 152, 167; "An Answer," 37; "The Axe-Helve," 11, 71, 72, 78, 80, 137, 150, 153, 154; "The Bear," 76, 115, 116, 126, 137; "Beech," 36; "Bereft," 29, 123, 131, 134; "Beyond Words," 39, 75, 118; "Birches," 22, 67, 75, 78, 79, 84, 86, 88, 90, 127, 129, 172; "The Birthplace," 28; "Blueberries," 159; "A Boundless Moment," 81, 122, 137, 148; "A Brook in the City," 117, 119,